Readings Between Animal Studies and the Environmental Humanities

Readings Between Animal Studies and the Environmental Humanities

Aesthetics, Ethics and Sustainable Transition

JOHN MILLER

BLOOMSBURY ACADEMIC
LONDON • NEW YORK • OXFORD • NEW DELHI • SYDNEY

BLOOMSBURY ACADEMIC
Bloomsbury Publishing Plc, 50 Bedford Square, London, WC1B 3DP, UK
Bloomsbury Publishing Inc, 1359 Broadway, New York, NY 10018, USA
Bloomsbury Publishing Ireland, 29 Earlsfort Terrace, Dublin 2, D02 AY28, Ireland

BLOOMSBURY, BLOOMSBURY ACADEMIC and the Diana logo are trademarks of Bloomsbury Publishing Plc

First published in Great Britain 2026

Cover design: Aisling Repp
Cover image: Set of bird silhouettes © tuffi_frutti/Adobe Stock, Utility pole silhouette © Bappi Creatives/Adobe Stock

A catalogue record for this book is available from the British Library.

A catalog record for this book is available from the Library of Congress.

ISBN: HB: 978-1-3502-5362-9
PB: 978-1-3502-5361-2
ePDF: 978-1-3502-5363-6
eBook: 978-1-3502-5364-3

Typeset by Newgen KnowledgeWorks Pvt. Ltd., Chennai, India
Printed and bound in Great Britain

For product safety related questions contact productsafety@bloomsbury.com.

For Lily, my ancient, hobbling, beloved companion, who sat with me – purring – while I wrote this book.

CONTENTS

ACKNOWLEDGEMENTS

This book is something like the culmination of two decades of thinking about animals and environments, shaped in too many conferences, seminars, lectures, libraries and conversations to mention. I am especially grateful to generations of students on Literature, Ecology, Capital; Radical Theory; and Humans, Animals, Monsters and Machines at the University of Sheffield for continually challenging and enriching my thinking. I am grateful to Ben Doyle at Bloomsbury for the initial suggestion that I write the book and for the patient support during its long evolution. Thanks too to Leigh Collins for diligent guidance.

Parts of Chapter 8 were published in earlier form in *The Palgrave Handbook of Literary Animal Studies*. I am grateful to Palgrave for permission to reprint this material. An earlier draft of Chapter 3 appeared in *The Edinburgh Companion to Vegan Studies*. Thanks to EUP for allowing me to republish that work here.

This book was completed in the most trying of circumstances. As my own crisis took hold, I was sustained by the fellowship, patience, kindness and wisdom of many dear friends and colleagues. Thank you for being with me Neil Allan, Matthew Cheeseman, Logan Collignon, Duncan Gillespie, Dug James, Hamish Mathison, Douglas Maxwell, Bob McKay, Seth Mehl, Adam Piette, Rachel van Duyvenbode and Graham Williams (not forgetting Mr Twinkles). My sister Louise Miller and mother Virginia Miller have always been the ground of my life: never more so than in the last year. My mind is continually rewilded by my lionhearted daughters, Martha and Peggy, whose boundless creativity, righteousness, pedantry and mischief are a mighty force for good in the universe. Their instinctive attunement to the world and its creatures – to the world the creatures have made; the creatures the world has made – is what this book aims to honour.

Introduction: Sustainable transition and the more-than-humanities

Perhaps the most extraordinary aspect of the twenty-first century's ecological emergency is how long global heating has been established as an urgent theme in political, intellectual and cultural life and how little has been accomplished in the attempts to address it. This is not to disparage the vast, disparate, continually evolving and often influential activist projects underway across the world or to belittle the achievement of researchers who have created precise understandings of complex issues and potential pathways away from catastrophe. The determination of these endeavours only emphasizes the paucity of meaningful large-scale action towards the creation of a genuinely ecological politics that directly and committedly addresses the challenge of holding on to a biosphere conducive to the flourishing of human and more-than-human life. Data on greenhouse gas emissions makes it clear that humanity remains locked into a disastrous trajectory. A consortium of climate scientists announced in 2024 that 'carbon emissions from fossil fuels have reached a record high' and noted that 'there is still "no sign" that the world has reached a peak in fossil CO_2 emissions'.[1] At the current rate of increase, the rise in global temperatures will exceed 1.5°C, widely advertised as a manageable if still dangerous limit, by around 2030.[2]

If the data looks bleak, it is hard to take encouragement about the future of the planet from the direction of mainstream political and corporate culture. Donald Trump's election to a second term as US president in 2024 came with the resuscitation of the Republican slogan 'drill, baby, drill'. As if in direct response, the story broke early in 2025 that BP would 'scale back renewable projects and increase oil and gas production following similar moves from rivals including Shell and Equinor'.[3] BP's plan may be alarming, but it isn't anything new. The world was already in the grip of what Andreas Malm and Wim Carton style a 'fossil fuel frenzy' that emerged in the wake of a relative lull in emissions during the COVID-19 pandemic.[4] Despite widespread appeals to leave fossil fuels in the ground, Malm and Carton note that 2022 saw new 119 oil pipelines, 477 gas pipelines and 432 coal mines enter development. The failure to limit fossil fuel extraction finds a counterpart in other, interlinked arenas of ecological degradation. A 2022 UN agreement to safeguard biodiversity by protecting 30 per cent of land and sea resulted in few concrete proposals. Nor is history reassuring; as Patrick Greenfield et al. note, 'Governments have never met a single target in the history of UN biodiversity agreements.'[5] Malm and Carton gloss the global picture of environmental policy as a 'monumental failure to adjust to reality',[6] a position that is mirrored in the continuing prominence of climate change denial in public debates around global futures. With penalties for protest and non-violent direct action becoming increasingly harsh in the UK, possibilities for resistance seem ever more limited.[7]

It would be premature, however, to say that global elites have given up on the climate. They haven't, at least, given up talking about it. Negotiations on ecological questions continue on the world stage, expressed most publicly in the annual Conference of Parties (COP) meetings held since 1995 to progress the objectives of the UN Framework Convention on Climate Change, signed at the 1992 Rio Earth Summit. At the centre of the 'new blueprint for international action on the environment' developed at Rio was 'sustainable development', an idea that is both utopian and universalizing.[8] As the UN explains, 'Sustainable development is how we must live today if we want a better tomorrow.' By balancing 'economic growth, social inclusion, and environmental protection', we can meet 'present needs without compromising the chances of future generations to meet their needs'.[9] Evidently, to progress this agenda the world needs to change.

Consequently, at the centre of the goal of sustainable development is the concept of sustainable or sustainability transition (sometimes also referred to as 'just transition'), which is to say, in the summary of J. Markard et al., 'long-term, multi-dimensional, and fundamental transformation processes through which established socio-technical systems evolve into more sustainable versions of production and consumption'.[10] The language here is telling. Rather than fostering alternative forms of ecological culture, the emphasis of sustainable transition here is its continuity with an 'established' system framed by the familiar economic priority of 'production and consumption'. Accordingly, at the forefront of sustainable transition are free market mechanisms (such as carbon trading or natural capital accounting) and technological innovations (geoengineering or a new generation of electric cars, for example). If any form of environmentalism might be said to have penetrated global political discourse, it has come via the formulation of sustainability as a discourse tied closely to the prevailing capitalist economic logic.

Herein lies the problem. Because mainstream international deliberations on climate breakdown are premised on the maintenance of the economic system that caused the issues in the first place, genuinely meaningful attempts to address ecological crisis have been thwarted from the start. This is why for all the bluster of successive COPs, the picture still looks bleak. The gap between high-profile international negotiations on global heating and a meaningful commitment to the foundation of an ecological politics gained emphasis from a story which broke in 2025 about a 'new four-lane highway cutting through tens of thousands of acres of protected Amazon rainforest ... being built for the COP30 climate summit in the Brazilian city of Belém'.[11] It is easy to find truth in Malm and Carton's joke that COP functions as a 'sideshow to Black Friday'.[12] What matters most it seems is not the world and its creatures but the ritualistic performance of political sincerity as a smokescreen for the continuation of business as usual under the aegis of sustainability.

Critiques of the function of 'sustainability' as a means for deepening capitalism's hold on the planet are a long-standing element of academic debates around environmental politics. Imre Szeman identifies sustainable transition as part of the toolkit for globalization, conceptualized as the moment 'when capital finally finds itself victoriously spread across the globe'.[13] In this way, environmentalism becomes part of the ideological contours of neoliberalism. For Adrian Parr, 'the popular catchphrase and slogan *sustainability* is being seamlessly integrated into dominant modes of economic production and normative forms of political and civic life' (original emphasis) so that green politics is incorporated into 'the very system of relations that the movement struggles against'.[14] Or, as Arturo Escobar puts it, sustainable development operates as 'a massive attempt to … to re-signify nature, resources, the Earth and human life itself', resulting in the 're-inscription of the Earth into capital via the gaze of science; the reinterpretation of poverty as an effect of destroyed environments; and the new lease on management and planning as arbiters between people and nature'.[15] Sustainable development, for Escobar, is merely 'capital in its ecological phase' or, in Parr's phrasing, an expression of 'the neoliberalization of life'.[16] As such, it represents a restriction of the kinds of value, meaning and experience available to the future world imagined on the other side of transition.

It is in this context that the significance of the humanities, and more specifically for my purposes here literary studies, comes into view. If the world appears locked into disaster, and the promised – and to date largely ineffectual – solutions are contained narrowly within the ideologies of global capital, then there is an urgent need for critical analysis of the formulation of sustainable transition and an expansion of its parameters beyond 'established socio-technical systems'. In Szeman's terms,

> what is genuinely lacking today is the imaginative vocabulary and narrative resources through which it might not only be possible to challenge the dominant narrative of globalization, but to articulate alternative modes of understanding these processes that have come to shape the present – and future.[17]

It is in this space, for Szeman, that it may be possible to discover 'new possibilities and even new political functions for literature and literary criticism'.[18] The widespread sense that the humanities are increasingly beleaguered – out of place in a marketized academy and running out of time in the face of swingeing cuts – only emphasizes their value as a position from which to the interrogate the dominant narratives of global capital and to contribute to the formation of alternative models of ecological politics beyond the hegemonic structures of sustainable transition.

From their inception, modes of literary-critical enquiry concerned with ecological crisis have been conceptualized as a means to transform scholarship into activism; in this sense the idea of 'new political functions for literature' has been established for some time. In the 1978 essay that coined the term 'ecocriticism', William Rueckert asks, 'How can we translate literature into purgative-redemptive biospheric action? ... how can we do something more than just recycle WORDS?'[19] The sentiment runs through ecocriticism's development and into the subsequent formation of a broader environmental humanities. Cheryl Glotfelty in the 'Introduction' to *The Ecocriticism Reader* (1996), billed as a 'landmark in literary ecology', and one of the earliest essay collections in the field, identifies ecocriticism's most 'important task' as 'consciousness raising' with an eye on the possibility of meaningful change: 'How can we solve environmental problems unless we start thinking about them?'[20] Some claims in early ecocriticism were more forthright. In *The Song of the Earth* (2000), Jonathan Bate suggested that 'poetry is the place we save the earth'.[21] Bate's view can be – and has been – turned against ecocriticism as an example of the hubris of an (at the time) minor critical field with an inflated sense of its own significance. But its potential as a contribution to material questions has not gone away. J. Andrew Hubbell and John C. Ryan, reflecting on the role of storytelling in the successful campaign to save Australia's Beeliar Wetlands in 2017, ask, 'Is the pen mightier than the bulldozer?'[22] Robert S. Emmett and David E. Nye's critical introduction to the environmental humanities retains this aspirational merging of scholarly and activist agendas: 'Clearly,' they argue, 'the humanities have a crucial role to play in understanding and in solving environmental problems.'[23] The foundational ethic behind ecocriticism and the environmental humanities is that the humanities matter in an era of unprecedented ecological peril. They contain within them a vast network of critical and historical perspectives and imagined futures beyond the market-based ideological determinations of mainstream sustainable transition.

Evidently, by the nature of a vast network of possibilities, work in ecocriticism and the environmental humanities does not evince a straightforward programme for action, nor a clearly defined set of ethical and political coordinates, nor even a cohesive critical methodology. Ecocriticism has developed significantly since Rueckert's formulation of the term. Early, or 'first-wave', ecocriticism is often characterized as a relatively narrow enterprise with a tendency, as Greg Garrard summarizes, to 'celebrate nature rather than query "nature" as a concept and to derive inspiration as directly as possible from wilderness preservation'.[24] Ecocriticism focused in this initial phase to a considerable degree on non-fiction nature writing and Romantic poetry as forms that express this ethos in exemplary form. 'Second-wave' ecocriticism saw an expansion of the historical and generic parameters of enquiry and an increasing interest in forms of critical theory that first-wave ecocritics tended to avoid or disapprove as ostensibly gesturing away from the material–ecological world. The 'third wave' has been characterized by an increasingly global focus beyond a Euro-American canon, an integration of the concerns of ecocriticism with those of postcolonial studies and the arrival of material ecocriticism, an endeavour which aims in Serenella Iovino and Serpil Oppermann's phrasing to 'couple ecocriticism's interest in revealing the bonds between text and world with the insights of the new materialist wave of thought'.[25] This stage leads into an increasing prominence of the concept of the Anthropocene (which may in some accounts characterize an emerging fourth wave). The field continues to expand exponentially, splitting into more specialized subfields and modes of enquiry, opening up new avenues for scholarship by deepening understandings of historical and cultural contexts, theoretical perspectives and textual forms in relation to the central interest in ecology. As Sam Solnick notes, 'One cannot speak about ecocriticism … in the singular any more.'[26] The continuing evolution of work under the umbrella of ecocriticism and/or the environmental humanities has inevitably involved critical tensions. Among the most prominent of these is the question of what to do about animals.

Animal studies is a distinct interdisciplinary field with a strong, if sometimes tense, connection with ecocriticism and the environmental humanities. Some early work in animal studies was explicitly conceived as part of the green humanities; the 2005 essay collection *Figuring Animals*, for example, announced in the blurb that the 'contributors draw on and complement the growing field of ecocriticism'.[27] Later work has tended, like Timothy Clark, to see animal studies as a 'distinct field of inquiry'.[28] Nonetheless, the continuities between animal studies and the environmental humanities are strong enough to risk the (admittedly awkward) convenience of lumping the two fields together as the more-than-humanities: a set of enterprises concerned variously with non-human entities, systems and processes and their relationship with human cultures, with the caveat that the idea of the 'human', or at least specific human activities, is also under scrutiny for its implication in the forms of violence that these fields address (and with the further caveat that much work in animal studies takes place in the social sciences, rather than the humanities). Like ecocriticism and the environmental humanities, animal studies consistently demonstrates a sense of critical purpose in relation to real-world ethical and political dilemmas. Peter Singer's *Animal Liberation: A New Ethics for Our Treatment of Animals* (1975) is often cited as a foundational text for animal studies' development with its energizing premise that 'we have to speak up on behalf of those who cannot speak for themselves'.[29] Singer's encouragement to advocate for animals has some specific applications. Most notably, to address animal suffering, 'we must change our own lives, to the extent of changing our diet'.[30] It is possible to see a connection between the development of pro-animal research and the rise of veganism and vegetarianism since the millennium as an example of the role of scholarship in social transformation, though the remit of animal studies is wider than the question of food. Nor does all work under the heading animal studies necessarily subscribe to the vegan politics stimulated by Singer and others. An essay by Garry Marvin in the influential early essay collection *Killing Animals*, for example, approves hunting as a 'ritual event that celebrates the wild animal and the human attempt to engage with it'.[31] Animal studies, notwithstanding a consistent emphasis on animal ethics, does not map completely onto animal liberation.

As animal studies gained increasing traction, it evinced, like ecocriticism and the environmental humanities, a commitment to reshaping the future. In a 2013 introduction to the field, Paul Waldau identified the central concern of animal studies as how humans 'are now interacting with and exploring other-than-human animals, in the past have engaged the living beings beyond our own species, and in the future might develop ways of living in a world shared with other animals'.[32] Summaries of the purpose of the literary wing of animal studies, often styled literary animal studies, echo this forward-looking ethos. Identifying a 'central motivation for the study of literary animals' as 'animal advocacy', Marianne DeKoven noted in 2009 that 'many literary, theoretical, and critical texts of the animal kind are motivated by a desire to mitigate cruelty to animals'.[33] Or, in a framing that echoes Szeman's call for an 'imaginative vocabulary ... to challenge the dominant narrative of globalization', Karen L. Edwards, Derek Ryan and Jane Spencer argue, 'The imaginative constructions allowed by literature help us remember that the orthodoxies that govern human and animal relations are the result of history rather than inevitability. Literature frees us to envision how those relations might be, could be different.'[34] The more-than-humanities, then, contain consistent reflections on their relation to futurity, although with different points of emphasis: a better future for the world or a better future for animals. Crucially, it is not easy to think of these straightforwardly as the same thing.

In what follows I explore the connections and tensions between the environmental humanities and animal studies and turn this intimate but fraught alliance towards our current crises as an extension of each field's explicit orientation towards reshaping the future. More specifically, this book asks how the *relationship* between animal-focused and ecologically oriented literary critical practices contributes to understandings of sustainable transition as an instrument of global capital. As such, this book is about the distinct ethical commitments of ecological and pro-animal scholarship, the expression of these ethics in approaches to politics and the central role of literary aesthetics in these connections. Evidently, foregrounding sustainable transition as the central context for this book creates an initial investment in discourses more directly linked to ecology than to animals. The logic of this is not to assert a critical hierarchy in which the environmental humanities is primary and animal studies is secondary. Rather, it echoes the structure of public discourse in which ecological issues are routinely afforded more gravity than animal issues, though, as we shall see, the distinction between these topics is in any case fluid and inconsistent. Ultimately, my aim is not to produce a partisan elevation of the environmental humanities over animal studies (or vice versa), or to simulate a glib reconciliation between them, but instead to offer critical readings of select texts that move *between* ecological and animal priorities in order to understand the ethical, ontological, political and aesthetic dimensions of sustainable transition. My premise, following Matthew Calarco, is that 'complete ideological alignment is not necessary for successful coalitions to be formed'; indeed, it is precisely the tensions between ecological and animal critical trajectories that energize a two-pronged interrogation of the limitations of current discourses of sustainable transition as a response to the manifold crises of the twenty-first century.[35]

The tense associations between environmental and pro-animal ethics and politics have drawn critical attention since the inception of the various strands of the more-than-humanities. Here is how the story runs in Garrard's summary of the conventional wisdom concerning the impasse between environmentalism and animal liberation movements. While they

> are united in opposition to anthropocentric morality, [a]nimal liberationists generally draw the line of moral consideration at the boundary of sentience or feeling ... Environmental ethics, on the other hand, places far less emphasis on the individual organism, but demands moral consideration for inanimate things like mountains, assuming pain and suffering to be a necessary part of nature.[36]

In what might be taken as a classical exemplification of this ethical tension, Garrard concludes that 'liberationists are generally opposed to hunting, whereas ecophilosophers argue that exploding populations of a certain species must be culled if they threaten environments as a whole'.[37] The antagonism between environmentalism and animal liberation might, from this perspective, appear intractable, but relatively clear, established in relation to what is often characterized as a question of scale. Environmentalism and environmental philosophy are concerned with the functioning of ecological systems and thus with the whole. Animal philosophy and advocacy are concerned with the meaning and value of specific lives, which is to say part of that whole. By extension, these distinct traditions of thought involve diverging approaches to the question of animal suffering as either a part of nature or a profound ethical challenge.

There are several good reasons for revisiting the pattern Garrard summarizes, some of which are themselves axiomatic elements of the tension between environmentalism and animal advocacy. Neither animal studies nor the environmental humanities is reducible to a framing of the debate in relation to animal liberation or rights, a point which Garrard is clear about from the outset. For Garrard, the study 'of the relations between animals and humans in the humanities is split between the analysis of the representation of animals in history and culture, or animal studies, and the philosophical consideration of animal rights'.[38] In Garrard's account, while an emphasis on animal rights facilitates an oppositional reading of the relationship between animal and environmental ethics, the focus on culture and history muddies the distinction: animal studies as cultural analysis, for Garrard, is 'close kin to ecocriticism'.[39] There are, however, caveats to add to Garrard's caveat; there is a significant tradition of cultural analysis in animal studies that involves close consideration of the philosophy of animal rights and which demonstrates the continuing relevance of such debates in the more-than-humanities.[40] At the same time, if there might still be reasons for holding on to this conceptualization of the division between ecological and animal ethics, there are also reasons to move beyond it. Any separation of animals and ecology into distinct ethical foci defies the self-evident evolutionary insight that species and environments are fundamentally conjoined. As Frederike Middelhof and Sebastian Schönbeck put it in their summation of the relationship between animal studies and ecocriticism, 'Animals … cannot be fully grasped without their environments, whereas, in turn, environments cannot be conceived without the animals living in and affecting them.'[41] In tune with this position, there are some contexts in which ecological and animal issues are essentially the same problem. Deforestation, for example, is an urgent problem in which environmental and animal ethics are inseparable. But the interdependence of animals and environments does not provide an answer to every ethical question raised by animal liberation or environmental movements. It does, however, reveal that both animal and environmental ethics, taken on their own, can only provide a partial account of the complex material issues with which both fields are concerned.

The inevitable insufficiency of each position to account for the totality of any issue has created a space in which partisan condemnations of the other side have, at times, taken shape. An evaluation of animal advocacy from an environmentalist position often characterizes the focus on animals as too limited, and inattentive, as James Radcliffe notes in strikingly generalized terms, to 'the importance of the rest of nature'.[42] Accordingly, although there are clear causal links between global heating and animal suffering, for example, it would be hard to understand climate crisis *just* by thinking about animals. In this spirit, animal advocacy has been represented not just as an incomplete but also as dangerously counterproductive way to approach ecological issues. One of the most frequently cited commentators on the ostensible limitations of pro-animal thought is J. Baird Callicott whose influential early work is scathing about animal liberation and animal rights as set out by Peter Singer, Tom Regan and others. Drawing on Aldo Leopold's conception of a land ethic in contradistinction to the 'humane ethic' of animal liberationists, Callicot argues that the 'value commitments of the humane movement seem at bottom to betray a world-denying or rather a life-loathing philosophy'.[43] Vegetarianism – a central prop of the 'humane ethic' – comprises for Callicott a form of separation from the natural world; on the other hand, an ecological carnism (which is to say 'sustainable' meat consumption) reaffirms 'our participation in nature' and 'rejoices in a recrudescence of wilderness and a renaissance of tribal cultural experience'.[44] An environmental humanities and an animal studies attuned to postcolonial critiques of the role of 'wilderness' in colonial ideologies would balk at the simplified construction of the tribal here, but the idea that violence against animals is 'natural' and expressive of an unalienated ecological existence, especially in the context of meat, remains part of the public discourse around animal ethics (as we shall see in more detail in Part 1). Callicott even goes so far as to level something like a charge of anthropocentrism at animal liberation. In making a 'firm distinction between those beings worthy of moral consideration and those not' (yes to cows but no to orchids), animal liberation has more 'in common' with a conservative humanism that insists on the ethical priority of the human than with the 'holistic' environmental ethics Callicott takes from Leopold in which humans are conceived as part of nature.[45] For Val Plumwood, writing in a similar vein, the choice between animal and environmental ethics is a question of whether to 'set human life apart from animals and ecology' or to 'emphasise human continuity with other life forms'.[46] Animal liberation, by this line of argument, is analogous with ecological alienation.

Conversely, animal advocates have often drawn attention to the limitations of a model of enquiry that fails to recognize the ethical, political and cultural weight of animal lives. An ecological approach to large-scale animal agriculture would highlight many important points (the meat industry's massive carbon and freshwater footprint, for instance), but without consideration of the experience of the billions of creatures killed each year for food, the analysis misses the fundamental premise behind this environmental damage: the idea that animals can be killed legitimately to satisfy human desires. Sue Donaldson and Will Kymlicka, in developing a 'new moral framework' for animal rights, affirm that ecological ethics can provide a 'critique of many human practices that are devastating to animals', but in a reversal of Callicott's position, they detect an underlying anthropocentrism in environmental thought.[47] The environmental perspective, they argue, prioritizes 'a particular view of what constitutes a healthy, natural, authentic, or sustainable ecosystem' which creates an imperative 'to sacrifice individual animal lives in order to achieve this holistic vision'.[48] Environmentalism, by this standard, is never an ideologically neutral commitment to a common ecological good but a much more troubled negotiation of different, sometimes opposing interests that tends to return to the 'same basic problem of elevating human interests over those of animals'.[49] Consequently, despite Garrard's opening gambit that 'environmentalism and animal liberation are united in opposition to anthropocentric morality', there is no universal agreement on what an opposition to anthropocentric morality means and how it might proceed across the gulf between environmental and pro-animal thinking.

Such divided intellectual history invites syncretic work that aspires to bring ecological and animal philosophy and ethics into closer dialogue as correctives to their respective blind spots: to forge a more ecologically attuned animal advocacy and a version of ecological thought that recognizes the ethical significance of all creatures. As attractive as this prospect seems, there remain significant obstacles to its attainment, not least because of the scale and diversity of the terrain. Negotiating the relationship between ecological and pro-animal thought involves navigating a relatively young but increasingly complex pair of critical fields neither of which is a unified enterprise. Cary Wolfe cautions that 'we should *not* try to imagine some super-discipline called "animal studies" ...

but rather recognize that it is only in and through our disciplinary specificity that we have something specific and irreplaceable to contribute to the "question of the animal"'.[50] Graham Huggan makes a similar point in identifying the environmental humanities as 'a constellation of discrepant practices, some of which run the risk of contradicting others, and virtually all of which run up against institutional obstacles of one kind or another – not least the pressures of working with different discipline-oriented sets of expectations'.[51] If the various disciplinary perspectives accommodated within the fields (across the humanities and into the social sciences with numerous points of connection to the natural sciences) mitigate against cohesion, the picture is further complicated by the proliferation of what James Chandler calls 'subdisciplinary field[s]' within and at the edges of the more-than-humanities, which significantly complicate understandings of the links and divisions between environmental and pro-animal thought.[52]

If ecocriticism is not singular then nor is animal studies. Rather, it abuts onto several other terms, most notably *critical animal studies (CAS)*, *human–animal studies (HAS)* and the more minor *animality studies*, each of which contains a distinct conceptualization of the task of thinking about animals and their relationships with human cultures. CAS in Anthony Nocella's summary is a 'radical, interdisciplinary field dedicated to establishing a holistic total liberation movement for humans, nonhuman animals and the Earth'.[53] The other two formulations are less explicit in their ethical and political commitments. HAS is, as Calarco notes, 'perhaps the most established version of animal studies'.[54] It constitutes, in Margot DeMello's words, 'an interdisciplinary field that explores the spaces that animals occupy in human social and cultural worlds and the interactions humans have with them' without necessarily shaping this into an animal liberationist activist agenda, though it remains consistently concerned with ethical and political questions.[55] The relationship between CAS and HAS (and between CAS and animal studies) has not always been easy; Nik Taylor and Richard Twine characterize it as 'increasingly fractious. With both "sides" locking horns over the overt political/activist ... stance of CAS.'[56] Animality studies, developed primarily by Michael Lundblad, is formulated precisely in its distance from animal activism. Lundblad sees '"animality studies" as a way to describe work that expresses no explicit interest in advocacy for various nonhuman animals, even though it shares an interest in how we think about "real" animals'.[57] The situation is complicated further by the development of *multispecies studies*, a field that emerges primarily from anthropology in the form of multispecies ethnography. The focus of multispecies ethnography, in Eben Kirksey and Stefan Helmreich's phrasing, on 'how a multitude of organisms' livelihoods shape and are shaped by political, economic, and cultural forces' is evidently in tune with the broad agenda of animal studies.[58] But it also, according to another essay co-authored by Kirksey (this time with Thom van Dooren and Ursula Münster), 'promises something a little bit different', taking up 'a broader taxonomic scope of inquiry' encompassing plants, fungi and other biota, focusing less on 'people's relationships with a given animal' and more on 'the multitudes of lively agents that bring one another into being through entangled relations'.[59] A multispecies studies approach creates in this way much stronger links between animals and ecology as critical foci.

The environmental humanities is more straightforward in its designation than animal studies, at least in its terminology. Both the *ecological humanities* and *green cultural studies* featured in the past but have largely been superseded. The environmental humanities' relation to ecocriticism, however, adds a degree of complexity to the development of a green humanities. On the one hand, the relationship between ecocriticism and the environmental humanities is clear. Ecocriticism is the specific literary-critical manifestation of the wider environmental humanities. But if the environmental humanities is broader, it is also later. It was not until 2010 that the environmental humanities came to widespread prominence, by which time ecocriticism was well established in academic culture.[60] In part the environmental humanities' emergence can be understood as a coalescence of discipline-specific enquiries with ecocriticism finding counterparts in environmental history and philosophy.[61] That said, the environmental humanities is more than an assemblage of autonomous pre-existing fields; rather, it has created a new context for the development of green disciplinary perspectives that has encouraged different inflections for ecocriticism. Ecocriticism may remain primarily focused on textual analysis, but the determination of the environmental humanities to look beyond the text has in turn encouraged ecocritics to reflect on what might constitute a text. Huggan cites a discussion of a trip to Lundy Island as an 'exemplary piece of ecocriticism' in its attention to 'issues of representation and discourse'.[62] Grounds for holding on to a differentiation between ecocriticism and the environmental humanities appear increasingly ambiguous. Huggan raises a number of possibilities. The environmental humanities is '*practice*-oriented, with field work – both biological and anthropological – often being seen as a prerequisite for research in the area', a trajectory that is seldom seen in ecocriticism.[63] Or, 'ecocriticism, for all its commitment to the field, remains at heart an individual enterprise, whereas environmental humanities require the types of collaborative work required to tackle large-scale problems that are beyond the scope of individual researchers or single disciplines'. Neither of these distinctions for Huggan are 'watertight'.[64] Ultimately, it is probably unhelpful to try at this point in their development to resolutely disentangle ecocriticism and the environmental humanities.

Despite the various terminologies in use within animal studies and the environmental humanities, it is still possible at this level to identify animals and ecology as two distinct foci, though they consistently impinge on one another. Recall how Nocella's definition of critical animal studies specifies it as a 'liberation movement for humans, nonhuman animals and *the Earth*'. Climate change is part of the contextual territory of animal studies with, in Calarco's summary, three primary topics within which this happens: meat's environmental footprint; the effect of climate change on animals; and the 'manner in which climate change transforms human–animal relations'.[65] Conversely, the environmental humanities from its inception has been intimately associated with the 'multispecies approach' derived from multispecies ethnography.[66] Ecocriticism always contained some engagement with the representation of animals too, largely along the lines formulated by van Dooren, Kirksey and Münster, which is to say thinking about animals within entangled ecological (and cultural) systems of relation. In essence these broad summaries of internally compartmentalized fields return us to the familiar pattern: animal studies is interested in ecological questions insofar as they touch on animal lives, and the environmental humanities is interested in animals as participants in ecological systems, which also involves many other life forms.

But beneath the umbrella of animal studies (with its various inflections) and the conjoined enterprise of ecocriticism and the environmental humanities, there is a giddying array of more specialized terms (yet more subdisciplinary fields) with different priorities and orientations. These tend to appear in one of three main formats, described by Cary Wolfe as 'fill-in-the-blank studies': either the '... humanities' (as in environmental humanities), 'critical ... studies' (as in critical animal studies) or the plainer '... studies' (think of vegan studies, more on which shortly).[67] The '... humanities' straightforwardly indicates a particular thematic focus in the humanities; '... studies' indicates a topic with a focus that extends beyond the humanities, most commonly into the social sciences. As Taylor and Twine outline in their delineation of critical animal studies, the modifier critical denotes both 'the urgency of our times' and a 'stance against an anthropocentric status quo'.[68] 'Critical' in this way announces a sense of both urgent relevance and ideological commitment to the object of study. The proliferation of such terms not only adds significant complexity to the overall task of assessing the interconnections and tensions between pro-animal and ecological discourses but also provides (in some cases) the opportunity for more precise and context-specific analysis of the relationship between them. Although this book has no pretensions to be an exhaustive encyclopaedia of more-than-human critical language, the explosion of terms that have taken hold since around 2010 is central to the current shape of the animals–ecology crux and its application to understandings of sustainable transition.

The environmental humanities has dispersed into a number of subfields that focus on particular topographies and in doing so create particular geographical contexts for thinking about the interplay of ecological and pro-animal perspectives. The *blue humanities* brings an oceanic focus into the domains of both animal studies and the environmental humanities (though *critical ocean studies* and *hydrocriticism* offer alternative nomenclatures); the *forest humanities* and the *desert humanities* have gathered some momentum too. Particular biological entities have encouraged specific fields. *Critical plant studies* aims to do for plants something like what animal studies has done for animals by thinking about vegetal ontology and agency and the evolutionary entanglement of plants with human cultures. Since the humanities are currently undertaking a *mycological turn*, it may well be that a *fungal humanities* is just around the corner. The *insect humanities* (along with its rival *critical insect studies*) has been mooted as well. If you can now take a degree in *Anthropocene studies*, how long before there will be programmes in Capitalocene studies or Cthulhucene studies (or the dozens of other neologisms for the current geological era)?

All of these are interdisciplinary fields in which literary analysis may operate, but there are also a range of terminologies specifically within literary studies that provide distinct foci in the more-than-humanities. Particular literary forms and genres have their own formulations: think of *ecopoetics* (or indeed *zoopoetics*) and the *ecoGothic* as elements of ecocriticism and literary animal studies (or *zoocriticism* if you prefer). This raises questions about the relationship of literary-critical practice to theoretical paradigms. *Ecofeminism* has long been part of debates around animals and ecology, as has *ecoMarxism*, both of which link intersectionally with *postcolonial ecocriticism*. *Posthumanism* not only has an intimate relationship to animal studies through a shared questioning of the idea of the 'human' and how it structures the idea of the 'animal' but also has a bearing on the environmental humanities through the realization that human life is structured, in Clark's phrasing, by 'multiple material conditions and relationships' that exceed the human.[69]

There are so many terms in, across and at the edges of animal studies and the environmental humanities that it is hard to resist the seductions of parody. Every creature and corner of the Earth deserves its forum for interdisciplinary enquiry; bring on the slug humanities and critical car park studies. A certain exasperation is apparent even within the work of those scholars responsible for forming this entangled critical vocabulary. In the very essay he coins the term 'ecocriticism', Rueckert bemoans the 'senseless creation of new models just to displace or replace old ones, or to beat out a competitor in the intellectual marketplace' (and this at a time when the range of isms was much more restricted than it is today).[70] Mark Bould is more charitable in surveying the propagation of new geological eras. After listing thirty-seven of the Anthropocene's rivals, Bould suggests that the 'proliferation of terms' is not 'the result of bandwagon-jumpers, coining career-making catchphrases for the heady fame and giddying royalties academic publishing bestows'.[71] While Bould's claim that 'changing the name changes the story' is of specific application to the politically loaded question of what to call the current moment, there is a wider relevance to his reflection on the 'power a name has to construe a narrative ...

indicate an orientation, shape perception'.[72] Rueckert's and Bould's diverging attitudes provide a salutary reminder that academic knowledge production is both stimulated by a sincere intention to tackle urgent material and intellectual issues and conditioned by the specific contexts of institutional cultures with all the compromises and limitations they create.

In what follows, I focus on three of the emerging fields within the wider more-than-humanities – *vegan studies*, *the energy humanities* and *extinction studies* – that serve as vantage points from which to think through the intersections and tensions between pro-animal and ecological approaches. Each of these critical fields has a different situation: vegan studies is intimately connected with animal studies; the energy humanities is closer to the environmental humanities; extinction studies is located more centrally between them though in a way that produces significant tensions. These fields are each, evidently, focused on a key theme in urgent academic and public debates around sustainable transition. In Part 1, vegan studies facilitates analysis of meat; the energy humanities explores automobility as an instantiation of the larger question of oil in Part 2; extinction studies provides a perspective on conservation in Part 3. More specifically, each of these approaches allows for analysis of a particular form of innovation that has come to the fore in the context of sustainable transition and which functions – though not always in a straightforward way – as a mechanism for the continuing absorption of imaginings of a more sustainable world into the hegemonic regime of global capital.

Consequently, this book serves as an analysis of three forms of neoliberal environmental salvation: cultured meat (CM) (which is to say meat grown in a laboratory) as a way to render animal protein sustainable; electric vehicles (EVs) as a way of moving mass, private transportation beyond fossil fuels; and developments in natural capital accounting as a way of securing the future of endangered species. Each of the book's three parts consists of three chapters, opening with a contextual analysis of its topic that situates it in relation to animal studies and the environmental humanities and sets out the aims and orientations of the more specific critical approach it is in dialogue with. Thereafter, I offer literary-critical case studies that demonstrate how the links between animal studies and the environmental humanities, expressed respectively in vegan studies, the energy humanities and extinction studies, provide a literary-critical perspective on the meaning of the forms of transition the book addresses.

The book begins with Part 1, 'Meat: Ecocarnism and Vegan Studies'. Food is an area of huge ecological and ethical anxiety. To Nora Castle and Graeme Macdonald, 'As a core element of both the problems with and solutions to the climate crisis, the global food system is the nexus of an array of future-oriented concerns.'[73] Meat, in particular, is a central element of discourses of sustainable transition. At the same time, meat, and its rejection in veganism, is perhaps the clearest articulation of the tension between pro-animal and ecological positions. Accordingly, Chapter 1: 'Eating well in the Anthropocene', reassesses the relationship between environmentalist and pro-animal positions on meat. Industrial animal agriculture as it is currently configured is a deeply unsustainable practice that is also responsible for enormous animal suffering; as such its repudiation constitutes a point of connection between environmental and animal ethics. Reading the harm perpetrated by meat-eating in relation to debates around the Anthropocene and Capitalocene as rival terms for the current era reveals, however, a significantly more complex picture. Is it the idea of the human or the machinations of capital that underpin the horrors of meat? A focus on capital suggests that – in ecological terms – not all meat is equally harmful. While the impacts of large-scale animal agriculture are devastating, certain forms of small-scale meat production, particularly those under the designation regenerative agriculture, are increasingly heralded for their positive environmental impact. Emerging technologies of CM – growing animal protein in a laboratory cell culture without the need to raise and kill an animal – make an even more robust ethical promise: sustainable meat which may even appeal to some vegans. In their commitment to sustainability, regenerative agriculture and CM are thus two versions of what Melanie Joy terms ecocarnism. At the same time, while many advocates have been keen to emphasize veganism's environmental credentials, it is also clear that a vegan diet is not exterior to networks of harm, especially in the context of the rise of what Eva Giraud calls 'plant-based capitalism' (think for example of plastic-wrapped, ultra-processed meat replacements). It is far from clear how to eat well in the Anthropocene. Given the centrality of narrative in these debates, literary studies offers a significant vantage from which to view the cultural and historical formation of these debates. The chapter ends by setting out the methodology that informs Chapters 2 and 3. Taking a vegan studies approach to the literary representation to two forms of ecocarnism – regenerative agriculture and CM – facilitates a critical assessment of the construction of the meanings of sustainable meat while also, conversely, asking questions of the contours of vegan studies.

Chapter 2, 'Wendell Berry's carnopoetics', explores regenerative agriculture through Berry's extensive, ecologically resonant writing, closely connected to his life as a farmer in Kentucky. Berry is notable for his implacable opposition to corporate power in farming and elsewhere, a position that translates to a sharp criticism of industrial animal agriculture. In contrast, small-scale animal husbandry embodies for Berry what it means 'to eat with understanding and with gratitude'.[74] Meat plays a significant role in the landscape aesthetics of Berry's poetry as a sign of an ecological connection between farmer and world. While Berry's writing can thus be read in relation to the established critical discourse of ecopoetics and the emerging field of zoopoetics (both of which are premised on the apprehension of more-than-human agency in the text), I posit carnopoetics as a term more exactly attuned to the ecocarnist ethos of pastoral poetry. This tradition is premised not just on the representation of food animals but also on the wider portrayal of flourishing, biodiverse landscapes that embody regenerative agriculture's recurrent claim of its hospitality to wild creatures, an ethos which I trace in two Berry poems: 'Work Song' (1977) and *The Farm* (1995). The depiction of the landscapes of meat in these texts displays a harmonious integration of human families, wild creatures and livestock, which connects with the conception of ecological holism, used in the work of J. Baird Callicott and Val Plumwood as a point from which to criticize plant-based diets. The well-established vegan counter-argument to this position focuses on the lives of animals against the ostensible harmony of the world, a theme which Berry addresses directly in 'For the Hog Killing' (1979). Although the poem focuses on the injunction to look a pig in the eyes when you kill it, Berry pivots away from the pig's individual experience to identify its death as a wider sign of the farmer's 'wedding with the world' with which the pig is apparently compliant. While my analysis of Berry's ecocarnism exemplifies a vegan studies critique of the cultural construction of carnivoracity, Berry's anti-capitalist agrarian politics and poetics also, however, make an intriguingly awkward fit with a vegan studies that aspires to be about more than diet.

Chapter 3, 'Cultured meat landscapes', juxtaposes the organic aesthetics of Berry's smallholding with a discussion of CM as an exemplary form of neoliberal technological innovation in the service of ethical eating. The enticements of speculation about the possible social, ecological and gastronomic impacts of the partial – or even complete – replacement of conventional meat with CM are considerable and have been underway at least since the late nineteenth century, flickering between utopian and dystopian imaginaries as a sign of perfected technological accomplishment and/or the sign of a world gone wrong. While much of the critical musing on CM to date has focused on the substance or 'body' of CM, this chapter explores the long relationship of CM to depictions of landscape and ecology in science and speculative fiction through an analysis of Mary Bradley Lane's 1881 utopian novel *Mizora: A Prophecy*, perhaps CM's first literary incarnation. *Mizora* is the tale of a woman taken by a whirlpool into a mysterious other domain beneath the North Pole, a feminist utopia in which agriculture has been replaced by the chemical production of food. So developed is Mizoran technology that food is pure and plentiful and central to a perfected society. The depiction of CM in this context is associated with a lush aesthetics that emerges both in the Mizora's lavish gastronomy and in the harmonious arrangement of the landscape. Without the need for agriculture, space is given over to parks and gardens in an idealized geography that also includes notable achievements in renewable energy and sustainable transport. This is no haven for creatures, however. Animals have been eradicated as part of a network of eliminations that has also seen the eradication of people of colour; in this way, Lane's CM is not so much utopian protein as eugenic protein. The limitations of Lane's utopia connect with the longer history of CM in which its artificiality produces a nostalgic fetishization for the lifeways of traditional agriculture. Consequently, I argue, CM and regen-ag can be read as conjoined elements of a carnist world, a connection that emphasizes the need for a vegan landscape aesthetics that moves beyond the ecocarnist formulation of the imbrication of ecology and ontology through meat and comprises a holistic form of resistance to a compromised neoliberal politics of sustainable food.

Part 2, 'Automobility: Animals, Oil and the Energy Humanities', explores the mass use of privately owned cars as one of the most visible, harmful and intractable elements of global petroculture. While the development of the energy humanities pivots on many of the foundational topics of the environmental humanities – most notably the dependence on fossil fuels – there has also been growing attention to oil, and particularly to the connected issue of automobility in animal studies, most notably in relation to the previously underexplored topic of roadkill. These three chapters examine the transition of automobility from petrol-fuelled vehicles to EVs, demonstrating how ecological and pro-animal perspectives taken in dialogue with one another shape a critique of the idea of car culture per se as a facet of neoliberalism that remains tied to networks of violence even in its supposedly sustainable form.

In Chapter 4, 'Carnism and motonormativity', I continue the thread of Part 1, and Chapter 3 in particular, by arguing that there is a close structural similarity between CM and EVs as ostensibly sustainable forms of technology that in effect serve to redeem ethically dubious practices for global capital. While the EV promises to liberate transportation from the devastation of petroculture (in the same way that CM liberates meat from the horrors of industrial animal agriculture), it remains linked to forms of 'car harm' that have taken a massive toll on human and animal life while contributing significantly to climate change and other interlinked ecological issues. If the readymade solution to the violence of the car would be to pursue alternative forms of transport beyond mass automobility (in the same way that the most obvious solution to the problem of meat is to eat plants), motonormativity, which is to say the deep-seated cultural and ideological attachment to cars, makes this outcome improbable. Animal studies' recent turn to the question of automobility, I argue, provides a forceful contribution to arguments against the hegemony of cars that energizes ecological critiques of car use with the aim of creating a critical movement for a post-automobile culture.

In a structure that mirrors Part 1, Part 2 offers two literary case studies based on contrasting approaches to the problem of automobility by investigating the fictional imagining of cars on either side of sustainable transition. Chapter 5, 'Roadkill in J. G. Ballard's autoscapes', explores the relationship between space and animal death in one of the most notable contributors to the literary representation of automobility. Ballard is a writer with a strong critical connection to the theme of environmental catastrophe, expressed notably in his early apocalyptic fictions from the 1960s but also developing in a loose trilogy of novels about automobility and oil in the 1970s: *Crash* (1973), *The Concrete Island* (1974) and *High Rise* (1975). Concentrating on the first and third of these, I examine the depiction of roadkill as an integral part of Ballard's imagining of Britain's 'autoscapes', which is to say landscapes structured around automobility. *Crash* – Ballard's infamous novel of the sexual allure of traffic accidents – unfolds in an environment devoid of more-than-human life; tellingly, animals are absent from the novel, except in three episodes in which dogs are run over and killed. These moments, I argue, are crucial to the meaning of Ballard's exploration of the psychosexual marriage of humans and technology (which resonates with the depiction of marriage in Berry's carnopoetics). *High Rise* picks up – from the first page – on the image of dead dogs in its imagining of social unrest in a luxury tower block. Although cars are less in the narrative foreground here than in *Crash*, the alienated lives of the novel's protagonists are structured by automobility. The nightmare visions of car culture in *Crash* and *High Rise* may not correspond to a straightforward anti-car politics or ethics, but there is, I argue, a significant consanguinity between Ballard's automobile ontologies and Matthew Calarco's radical vegan critique of automobility, which in turn inflects Ballard's environmental imagination.

Chapter 6, 'Multispecies automobilities in Nnedi Okorafor's Africanfuturism', explores the process of transition away from oil in *Lagoon* (2014) and *The Shadow Speaker* (first published in 2007 and revised in 2023). If Ballard's work can be taken as exemplary of oil ontologies, Okorafor's fiction is premised on an imaginative explosion of categories of being. Her work involves, as Eugenia Ossana summarizes, 'an expansive interplanetary macro cosmos where human, botanical, animal, mythical, and technological beings are entangled and hybridized at will'.[75] Integral to this is a sustained criticism of global, and specifically Nigerian, petroculture that contributes to a long engagement with questions around energy in Afro- and Africanfuturism. In imagining the end of oil – or at least the beginning of its end – Okorafor showcases a range of automobile speculations, through EVs in *Lagoon* and via a more fantastic vision of green transport in *The Shadow*

Speaker. Although Okorafor's post-oil imaginings consistently involve multispecies perspectives (in contrast to Ballard's sterile autoscapes), this element of her depiction of automobility is closer to an ecological holism than it is to a species justice position. In this way, the redemption of car culture for an alternative future after petrocapitalist hegemony can also, at times, sound a jarring note through the obfuscation of the extractive regime behind EVs and a narrative link between the escape from petroculture and the celebration of meat.

Part 3, 'Conservation: Neoliberalism and Extinction Studies', moves from technological innovations to financial mechanisms as the key context for sustainable transition in the context of the global biodiversity crisis. In this way, the book's final part provides the clearest account of the structuring of urgent questions in ecological and animal ethics in relation to economic imperatives. Chapter 7, '(Un)natural capital and endangered species', offers an account of the development of discourses of natural capital and biodiversity offsetting as increasingly prominent ways for governments to balance the demands of corporations with the exigencies of global ecological crisis. While proponents of these policies often identify them as part of a portfolio of diverse approaches to the natural world, critics have highlighted their tendency to overwhelm or sideline non-economic forms of value. Biodiversity offsetting by this argument risks the reduction of beings to exchangeable elements of a system that empties them – and the landscapes and environments they inhabit – of their own specific significance by undermining any sense of their particularity or intrinsic value. It is precisely the interplay between these conflicting rationales for conservation that highlights the significance of extinction studies as a multidisciplinary field that endeavours to understand the 'profound implications of [the] cascade of loss' of the current extinction crisis.[76] Evidently extinction bestrides animal studies and the environmental humanities as a key ecological symptom of global crisis that proceeds through the death of animals. Extinction is also one of the themes in which environmental and animal ethics find themselves locked into an intractable quandary. Should invasive species be culled to allow endangered creatures to flourish? While questions such as this emphasize the divergence of environmental and animal ethics in this context, the question of neoliberalism's absorption of conservation through biodiversity offsetting encourages a more positive sense of an alliance between them in formulating points of resistance to green capitalism.

The literary-critical case studies that follow pair an early anticipation of neoliberal economic discourses of conservation with a more recent, explicit narrative of the intricate machinations of offset ideology. Chapter 8, 'Comedy, capital and the poetics of encounter in Douglas Adams and Mark Cawardine's *Last Chance to See*', explores the (neo)colonial origins of the conservation travel narrative as a key part of the ideological contours of this textual form. As the account of a series of journeys to the tropical world in the quest to witness endangered species, *Last Chance to See* is a text squarely in this tradition but one that derives much of its comedy from a knowing engagement with its own ideological implications. Drawing on Douglas Adams's credentials as the author of *The Hitch Hikers' Guide to Galaxy* series – a set of novels that unravel the logics of anthropocentrism and bureaucracy – this chapter argues for *Last Chance to See* as a text that accommodates both ecological and pro-animal arguments against the commodification of animal life in the context of extinction. To reach this point I argue against Ursula Heise's reading of the text as a justification for an ecological over an animal studies approach to the question of extinction by examining the text's quirky representation of non-endangered creatures alongside the charismatic fauna that form the book's central focus.

The final chapter of Part 3 is 'Disentangled creatures in Ned Beauman's *Venomous Lumpsucker*'. Beauman's 2022 novel is perhaps the first to focus directly on the application of natural capital approaches to the question of extinction in a comedy eco-thriller that focuses on the plight of an endangered but highly intelligent fictional fish. At the centre of the novel are the contrasting reasons for seeking the lumpsucker's continued survival, represented by Beauman's two main protagonists: Halyard who works for a mining company, navigating the world's new system of extinction credits, and Resaint a biologist whose job is to evaluate the intelligence of threatened species. For Halyard, conservation is all about money; for Resaint there are darker and more complex reasons for ensuring the lumpsucker's survival. Beauman's novel involves explicit reference to the field of extinction studies – Thom van Dooren's work is an acknowledged influence – which unfolds through the theme of entanglement and more particularly the disentanglement inherent to the abstract domain of extinction accounting. There are also moments that are reminiscent of Jacques Derrida's pivotal work on animals that emerge in relation to a contrast between wonder and calculation integral to Resaint's angsty reflections on extinction which lead her to fantasize sacrificing herself to animals as an act of retributive justice which also stands as a manifestation of and comment on the idea of ecological holism. In its attention to both the system of global capital and the flesh of its victims, *Venomous Lumpsucker*, I argue, illustrates a close conjunction between the concerns of animal and ecological ethics in the context of extinction.

The conclusion picks up on the reference to Derrida in Chapter 9 to explore the operations of green capitalism as a form of calculation against which literary reading serves as an instantiation of the undecidable, marking the possibility of a free decision that isn't determined by any pre-existing programme. Connectedly, the relationship between animal and ecological ethics might be taken as an aporia in which contradictions are not resolved by the subordination of one term to the other but held onto as an integral element of justice. I end, in more personal mode, by reflecting on the hermeneutics of suspicion which shapes my response to hegemonic conceptions of sustainable transition and by gesturing towards different forms, ideologies and practices of transition in grass roots activism.

Notes

1 Global Carbon Project, 'Fossil Fuel CO_2 Emissions Increase Again in 2024', https://globalcarbonbudget.org/fossil-fuel-co2-emissions-increase-again-in-2024/, accessed 14 February 2025.

2 Global Carbon Project', 'Fossil Fuel CO_2 Emissions'.

3 Tom Espiner, 'BP Set to Scale Back Green Investments as Profits Drop sharply', *BBC News*, 11 February 2025, https://www.bbc.co.uk/news/articles/c30d4ernzqjo, accessed 14 February 2025.

4 Andreas Malm and Wim Carton, *Overshoot: How the World Surrendered to Climate Breakdown* (London: Verso, 2024), 13.

5 Patrick Greenfield, Daisy Dunne and Giuliana Viglione, 'More Than Half of Countries Are Ignoring Biodiversity Pledges', *The Guardian*, 24 February 2025, https://www.theguardian.com/environment/2025/feb/24/countries-biodiversity-pledges-rome-cop16-aoe, accessed 27 February 2025.

6 Malm and Carton, *Overshoot*, 24.
7 See, for example, Attracta Mooney and Jim Pickard, 'UK Climate Activists Jailed for At Least Four Years over Road Blocks', *The Financial Times*, 18 July 2024, https://www.ft.com/content/efa11ff6-555d-44a4-84f9-469e5e58c37d, accessed 14 February 2025.
8 United Nations, 'United Nations Conference on Environment and Development, Rio de Janeiro, Brazil, 3–14 June', https://www.un.org/en/conferences/environment/rio1992, accessed 27 February 2025.
9 United Nations, 'What Is Sustainable Development?', https://www.un.org/sustainabledevelopment/blog/2023/08/what-is-sustainable-development/, accessed 14 February 2025.
10 Cited in Katariina Koistinen, Anna Kuokkanen, Mirja Mikkilä, Jarkko Levänen and Lassi Linnanen, 'Sustainable Transition', *Encyclopedia of Sustainable Management*, https://link.springer.com/referenceworkentry/10.1007/978-3-031-25984-5_434, accessed 14 February 2025.
11 Ione Wells, 'Amazon Forest Felled to Build Road for Climate Summit', *BBC News*, 12 March 2025, https://www.bbc.co.uk/news/articles/c9vy191rgn1o, accessed 30 April 2025.
12 Malm and Carton, *Overshoot*, 90.
13 Imre Szeman, *On Petrocultures: Globalisation, Energy, and Culture* (Morgantown: West Virginia University Press, 2019), 80.
14 Adrian Parr, *The Wrath of Capital: Neoliberalism and Climate Change Politics* (New York: Columbia University Press, 2013), 19, 20.
15 Arturo Escobar, *Encountering Development: The Making and Unmaking of the Third World* (Princeton, NJ: Princeton University Press, 2011), 202.
16 Escobar, *Encountering Development*, 205; Parr, *The Wrath of Capital*, 72.
17 Szeman, *On Petrocultures*, 86.
18 Szeman, *On Petrocultures*, 71.
19 William Rueckert, 'Literature and Ecology: An Experiment in Ecocriticism', *The Iowa Review* 9.1 (1978), 71–86, 85.
20 Cheryl Glotfelty, 'Introduction: Literary Studies in an Age of Environmental Crisis'. In *The Ecocriticism Reader: Landmarks in Literary Ecology*. Edited by Cheryll Glotfelty and Harold Fromm, xv–xxxvii, xxiv (Athens: University of Georgia Press, 1996).
21 Jonathan Bate, *The Song of the Earth* (London: Pan Macmillan, 2001), 283.
22 J. Andrew Hubbell and John C. Ryan, *Introduction to the Environmental Humanities* (London: Routledge, 2021), 170.

23 Robert S. Emmett and David E. Nye, *The Environmental Humanities: A Critical Introduction* (Cambridge, MA: MIT Press, 2017), 2.
24 Greg Garrard, 'Introduction'. In *The Oxford Handbook of Ecocriticism*. Edited by Greg Garrard, 1–24, 1 (Oxford: Oxford University Press, 2014).
25 Serenella Iovino and Serpil Oppermann, 'Introduction: Stories Come to Matter'. In *Material Ecocriticism*. Edited by Serenella Iovino and Serpil Oppermann, 1–21, 2 (Bloomington: Indiana University Press, 2014). On ecocriticism's waves see Scott Slovic, 'On the Third Wave of Ecocriticism', *Ecozon@* 1.1 (2010), 4–10; and Mohammed Ataullah Nuri, 'Three Waves of Ecocriticism: An Overview', *Horizon* 2.5 (2020), 253–68.
26 Sam Solnick, *Poetry and the Anthropocene: Ecology, Biology and Technology in Contemporary British and Irish Poetry* (Abingdon: Routledge, 2016), 26.
27 Mary Sanders Pollock and Catherine Rainwater, *Figuring Animals: Essays on Animal Images in Art, Literature, Philosophy and Popular Culture* (New York: Palgrave Macmillan, 2005).
28 Timothy Clark, *The Value of Ecocriticism* (Cambridge: Cambridge University Press, 2019), 13.
29 Peter Singer, *Animal Liberation: A New Ethics for Our Treatment of Animals* (London: Pimlico, 1995 [1975]), xiii.
30 Singer, *Animal Liberation*, 23.
31 Garry Marvin, 'Wild Killing: Contesting the Animal in Hunting'. In *Killing Animals*. Edited by The Animal Studies Group, 10–29, 26 (Urbana: University of Illinois Press, 2006).
32 Paul Waldau, *Animal Studies: An Introduction* (Oxford: Oxford University Press, 2013), 1.
33 Marianne DeKoven, 'Why Animals Now?, *PMLA* 124.2 (March 2009), 361–9, 364.
34 Karen L. Edwards, Derek Ryan and Jane Spencer, 'Introduction', *Reading Literary Animals: Medieval to Modern* (London: Routledge, 2020), 1.
35 Matthew Calarco, *Animal Studies: The Key Concepts* (London: Routledge, 2021), 62.
36 Greg Garrard, *Ecocriticism*, 2nd edn (Abingdon: Routledge, 2012), 148–9.
37 Garrard, *Ecocriticism*, 149.
38 Garrard, *Ecocriticism*, 150.
39 Garrard, *Ecocriticism*, 150.
40 See, for example, John Simons, *Animal Rights and the Politics of Literary Representation* (London: Palgrave, 2002).

41 Frederike Middelhof and Sebastian Schönbeck. 'Coming to Terms: The Poetics of More-Than-Human Worlds'. In *Texts, Animals, Environments: Zoopoetics and Ecopoetics*. Edited by Frederike Middelhof and Sebastian Schönbeck, 11–40, 14 (Berlin: Rombach Verlag, 2019).
42 James Radcliffe, *Green Politics: Dictatorship or Democracy?* (Basingstoke: Macmillan, 2000), 117.
43 J. Baird Callicott, 'Animal Liberation: A Triangular Affair', *Environmental Ethics* 2.4 (1980), 311–38, 333.
44 Callicot, 'Animal Liberation', 334.
45 Callicott, 'Animal Liberation', 318.
46 Val Plumwood, 'Animals and Ecology: Towards a Better Integration', https://openresearch-repository.anu.edu.au/bitstream/1885/41767/3/Vegpap6.pdf, 1, accessed 27 February 2025.
47 Sue Donaldson and Will Kymlicka, *Zoopolis: A Political Theory of Animal Rights* (Oxford: Oxford University Press, 2011), 3.
48 Donaldson and Kymlicka, *Zoopolis*, 4.
49 Donaldson and Kymlicka, *Zoopolis*, 4.
50 Cary Wolfe, *What Is Posthumanism*? (Minneapolis: University of Minnesota Press, 2010), 115.
51 Graham Huggan, 'Editorial', *Green Letters* 23.1 (2019), 1–4.
52 James Chandler, 'Critical Disciplinarity', *Critical Enquiry* 30.2 (2004), 355–60, 358. For an application of Chandler's work to animal studies see Cary Wolfe, 'Human, All Too Human: "Animal Studies" and the Humanities', *PMLA* 124.2 (2009), 564–75, 569.
53 Anthony J. Nocella II, John Sorenson, Kim Socha, and Atsuko Matsuoka, 'Introduction: The Emergence of Critical Animal Studies'. In *Defining Critical Animal Studies: An Intersectional Social Justice Approach for Liberation*. Edited by Anthony J. Nocella II, John Sorenson, Kim Socha and Atsuko Matsuoka, ix–xxxvi, xxvi (New York: Peter Lang, 2014).
54 Calarco, *Animal Studies*, 43.
55 Margo DeMello, *Animals and Society: An Introduction to Human–Animal Studies* (New York: Columbia University Press, 2012), 4.
56 Nik Taylor and Richard Twine, 'Introduction: Locating the "Critical" in Critical Animal Studies'. In *The Rise of Critical Animal Studies*. Edited by Nik Taylor and Richard Twine, 1–15, 2 (Abingdon: Routledge, 2014).
57 Michael Lundblad, 'From Animal to Animality Studies', *PMLA* 124.2 (2009), 496–502, 497.
58 Eben Kirksey and Stefan Helmreich, 'The Emergence of Multispecies Ethnography', *Cultural Anthropology* 25.4 (2010), 545–76, 545.

59 Thom van Dooren, Eben Kirksey and Ursula Münster, 'Multispecies Studies: Cultivating Arts of Attentiveness', *Environmental Humanities* 8.1 (2016), 1–23, 3.
60 See Emmett and Nye, *Environmental Humanities*, 5.
61 Emmett and Nye, *Environmental Humanities*, 8.
62 Huggan, 'Editorial', 3.
63 Huggan, 'Editorial', 2.
64 Huggan, 'Editorial', 2–3.
65 Calarco, *Animal Studies*, 43.
66 Van Dooren et al., 'Multispecies Studies', 3.
67 Wolfe, *What Is Posthumanism?*, 123.
68 Taylor and Twine, 'Introduction', 2.
69 Clark, *Value of Ecocriticism*, 14.
70 Rueckert, 'Literature and Ecology', 72.
71 Mark Bould, *The Anthropocene Unconscious: Climate, Catastrophe, Culture* (London: Verso, 2021), 8.
72 Bould, *Anthropocene Unconscious*, 9.
73 Nora Castle and Graeme Macdonald, 'Introduction: Food Futures', *Science Fiction Studies* 49.2 (2022), 209–16.
74 Wendell Berry, 'The Pleasures of Eating'. In *What Are People For?*, 145–52, 151 (Berkeley, CA: Counterpoint, 2010).
75 Eugenia Ossana, 'Decolonizing the Desert: From Necropolitical Dynamics to Ubuntu Communal Re-Imaginings in Nnedi Okorafor's *Noor* (2021)', *ISLE* 32.3 (2024), 1–20, 1.
76 The Extinction Studies Working Group, 'About Us', http://extinctionstudies.org/about/, accessed 2 May 2025.

PART ONE

Meat: Ecocarnism and vegan studies

CHAPTER 1

Eating well in the Anthropocene

It has become an axiomatic element of debates about the relationship between pro-animal and ecological thought to claim that, despite the tensions between them, they are united in their opposition to industrial animal agriculture.[1] It is easy to see why. The number of land animals killed for food in 2020 was calculated by the UN Food and Agriculture Organisation at 73,162,794,213 (seventy-three billion, one hundred sixty-two million, seven hundred ninety-four thousand, two hundred and thirteen); the figure for aquatic species was considerably higher, possibly over two trillion.[2] This vast enterprise comes at a substantial ecological cost: animal agriculture is responsible for 14.5 per cent of global greenhouse gas emissions,[3] functions as the 'single largest driver of habitat loss'[4] and creates water scarcity and pollution in many locations.[5] Meat, and the question of food more widely, is thus integral to the project of sustainable development; as the UN Development Programme summarizes, food systems 'are in crisis and need to be radically transformed'.[6] If there is ample ground for an animal–environmental alliance and an integration of these perspectives with hegemonic conceptions of sustainable transition, a wider scrutiny of the culture and politics of meat-eating indicates a shared antipathy to factory farming as part of a more contradictory picture that emphasizes the fault-lines between animal and environmental ethics as well as a complex relationship to capitalist foodways.

One way to gloss the extensive violence of industrial animal agriculture would be to agree with George Monbiot that meat is 'consuming the planet'.[7] Framing animal agriculture in these terms evokes meat's involvement with the conception of the Anthropocene, one of the most prominent – if contested – conceptual hooks of the environmental humanities and a vantage point from which cracks start to appear in a green–animal pact around meat. The Anthropocene names the realization that, as John Parham puts it, 'humanity's indelible alteration of the Earth' is sufficiently profound to constitute a 'new geological era'.[8] Industrial meat production has contributed significantly to this alteration. In an example of what Heather Anne Swanson calls the Anthropocene's 'banality', it may be chicken bones that constitute the clearest geological signature of global meat culture.[9] Carys Bennett et al. note how broiler chickens (the 'most numerous vertebrate ... species on land') comprise a 'vast bird biomass ... unprecedented ... in Earth's geological history' with a growth rate that is 'five times faster than meat chickens from the 1950s' and bones that are 'often deformed'.[10] As these denatured birds 'become fossilised markers of the time when humans reigned the planet', the commodification and destruction of animal lives becomes an integral part of the story of the Anthropocene.[11]

Any sense that the concept of the Anthropocene anchors the connection between animal studies and the environmental humanities in the context of meat is pressurized, however, by the weight of ongoing debates around the naming of the present geological moment. Contestations of the idea of the Anthropocene often hinge on its reification of the generalized figure of the *Anthropos*. Jason W. Moore's influential rejection of Anthropocene in favour of Capitalocene is based on the assertion that it is not the figure of the *Anthropos* (which is to say 'humanity as an undifferentiated whole') that underpins ecological emergency but rather 'the endless accumulation of capital'.[12] After all, humans are not all equally responsible for climate change; culpability is strongly linked to economic privilege. One of the consequences of Moore's rebranding of the Anthropocene most pertinent to the question of meat is the shift he institutes from ontology to economics as the main cause of planetary harm. These domains are not necessarily easy to separate; think, for example, of the conception of *Homo economicus* as a model for the internalization of a capitalist ethos. Nonetheless, Moore's focus on economics over ontology is significant because it provides a limit point to the implication of meat in the formulation of the Anthropocene as a signifier of global catastrophe.

Debates around the relationship between meat and the idea of the human – the ontology of meat-eating to put it another way – are a key battleground in debates around dietary ethics. Is it natural for humans to eat meat? Or, as People for the Ethical Treatment of Animals (PETA) contends, is 'a natural diet ... in fact, vegan'?[13] The role of the 'natural' will surface again later in this and subsequent chapters, but for now, in deference to Moore's position, a simpler point will suffice. Some people eat meat and some people do not eat meat, so it is unhelpful to point the finger at the dietary predilections of a generalized *Anthropos* to account for meat's role in ecological crisis. The problem is not a human appetite for meat per se (which is in any case disputed) but rather the damage perpetrated by the corporations behind most global meat production. Nor indeed, by this argument, is the refusal of meat a complete solution to the challenge of ethical eating in the Anthropocene if it ultimately serves to buttress the dominant economic system with all the damage and injustice that entails. Accordingly, the increasing availability of vegan products in mainstream consumer culture has given rise to critical analysis of what Eva Haifa Giraud calls 'plant-based capitalism', an ideological process through which veganism is incorporated into the economic regime it is often taken to contest.[14]

Moreover, the identification of capital (rather than the *Anthropos*) as the key driver of planetary harm in turn connects to an idealization of supposedly pre-capitalist and/or pre-colonial foodways that increasingly feature in defences of smaller-scale forms of animal agriculture and meat consumption. Rob Percival's exploration of the ethical complexities of meat in the modern world devotes extended, approving attention to the sustainable and respectful use of animal food in Indigenous cultures.[15] Notwithstanding the urgent necessity of standing as allies with Indigenous causes, such approaches carry some risk: detaching culturally specific dietary practices from their contexts to make broader claims for the virtues of meat-eating oversimplifies the range of historical and environmental factors in play while also potentially revivifying colonial myths of the 'ecological Indian'. Even so, there are clear disparities between the ecological impact of different methods and kinds of meat consumption that complicate the relationship between pro-animal and environmental food politics. Meat is not reducible to the global industrial machine of animal agriculture in the twentieth and twenty-first centuries. Certain forms of local, principally organic, animal agriculture have been heralded by meat advocates for their positive contribution to sustainability. Not all meat, by this argument, is consuming the planet.

Consequently, the idea of the Anthropocene and its repudiations reveal a more complex and divisive set of discourses around meat in and between pro-animal and ecological discourses than that suggested by their shared opposition to factory farming. In other words, the problem of factory farming may bring ecological and pro-animal positions together, but what to do about it exacerbates the tensions between them. To frame the question in terms taken from Jacques Derrida's influential reflections on food, how to 'eat well' in the Anthropocene? For Derrida, the question is not a matter of nourishment or pleasure but of recognizing the complex set of relationships food initiates: 'One never eats entirely on one's own: this constitutes the rule underlying the statement, "One must eat well". It is a rule offering infinite hospitality.'[16] Derrida's conception of an unlimited hospitality encourages attentiveness to all other beings, though his position does not straightforwardly equate ethical eating with vegetarianism (or veganism). In a phrase that could be taken as prescient of the emergence of 'plant-based capitalism', Derrida asserts that 'vegetarians, too, partake of animals'.[17] In this way, Derrida's formulation of 'eating well' encapsulates the ethical dilemmas that structure the interplay between ecological and species justice in relation to meat.

In what follows in this chapter, I explore three of the most influential current answers to the dilemma of ethical eating in an era of planetary crisis: veganism, regenerative agriculture and cultured meat (CM). These options by no means exhaust the possibilities for a new food politics, but they do allow for an assessment of debates around the future of meat that illustrates the schism – and some points of connection – between environmental and pro-animal positions in the context of sustainable transition. This initial summary of the state of field provides a material and critical context for the analysis of the literary representation of meat later in Chapters 2 and 3, while also illustrating that debates around sustainable eating in academic and popular discourse are always already closely linked to literary frames of reference.

To take plant-based diets first, it is hardly surprising given industrial meat production's ecological consequences that, in Giraud's words, 'environmental politics has been a key driver of veganism's popularisation'.[18] Statistical analysis of the 'greenhouse gas emissions, land use, water use, eutrophication risk and potential biodiversity loss' of different dietary practices shows that 'the relationship between environmental impact and animal-based food consumption is clear'.[19] Veganism's moment appears to have arrived. For Ed Winters 'going vegan really is our best chance to save the planet'.[20] To PETA, 'all signs point to a vegan future ... like a benevolent person's utopian dream'.[21] The double fix promised by the link between veganism and sustainability is alluring – end cruelty and begin a new epoch of ecological eating with one seismic shift in global food culture – but rebuttals of vegan utopianism remain a staple ingredient of the public discourse around food politics. There has been a notable carnist backlash against what the meat advocate Jayne Buxton calls the 'plant-based juggernaut'.[22] Evidently, a product's vegan certification does not necessarily mean that it is free from implication in wider networks of harm. Think (in the spirit of a critical analysis of 'plant-based capitalism') of plastic packaging, fossil fuel-laden supply chains, petrochemical fertilizers, the freshwater footprint of crops like almonds or avocados or the small creatures accidentally killed in crop harvesting. As Alexis Shotwell contends, there 'is no food we can eat ... without deepening our ties to complex webs of suffering', a point which is not lost in self-reflective accounts of vegan ethics.[23] Emilia Quinn, for example, formulates the concept of 'vegan camp' as a 'way of working through horror and continuing to fight for change in the face of the seeming impossibility of living an ethical life'.[24] Such acknowledgements do not prevent recurrent accusations of vegan hypocrisy and assertions of carnism as a form of realpolitik. Shotwell's position picks up on Donna Haraway's insistence that there is 'no way to eat and not kill ... no way to pretend innocence, transcendence or a final peace'.[25] While Haraway sees veganism as an important form of 'witness to the extremity of the brutality in our "normal" relations with other animals',[26] her position is ultimately supportive of carnism. For Haraway, we should 'face nurturing and killing as an inescapable part of mortal companion species entanglements' so that we 'figure out how to honor the entangled labor of humans and animals together ... including animal husbandry right up to the table'.[27] To adapt a much-quoted phrase of Haraway's, we should 'stay with the trouble' of meat, rather than seeking to abolish it.[28]

Haraway's formulation is sustained by the trope of entanglement, a term which has become a dominant conceptual model for the environmental humanities, grounded in Darwin's foundational image of the 'tangled bank' as an image of evolutionary interdependence.[29] Among the many applications and dimensions of the idea of entanglement is a carnivorous environmentalism that reaches beyond industrial animal agriculture towards a sustainable global food system that includes meat. Melanie Joy terms this emergent confluence of carnism and sustainability discourses 'ecocarnism'. By this position, the solution to the problems of industrial animal agriculture 'is not to stop eating animals, but to eat animals who have been raised and killed "sustainably"'.[30] 'It's not the cow, it's the how' as the carnist slogan expresses it. Accordingly, there has been a surge of academic and public interest in forms of 'regenerative agriculture' celebrated for their potentially positive ecological contribution, playing a role in carbon sequestration, soil restoration and the increase of biodiversity. Regenerative agriculture is not just about producing meat – it is also a method for producing plant crops – but the integration of ruminants into the landscape is usually seen as key for their positive effect on soil. Agricultural systems such as silvopasture, an ancient 'integrated land use practice that combines trees, forage and livestock',[31] represent the ecological redemption of meat (at least locally sourced, organic meat) so that animal flesh has found a place (albeit often with a recommendation for reduced consumption) in the emerging phenomena of the climatarian and planetary health diets.[32] Just as veganism holds a utopian promise for some, regenerative agriculture also has a utopian flavour: imagine the happy critters, living free in the flourishing woods and meadows, expressing the ancient entanglement of humans, animals and the land. Such visions are profoundly nostalgic, comprising a 'future-past',[33] by which the development of sustainable animal agriculture mimics a primeval ecology characterized by vast herds of herbivores roaming across the Earth.

For all the optimism around regenerative agriculture, you still need to kill the animals before you eat them (even if welfare standards are characteristically higher than in factory farms). In this way, there are clear ethical limitations to the idea of entanglement, an argument that is energized by Giraud's work. In Giraud's analysis, while 'narratives of entanglement grasp something important about the world', attention 'also needs to be paid to the frictions, foreclosures and exclusions that play a constitutive role in the composition of lived reality'.[34] To celebrate meat as an enactment of the evolutionary entanglement of humans and animals is thus to foreclose or exclude consideration of the possibility of more rigorous care for other creatures. Evidently, vegan and regenerative utopias do not fit easily together. The development of CM, however, promises to take animal death out of the equation in a revolutionary leap for the world food system that adds a disruptive new element to debates around the ethics and politics of meat and its refusal. By growing animal protein in a laboratory cell culture, without the need to raise and slaughter an animal, CM entrepreneurs aspire to solve meat's multiple detriments through biotechnological innovation. We are on the cusp, it seems, of clean, green meat that takes ethical consumption to the next level: with greatly reduced land use, there would be no need to destroy habitat for cattle ranching. If regenerative agriculture represents one form of ecocarnism, CM is another.

Despite the scale of investment in CM since the first cultured hamburger was trialled in 2013 (some $3 billion between 2016 and 2022 alone), at the time of writing the success of this agricultural 'moonshot' is not assured. Indeed, some of the initial positivity around CM has edged towards despondency.[35] Even if CM production can be scaled up efficiently enough to make it affordable and profitable (which is by no means guaranteed), there are unanswered questions about the public appetite for lab meat and uncertainties about its ecological and animal justice prognosis. Joe Fassler notes that cultured chicken nuggets created in 2021 by UPSIDE foods, one of the key players in CM's development, generated 'more plastic waste than meat'.[36] Will CM be as green as its producers hope? How much energy will be required to make it? Will it really remove animal suffering from meat? Despite such lingering doubts, early marketing campaigns have emphasized CM's appeal as an antidote to mass animal slaughter and to wider ecological violence. Publicity for UPSIDE foods emphasizes the point, 'We love meat. We also love animals and the blue–green planet we share.' 'It's easy to be on the same side when we look for the UPSIDE', they pun.[37] Imagine a world (the logic runs) in which animal liberationists and environmental activists – whether vegans, vegetarians, omnivores or flexitarians – will sit down with a clear conscience to share a plate of cultured chicken nuggets. CM by this argument is the point at which ideological differences dissolve through the machinations of techno-capitalist speculation.

CM's connections to global capital are a prominent part of its ideological texture. Behind the glitz of its hypermodernity, CM is tied to the prevailing economic regime, as techno-capitalism aims to transcend the planet's material limits, offering boundless horizons for economic growth. The point is not just, as its manufacturers consistently note, that CM potentially allows meat-eating to continue unabated; it also supports a historical process by which, to borrow a phrase of Melinda Cooper's, 'the realms of biological (re)production and capital accumulation move closer together'.[38] Cooper's study of the wider domain of biotechnology as the expression of capitalist 'delirium' – the project of 'reinventing life beyond the limit' when the world's resources are close to exhaustion – makes it tempting to conclude that the reproduction of animal flesh in vitro is synonymous with the reproduction of capital itself. There is a counter-argument. Jan Dutkiewicz imagines a decoupling of CM and global capital. His call to 'socialize lab meat' insists that it is conceivable that a policy of 'lab-grown hamburgers for all' could 'make the benefits of a more just society ... more readily available to every member of society'.[39] Dutkiewicz is quick to admit that the task of wresting CM 'from corporate control' can seem 'far-fetched': the idea that the 'intellectual property' of a product funded by venture capital could be transferred into a 'public trust' flies in the face of established economic and political practices and assumptions.[40] Ultimately, it is easier to see CM as an exemplary strategy of neoliberalism – one that promises a better world by reframing 'consumption as virtue', as Fassler notes – than it is to see it as a contribution to a new turn in green and/or pro-animal socialism.[41]

An involvement with the power dynamics of global capital is one of a number of CM's associations that have encouraged dissent. Buxton's pro-meat tract sees CM as a form of corporate social control antithetical to her ecocarnist vision of rural community: 'saving the planet one cow at a time' through the adoption of forms of regenerative agriculture that work 'in harmony with nature'.[42] 'Nature' is a pivotal element of the conventional meat industry's defence against CM. While CM start-ups routinely insist their product *is* real meat, many meat advocates insist on a fundamental difference between lab meat and meat that comes from an animal; a 'fight against "fake" meat' has begun in order to enshrine this distinction in law.[43] In 2018, the US Cattleman's Association wrote to the US Department of Agriculture, Food Safety and Inspection Service (FSIS) to petition that

> products, which are not derived from animals born, raised, and harvested in the traditional manner, should not be permitted to be marketed as 'beef', or more broadly as 'meat' products. The labels of 'beef' or 'meat' should inform consumers that the product is derived naturally from animals as opposed to alternative proteins ... artificially grown in a laboratory.[44]

The key ingredients of the association's claim are the 'traditional manner' of meat production they support and the opposition between the natural and the artificial that CM is taken to embody. Legislation in Italy passed in 2023 'to pre-emptively ban cultured meat products in a bid to preserve its cultural heritage' emphasizes that anti-CM movements framed in these terms are developing global momentum.[45] Raising and killing animals for food, by this token, is sanctified by history (the continual reiteration of a practice that constitutes tradition) and by a conception of nature that such a history ostensibly articulates. There are clear objections to the familiar association of meat production with nature as a self-generated order of being – think again of the unnatural life of a broiler – but the key point here is a more basic one: meat 'naturally' comes from a creature not a lab.

Meat-eating's supposedly 'natural' appeal thus forms part of its enduring cultural legitimation; that meat is 'natural' comprises one of Melanie Joy's influential 'three ns of justification' (the others being that meat is 'normal and necessary').[46] For all its apparent self-evidence, the conception of meat as 'natural' involves notable philosophical tensions. Despite its centrality to popular discourses around food, the idea of the 'natural' has little credence in critical debates in animal studies and the environmental humanities. As Timothy Morton notes, for example, '*Anthropocene* ends the concept *nature*' (original emphasis).[47] In any case, the idea of 'nature' has long been understood to have an ambivalent connection to meat.

If meat-eating signifies participation in 'nature', it also embodies, in Nick Fiddes's account of the topic, the 'power over nature'.[48] Meat is a substance through which humans simultaneously connect with and transcend nature. Consequently, the 'natural' works for and against CM. On the one hand, CM is ostensibly protein at its most *un*natural: a Frankenfood which threatens centuries of agricultural practice. On the other hand, the rationale for its creation relies on the assumption that, as Believer Meat's CEO Nicole Johnson-Hoffman claims, 'people are biologically conditioned to crave meat'.[49] While an easier answer to the ethical problems of meat is to just eat plants, this is often ruled out as a solution based on assumptions about meat's overriding status as an object of desire, behind which resides the essentialist position Johnson-Hoffman articulates. If carnist desire cannot be vanquished, and meat-eating cannot continue in its current form in the era of runaway global heating, then the only solution to this natural urge is to make meat differently, either regeneratively or biotechnologically, though these versions of ecocarnism function as something like polar opposites: the former suggesting a movement *back* to the land and its history; the latter a movement away from it into a technocultural *future*.

There might seem good reasons for vegans to support CM's development. CM may not be perfect in animal liberationist terms (concerns remain, for instance, about the use of bovine foetal serum in its manufacture), but it is easy to see it as preferable to the current system of animal agriculture. Josh Milburn – one of the most prominent vegan supporters of CM – looks forward to a 'possible future in which animals are not hurt in the pursuit of food, but where meat is available for those who value it'.[50] Milburn's position exemplifies what Catherine Oliver calls techno-veganism: 'the coming together of vegan ethics and practices with scientific innovation'.[51] Contra Milburn's techno-vegan stance, a concerted attempt to discredit CM from a pro-animal perspective has emerged from the collective Clean Meat Hoax, which sees CM as a way 'to attack animal advocacy' and to strengthen the meat industry's long-term strategy of creating a diverse 'protein market' that includes 'meat from live animals'.[52] According to Clean Meat Hoax, if you buy into CM, you are 'helping destructive corporations greenwash and veganwash their products and reputations'. Because CM is often linked with the world's 'agribusiness giants' – 'ruthless, earth-destroying corporations' – its claims towards sustainability will always be compromised.[53] Clean Meat Hoax hold on to veganism as a radical force that resists meat and global capital in one breath, though somewhat paradoxically they find themselves in a position adjacent to Buxton's regenerative ecocarnism through a shared suspicion of the motives of global food corporations.

This summary of the state of debate on the future of meat is necessarily partial (the prospect of feeding the world with insects is another direction that has garnered increasing support), but it allows for a number of initial conclusions. First, and most generally, there is little prospect of consensus about the relationship between meat and a sustainable future, except a conviction that the current configuration of animal agriculture needs to change. The three versions of meat (or non-meat) future sketched here – veganism, regenerative agriculture and CM – indicate the deeply entrenched and seemingly irreconcilable ideological tensions that surround the question of meat. Second, the varied relationships to global capital across these approaches to ethical eating provide an important adjunct to the debate; as Nora Castle and Graeme Macdonald summarize, 'Different visions of the future of food put power into very different hands.'[54] How, then, do forms of meat-eating or its refusal constitute political positions that are imbricated in wider systems of power and violence? What would an anti-capitalist menu look like? Third, debates around meat futures recurrently involve questions around what is natural or proper to the human, a position that brings into focus the essentialized figure of the *Anthropos*. Last, the cultural meanings of ecocarnist solutions are notable for their contradictory temporalities: the nostalgic appeal of regenerative agriculture versus CM's giddying hypermodernity (veganism meanwhile is less straightforwardly locatable on this temporal axis).

The key overarching point is that it is by no means certain how best to approach the urgent issue of eating sustainably in the Anthropocene. The language of public debates around food futures reveals the insufficiency of technical or scientific perspectives to account for the complex, seemingly intractable conflicts between different dietary perspectives. Food ethics is not simply a case of calculating which diet has the lowest carbon footprint. Meat – whether cultured or not – is always necessarily a cultural issue as the centrality of conceptions of tradition and the natural to debates around CM and regenerative agriculture emphasize.

Critical reflections on carnism consistently support the overarching premise of this book that literary studies potentially has a key role in elucidating global crisis, the compromises of neoliberal discourses of sustainable transition and the contours of possible forms of resistance. Monbiot, for example, emphasizes narrative as integral both to the diagnosis and amelioration of damaging food politics: 'Our beliefs about food and farming are dominated by fables and metaphors that describe the world not as it is, but an idealized, simplified planet.'[55] Consequently, he concludes, 'We need stories that tell us where we are, how we got here and where we need to go.'[56] Accordingly, a literary register surfaces time and again – if often subtly – in the discourse of flesh-eating and its refusal. When Buxton lauds regenerative agriculture as 'farming poetry', her phrasing conveys not just the vernacular sense of the poetic as a synonym for harmony but also (perhaps unwittingly) an acknowledgement that her vision of rural tradition depends on the literary and wider cultural imagination.[57] Conversely, the association of CM with science fiction is so routine that one of the legions of lab meat start-ups has taken the name SciFi Foods.[58] Recall too the extensive gesturing to Mary Shelley through the spectre of Frankenfoods. PETA's 'utopian dream' of a vegan future articulates another, connected branch of literary history: the long tradition of imagining a perfected politics.

The central aim of Part 1 is to explore how the meanings of meat in veganism, regenerative agriculture and CM contribute to a deeper understanding of the tension between animal studies and the environmental humanities by applying a critical perspective based in the emerging field of vegan studies to the literary depiction of the two forms of ecocarnism at issue here. The focus on ecocarnism, conversely, allows for a critical reflection on the methods, politics and ethics of vegan literary studies as a mode of analysis centred on animal advocacy. Although this trajectory will not involve systematic analysis of the Capitalocene or Anthropocene (or indeed any of the many other proliferating -cenes), capital and the *Anthropos* will appear throughout as key contexts through which the meanings of meat are imagined. In turn, this task refracts back onto the context of sustainable transition.

The academic field of vegan studies is intimately linked with the wider project of animal studies, and especially with critical animal studies, which, given its explicit commitment to animal liberation, is a clear precursor to vegan studies. There are also explicit links between vegan studies and elements of the environmental humanities. While vegan studies emerges from and remains concerned with questions around the commodification, consumption and objectification of non-human creatures, it promises a consistent commitment to explore veganism in Giraud's words, as 'more than a diet' and (potentially) as a 'marker of resistance to other capitalist and patriarchal norms', an agenda that is brought into sharpened focus by the rise of 'plant-based capitalism'.[59] In conceptualizing veganism as 'a form of counter conduct' that transcends food to construe broader forms of resistance to the determinations of global capital, vegan studies intersects with modes of environmentalist thought and praxis antithetical to global capital (an ethos present in wider animal studies work too).[60] Inevitably, however, the vegan–eco allegiance only goes so far. There are clear points of tension between vegan studies and the environmental humanities created, for example, by ecocriticism's long-standing investment in the pastoral landscapes of traditional agriculture which links in turn to the more recent emphasis in the environmental humanities in forms of entanglement. This critical context provides a multifaceted perspective on an ecocarnist anti-capitalism materialized through the imagining of independent smallholdings outside the reach of global agribusiness. In this vein, Chapter 2 opens the literary discussion by focusing on regenerative agriculture in the work of the American poet, essayist and novelist Wendell Berry.

Notes

1 See, for example, Greg Garrard, *Ecocriticism*, 2nd edn (London: Routledge, 2012), 149.

2 Faunalytics, 'Global Animal Slaughter, Statistics and Charts: 2022 Update', https://faunalytics.org/global-animal-slaughter-statistics-charts-2022-update/, accessed 17 April 2023; for the statistics on aquatic species, see Ed Winters, *This Is Vegan Propaganda: And Other Lies the Meat Industry Tells You* (London: Vermillion, 2022), 86.

3 UN Food and Agriculture Organization, 'Key Facts and Findings', https://www.fao.org/news/story/en/item/197623/icode/, accessed 17 April 2023. The statistics of meat's greenhouse gas emissions have long been contested by the meat industry and its supporters. For a helpful summary of the case, see Nicolette Hahn Niman, *Defending*

Beef: The Case for Sustainable Meat Production (White River Junction, VT: Chelsea Green, 2014), 9–25.

4 Brian Machovina et al., 'Biodiversity Conservation: The Key Is Reducing Meat Consumption', *Science of the Total Environment* 536 (December 2015), 419–31, 419.

5 See Feeding Ourselves Thirsty, 'Meat: Overview', https://feedingourselvesthirsty.ceres.org/index.php/industry-scorecards/meat, accessed 23 June 2023.

6 United Nations Development Programme, 'Food Systems Transformation', https://www.undp.org/facs/food-systems-transformation, accessed 15 September 2025.

7 George Monbiot, '"Let Them Eat Lentils" Won't Save Us from Animal Farming – We Must Embrace Meat Substitutes', https://www.theguardian.com/commentisfree/2023/feb/01/environmentalists-animal-free-meat-livestock-farming, accessed 17 April 2023.

8 John Parham, 'With or Without Us: Literature and the Anthropocene'. In *Cambridge Companion to Literature and the Anthropocene*. Edited by John Parham, 1 (Cambridge: Cambridge University Press, 2021).

9 Heather Anne Swanson, 'The Banality of the Anthropocene', *Fieldsights*, 22 February 2022, https://culanth.org/fieldsights/the-banality-of-the-anthropocene, accessed 1 May 2025.

10 Carys Bennett, Jan Zalasiewicz, Mark Williams and Richard Thomas, 'How Chickens Became the Ultimate Symbol of the Anthropocene', *The Conversation*, 12 December 2018, https://theconversation.com/how-chickens-became-the-ultimate-symbol-of-the-anthropocene-108559, accessed 17 April 2023; Bennett et al., 'The Broiler Chicken as a Signal of a Human Reconfigured Biosphere', *Royal Society Open Science* 5 (2018), 180325.

11 Bennett et al., 'How Chickens Became'.

12 Jason W. Moore, 'The Capitalocene, Part I: On the Nature and Origins of Our Ecological Crisis', *Journal of Peasant Studies* 44.3 (2017), 594–630, 595, 596.

13 PETA, 'Is It Really Natural? The Truth about Humans and Eating Meat', https://www.peta.org/living/food/really-natural-truth-humans-eating-meat/, accessed 1 August 2023.

14 Eva Haifa Giraud, *Veganism: Politics, Practice and Theory* (London: Bloomsbury, 2021), 105.

15 Rob Percival, *The Meat Paradox: Eating, Empathy and the Future of Meat* (London: Little, Brown, 2022), 42–61.

16 Jacques Derrida, '"Eating Well", or the Calculation of the Subject: An Interview with Jacques Derrida'. In *Who Comes after*

the Subject? Edited by E. Cadava, P. Connor and J.-L. Nancy, 115 (New York: Routledge, 1991).

17 Derrida, '"Eating Well"', 114–15.

18 Giraud, *Veganism*, 140.

19 Peter Scarborough, Michael Clark, Linda Cobiac, Keren Papier, Anika Knuppel, John Lynch, Richard Harrington, Tim Key and Marco Springmann, 'Vegans, Vegetarians, Fish-Eaters and Meat-Eaters in the UK Show Discrepant Environmental Impacts', *Nature Food* (2023), 1–10, 1.

20 Ed Winters, *This Is Vegan Propaganda* (London: Ebury, 2022), 127.

21 PETA Prime, 'The Future of Food', https://prime.peta.org/news/the-future-of-food-is-vegan/, accessed 17 April 2023.

22 Jayne Buxton, *The Great Plant-Based Con* (London: Piatkus, 2022), 18. See also Dominique Lestel, *Eat This Book: A Carnivore's Manifesto* (New York: Columbia University Press, 2016); and Nicolette Hahn Niman, *Defending Beef: The Case for Sustainable Meat Production* (White River Junction, VT: Chelsea Green, 2021).

23 Alexis Shotwell, *Against Purity: Living Ethically in Compromised Times* (Minneapolis: University of Minnesota Press, 2016), 5.

24 Emilia Quinn, 'Notes on Vegan Camp', *PMLA* 135.5 (2020), 916.

25 Cited in Shotwell, *Against Purity*, 114.

26 Donna J. Haraway, *When Species Meet* (Minneapolis: University of Minnesota Press, 2007), 105.

27 Haraway, *When Species Meet*, 105, 80.

28 Donna J. Haraway, *Staying with the Trouble: Making Kin in the Chthulucene* (Durham, NC: Duke University Press, 2016).

29 Charles Darwin, *On the Origin of Species* (New York: Collier and Sons, 1909 [1859]), 528.

30 Melanie Joy, 'Understanding Neocarnism: How Vegan Advocates Can Appreciate and Respond to "Happy Meat", "Locavorism" and "Paleo Dieting"', https://www.onegreenplanet.org/lifestyle/understanding-neocarnism/, accessed 1 August 2023.

31 Shibu Jose and Jeanne Dollinger, 'Silvopasture: A Sustainable Livestock Production System', *Agroforestry Systems* 93 (2019), 1–9, 1.

32 On the climatarian diet, see Winters, Vegan Propaganda, 105, 109. On the planetary health diet, see the 'EAT-Lancet Commission Brief for Everyone', https://eatforum.org/lancet-commission/eatinghealthyandsustainable/, accessed 1 August 2023.

33 DeSilvey and Bartolini, cited in George Cusworth et al., 'Green Rebranding: Regenerative Agriculture, Future-Pasts, and the Naturalisation of Livestock', *Transactions of the Institute of British Geographers* 47.4 (2022), 1009–27, 1010.

34 Eva Haifa Giraud, *What Comes after Entanglement? Activism, Anthropocentrism, and an Ethics of Exclusion* (Durham, NC: Duke University Press, 2019), 2–3.
35 Joe Fassler provides the statistics on investment in CM before giving a bleak prognosis of the possibility of its realization as a mainstream food source: 'The Revolution That Died on Its Way to Dinner', *New York Times*, 9 February 2024, https://www.nytimes.com/2024/02/09/opinion/eat-just-upside-foods-cultivated-meat.html, accessed 24 June 2024. See Jan Dutkiewicz for the idea of CM as a 'moonshot', 'Socialize Lab Meat', *Jacobin*, 8 November 2019, https://jacobin.com/2019/08/lab-meat-socialism-green-new-deal, accessed 9 January 2023.
36 Fassler, 'The Revolution That Died'.
37 'Meet the New Meat', Upside Foods, https://upsidefoods.com/, accessed 1 August 2023.
38 Melinda Cooper, *Life as Surplus: Biotechnology and Capitalism in the Neoliberal Era* (Seattle: University of Washington Press, 2008), 3.
39 Dutkiewicz, 'Socialize Lab Meat'.
40 Dutkiewicz, 'Socialize Lab Meat'.
41 Fassler, 'The Revolution That Died'.
42 Buxton, *Plant-Based Con*, 321, 315.
43 Jaden Urbi, 'The Fight against "Fake Meat" Has Officially Begun', *CNBC*, https://www.cnbc.com/2018/02/23/the-fight-against-fake-meat-has-officially-begun.html, accessed 1 August 2023.
44 FSIS Case No. 2018, https://downloads.regulations.gov/FSIS-2018-0016-0001/content.pdf, p. 1., accessed 1 August 2023.
45 Elena Valeriote, 'Italy's Ban on Cultured Meat Raises Questions about Innovation versus Tradition', *Modern Farmer*, https://modernfarmer.com/2023/05/italys-ban-on-cultured-meat/, accessed 1 August 2023.
46 Melanie Joy, *Why We Love Dogs, Eat Pigs and Wear Cows* (San Francisco, CA: Conari Press, 2010), 96.
47 Timothy Morton, 'How I Learned to Stop Worrying and Love the Term *Anthropocene*', *Cambridge Journal of Postcolonial Literary Inquiry* 1.2 (2014), 257–64, 258.
48 Nick Fiddes, *Meat: A Natural Symbol* (London: Routledge, 1991), 48.
49 Rachael Oatman, 'Future Meat Rebrands to Believer Meats, *Food Business News*, https://www.foodbusinessnews.net/articles/22657-future-meat-rebrands-to-believer-meats, accessed 1 August 2023.
50 Josh Milburn, 'Is Lab-Grown Meat Good News for Animals', *The Conversation*, https://theconversation.com/

is-lab-grown-meat-good-news-for-animals-151610, accessed 1 August 2023.

51 Catherine Oliver, *What Is Veganism For?* (Bristol: Bristol University Press, 2024), 101.

52 'About Us', Clean Meat Hoax, https://www.cleanmeat-hoax.com/about.html, accessed 1 August 2023.

53 'Green-Washing & Vegan-Washing Evil Companies', Clean Meat Hoax, https://www.cleanmeat-hoax.com/green---vegan-washing.html, accessed 1 August 2023.

54 Nora Castle and Graeme Macdonald. 'Introduction: Food Futures', *Science Fiction Studies* 49.2 (2022), 209–16.

55 George Monbiot, *Regenesis: Feeding the World without Devouring the Planet* (London: Allen Lane, 2022), 25.

56 Monbiot, *Regenesis*, 225.

57 Buxton, *Plant-Based Con*, 276.

58 SciFi Foods, https://scififoods.com/, accessed 1 August 2023.

59 Giraud, *Veganism*, 2, 65.

60 Dinesh Wadiwel, cited in Giraud, *Veganism*, 9.

CHAPTER 2

Wendell Berry's carnopoetics

Wendell Berry is among the most prolific and influential voices in American environmental literature: one of the 'harbingers of contemporary ecopoetry', as Angela Hume and Gillian Osborne describe him.[1] His significance derives from the depth of his engagement with the land and creatures of his farm in Kentucky and the wider ecological politics that his literary, agricultural and activist work expresses. Central to Berry's world-view is a forthright antipathy to the processes and effects of global capital, particularly in relation to farming, a dimension of his thought that emerges explicitly in his essays. In 'The Unsettling of America' (1977), Berry lambasts the 'mechanization and chemicalization of farming' as a form of 'corporate totalitarianism'.[2] Similarly, 'In Distrust of Movements' (1999) sees Berry lamenting 'the attempt of the great corporations to own and control all of creation'.[3] The domination of American agriculture by big business thus represents for Berry part of a wider absorption of culture into a hegemonic socio-economic paradigm. As he phrases it in 'Economy and Pleasure' (1988), 'We have been reduced almost to a state of absolute economics, in which people and all other creatures may be considered as economic "units".'[4] In these terms, Berry's agricultural politics stands as an implicit critique of the market-based, neoliberal environmentalism that underpins such innovations as natural capital accounting (a topic that will resurface in Part 3 in the context of extinction). The alternative, for Berry, is the encouragement of 'local land-based economies' that stand against the relentless drive of corporate agriculture.[5]

A key element of this anti-capitalist stance is a distinctive rejection of many forms of technology. To turn away from 'corporate totalitarianism', it is also necessary to refuse the 'technological fundamentalism' that goes along with it and thereby to resist an assumption by which the 'world is made safer for corporations': namely that the past was 'servile, meaningless and slow' and the present is 'meaningful, bright, lively, centralized and fast'.[6] As Bill McKibben puts it, Berry appears to be in an 'argument with the modern world', a position which extends equally across his writing and his farming.[7] The essay 'Why I Am Not Going to Buy a Computer' (1987) could be taken as a manifesto of Berry's luddism. As he explains at the start, 'As a farmer, I do almost all my work with horses. As a writer, I work with a pencil or a pen and a piece of paper.'[8] It is tempting to see him, as Paul Kingsnorth suggests, as a 'relic from the past'. Certainly, Berry's agricultural, political and ecological philosophy fits coherently with the nostalgic tendency present in much advocacy for regenerative farming. It is this tradition of thought – a commitment to pre- or, perhaps more accurately, counter-industrial relationships to the land – that represents the key element of Berry's reflections on meat.

It is no surprise that Berry is an opponent of factory farming. Taking the example of a 'hog factory' in the essay 'Two Minds' (2003), he criticizes industrial animal agriculture on grounds that connect with both environmental and pro-animal politics. In the first case, 'a hog factory exists in utter indifference to the landscape'. In the second case, Berry insists on the incompatibility of factory farming and compassion: 'If compassion were to be admitted to consideration, such a "farm" could not exist.'[9] Such discomfort with violence against animals (or at least an aspiration to limit violence) also finds expression in the 'dissatisfactions with hunting' he relates in 'A Native Hill' (1968–9).[10] For Berry, 'the eagerness to kill something I did not need to eat' through hunting creates 'an artificial relation to the place'. Note the priority here of the habitat over the creature. It is this emphasis that informs Berry's carnist ethos. Set against his rejection of factory farming and hunting, raising, killing and eating animals through small-scale agriculture is central to how Berry envisions an ethical and fulfilling relationship to the land and – problematically from a vegan perspective – to the animals themselves.

Setting out this agenda more fully in 'The Pleasures of Eating' (1990), Berry engages directly with meat refusal: 'Some, I know, will think it bloodthirsty or worse to eat a fellow creature you have known all its life. On the contrary, I think it means that you eat with understanding and with gratitude.'[11] The 'politics, ethics and aesthetics of food' that informs Berry's carnism is, he asserts, 'perhaps the profoundest enactment of our connection with the world'.[12] Berry's defence of meat – a specific form of meat at any rate – thus operates through a linkage between ontology and ecology: to raise and consume your own animals on a small farm is to *be* ecological. Consequently, while elements of Berry's philosophy – his anti-capitalist ethos and commitment to local communities of labour most notably – cohere with the ideological contours of much work in vegan studies, his pro-meat stance evidently compromises this attunement and provides a test case for understanding the interaction of veganism with carnist versions of ecological politics. Specifically, at the heart of Berry's vision of meat are the landscape aesthetics of his poetry through which he prioritizes a conception of 'world' which necessitates the killing and consumption of animals as the grounds of ecological existence. While the tension between veganism and regenerative agriculture remains irresolvable, a vegan reading of Berry's poetry suggests some telling blind spots in the cultural expression of each of these contrasting dietary politics.

Berry's voluminous poetic output is premised to a significant extent on the intimacy between writing and agriculture that emerges in his essays – 'living in one's subject' he calls it in 'The Making of a Marginal Farm' (1981).[13] This connection between farm and poem is central to what Scott Knickerbocker calls a 'conventional ecopoetry' that operates through 'the experiential, authorial presence of the poet-prophet who … wants to affect his audience ethically'.[14] Meat is part of this pattern in Berry's poetry – sometimes directly, often more subtly – in a way that situates his work in relation to critical interventions that explore both ecopoetics and zoopoetics. Broadly speaking, the formulation of ecopoetics and zoopoetics in the critical lexicon of the environmental humanities and animal studies (respectively, though inevitably with some crossover) emphasizes the agency of the more-than-human world in the creation of human cultural artefacts. This understanding of poetics exists between creative composition and critical analysis; ecopoetics and zoopoetics are part of the practice of poetic composition and a perspective that criticism explores. Texts do not, from this standpoint, express only a limited anthropomorphic perspective but are forged in a relationship with a dynamic world that includes the activities of other creatures. Frederike Middelhoff and Sebastian Schönbeck use Kate Rigby's definition of ecopoetics and Aaron Moe's definition of zoopoetics to highlight the connection between the terms. Rigby describes ecopoetics, with a Romantic flourish, as 'a mode of participation in the more-than-human song of an ever-changing earth'.[15] Similarly, for Moe the concept of zoopoetics 'recognizes that nonhuman animals (*zoion*) are makers (*poiesis*), and they have agency in that making'. A poem can be conceived, for Moe, as a 'multispecies event'.[16] To solidify the linkages between these two conceptions, Middelhoff and Schönbeck posit a syncretic 'eco-zoopoetics' that comprises 'the study of the relationships between and the agencies of literature, animals, and environments'.[17] This formulation encompasses the processes, spaces and experiences of meat production but only in broad terms that are insufficient for a more specific analysis of carnism, a point that gains emphasis from an idealizing tendency that appears in some conceptions of more-than-human poetics. Moe's understanding of zoopoetics, for example, is directed towards 'poems borne out of respect, wonderment and care for animals', an orientation that could only link with meat through an avowedly carnist lens.[18] Berry's ecocarnist ethos – with the intimacy it relies on between writing and farming – encourages reflection on the possibilities of a third, more specific term than ecopoetics or zoopoetics: carnopoetics. This coinage foregrounds meat's role in the entangled agencies of eco-zoopoetics, stressing the violence that haunts the unfolding of the 'more-than-human song of an ever-changing earth' and the 'multispecies event' of poetic creation. Carnopoetics allows for a recognition that the agency of food animals is routinely coerced and that the landscapes in which their lives are created and ended have also been subject to many centuries of anthropogenic environmental change. Animals and environments may feed into poetic creation, but they also themselves exist in relation to complex and long-standing forms of human manipulation. Their bodies are the result of the *poeisis* of centuries of genetic manipulation. In this way, carnopoetics helps to formulate a vegan revision of literary history.

The idea of carnopoetics has a strong link with the pastoral as a mode of poetry that is premised on animal agriculture (with 'pastoral' signifying both a form of writing and a form of farming). Early ecocriticism's extensive engagements with the pastoral, and its relative the Georgic, tended to minimize the topic of meat, despite the centrality of animal agriculture to the classical foundations of both these modes. Opening with a dialogue between a shepherd and a goatherd, Theocritus's *Idylls* – widely conceived as inaugurating the pastoral tradition – revolves around ruminants, as does Virgil's *Georgics* in beginning with a reflection on 'what care the cows, what care/ the flocks require'.[19] Critical debates around the pastoral and Georgic are extensive and ongoing and incorporate a strand of critique of the dematerializing effect of many examples of these modes. As Garrard points out, following Raymond Williams, much pastoral poetry 'obscures the realities of labour and hardship'.[20] This Marxist critical direction potentially directs attention towards the animals that are necessarily part of the pastoral scene (a point which Garrard emphasizes), though early ecocriticism (as well as the wider pastoral criticism) is usually more interested in shepherds than sheep.[21] Paul Alpers, for example, in wrestling with the task of defining pastoral describes a key element of the mode's history as its presentation of 'different accounts of nature as the "scene" of shepherds' lives' with the sheep not meriting a mention.[22] In reinstating the significance of meat – and animals more broadly – in pastoral and Georgic (though that larger task is beyond the reach of this book), the conception of carnopoetics is gauged to form part of the emerging critical language of vegan literary studies, though it also highlights some key areas of tension in the wider debates around ethical diets.

The role of animals in evocations of farming is not only restricted to depictions of livestock destined for consumption (or for use in related forms of commodification in the dairy or wool industries, for example) but also involves the representation of other creatures that make their homes in agricultural landscapes, a key feature of Berry's poetic mis-en-scène and of his ecocarnist ethos more broadly. While Berry notes that the 'clear tendency of industrial agriculture ... has been to destroy any living thing that cannot be sold', a central ingredient of his agricultural aesthetics is the representation of wild and domesticated species together.[23] In this regard, Berry's thought owes a significant debt to Aldo Leopold (another American farmer-author and a recurrent reference point for Berry). Leopold's vision of farming is committed to diversity as a means 'to harmonize the wild and the tame in the joint interest of stability, productivity, and beauty'.[24] So, Berry's poetry embodies one of the key claims of advocates for regenerative farming: the idea that sustainable, organic animal husbandry promises considerable wider benefits for biodiversity (expressed in the representation of non-food animals) and constitutes a form of unalienated labour that enacts the positive imbrication of humans in ecological systems.

Berry's carnopoetics emerges in exemplary form in 'Work Song' from the 1977 sequence *Clearing* and particularly in the poem's second section, 'A Vision', in which the utopian allure of regenerative agriculture is depicted through the revival of a 'ruined place'. In the future domain Berry depicts, alienating and extractive economic regimes have given way to an intimately connected human and natural flourishing; humans will learn to live on the land 'like slow-growing trees', 'asking not too much of earth or heaven', taking 'nothing from the ground they will not return'.[25] As Berry's vision develops, meat is woven into the texture of ecological redemption:

> The river will run
> clear, as we will never know it,
> and over it, birdsong like a canopy.
> On the levels of the hills will be
> green meadows, stock bells in noon shade.
> on the steeps where greed and ignorance cut down
> the old forest, an old forest will stand ...
> Families will be singing in the fields.
> In their voices they will hear a music
> risen out of the ground.[26]

The role of meat in Berry's regen-ag vision is initially easy to miss, though the subtlety of its involvement with the successive facets of ecological flourishing the passage contains is central to the poem's carnopoetics. Meat is integrated into the scene through the synecdoche of 'stock bells in noon shade' that contributes to the poem's extended sonic patterning: the sound of the cattle bells connects with the canopy of birdsong that precedes it and to the ensuing image of the families 'singing in the fields'. Berry unifies three aspects of the rural scene into the poem's soundscape: wild creatures, livestock and human families. The incorporation of animal agriculture into the scene without explicit attention to slaughter or consumption creates a wide angle that foregrounds landscape rather than individual creatures as the conceptual and ethical focus. At the risk of reading the passage in too straightforwardly an agricultural way (though it is a risk that is in tune with the ethos of Berry's work), raising livestock facilitates a wider ecological and social flourishing expressed by the song of the birds and the human families. Meat in 'A Vision' is represented as part of an organic whole that exemplifies the trope of entanglement. Note how the families' voices are a 'music/ risen out of the ground' as human culture emerges from harmonious relationships with the natural world. If this seems an overly idealized Arcadia, Berry anticipates the objection at the end of the section: 'This is no paradisal dream./ Its hardship is its possibility.'[27] An ecocarnist conception of labour is what brings humans, animals and land into alignment in Berry's ecological future.

Berry's book-length agricultural verse almanac *The Farm* (1995) provides an extended gloss on the spirit of this vision. Recommending that a smallholder keeps cows, pigs and hens, Berry's advice is to 'Eat these good beasts' and

        Be thankful
To them and to the plants,
To your small, fertile homeland,
To topsoil, light, and rain
That make you what you are.[28]

Ecology and ontology again entwine in the context of meat; human being is structured on the consumption of animals as part of what makes 'you what you are'. This, in turn, as the poem continues, is understood to be how 'You make yourself a place;/ You make yourself a way/ For love to reach the ground'.[29] The pastoral landscape's expression of a carnist conception of ontology includes a consistent sense of hospitality towards other non-domesticated creatures. Berry advises the farmer that a coyote may 'Become your supper guest ... / He'll just excerpt a lamb/ And dine before you know it' but goes on to counsel 'don't, because of that,/ Make war against the world/ And its wild appetites'. Rather than framing the relationship between smallholder and coyote as one of enmity, the image of the 'supper guest' expresses a shared participation in a network of carnivoracity. The clinching point for Berry is once again delivered through an evocation of sound: 'Coyote's song at midnight/Says something for the world/ The world wants said'.[30] Meat – and the farmer's link to the coyote – is represented as the world's imagined self-fulfilment. To frame this in terms of wider critical debates, Berry's coyote is exemplary of a form of ecological sensibility that weighs against animal studies' and vegan studies' insistence on the ethical meaning of individual creature's experience. It is not, for Berry, what the *coyote* wants to say for *themself* that provides the moment's central significance but rather the way that its voice manifests the world's larger agency; observe how the term is reiterated in the injunction not to 'Make war against the world' and in the idea of the coyote's song saying 'something for the world/The world wants said'. The emphasis on sound in this context operates as a form of disembodiment that subordinates the bodily feeling of the animal to the aesthetic effects of their call. The apprehension of the soundscape is more significant than the creature's lived experience.

What matters most in this framing is the ethical and aesthetic force of a larger system of ecological relationships that is often referred to in environmental thought as holism: the integration of beings and environmental processes in their shared place. Significantly, holism is a key conceptual element in a tradition of environmentalist disapproval of animal rights discourses and, more specifically, veganism and vegetarianism. Here J. Baird Callicott's application of Leopold's thought as a critique of animal liberation comes back into view. Callicott lauds the 'beauty, integrity and stability' of ecological holism. As Berry summarizes in a foreword to Leopold's best-known work *A Sand County Almanac*, 'Leopold understood carefully that we and the world, the land and its places, are ultimately gathered into a single membership.'[31] This, for Callicot, is a central problem of meat refusal: a failure to appreciate the role meat plays in a wider network of natural and social relationships. The allure of holism, Callicot claims, 'may simply not have penetrated the thinking of the animal liberationists'.[32] Rather, Callicott claims that the 'vegetarian' ethics of pro-animal thought and the concomitant emphasis on domesticated animals over wild species means that 'animal liberation, if pursued at the practical as well as the rhetorical level, would have ruinous consequences on plants, soils and waters' (due to the supposed overpopulation of livestock in a world after the mass consumption of meat).[33] Val Plumwood – again an important environmental philosopher with reservations about veganism – provides another philosophical companion to Berry's poetry. Berry's carnopoetics exemplifies what Plumwood calls 'ecological animalism', a position which 'supports and celebrates animals and encourages a dialogical ethics of sharing and negotiation or partnership between humans and animals, while undertaking a re-evaluation of human identity that affirms inclusion in animal and ecological spheres'.[34] (Think back to the predatory coyote and the 'stock bells in noon shade'.) For Plumwood, ecological animalism should be read in opposition to 'ontological veganism', a 'theory that advocates universal abstention from all use of animals as the only real alternative to mastery', as she puts it.[35] Plumwood's argument is that veganism fails in a necessary task of 'situating human life in ecological terms'; by denying the edibility of animals, vegans reinforce the 'human/nature dualism' that necessarily exists in alienation from the natural world.[36]

The obvious starting point for vegan counter-arguments to these aesthetic and philosophical bulwarks of carnism is to return to the lives of the individual animals as a point from which to critique the insistence on the holistic. If it is the 'world' that matters, where does that leave the lives of individual creatures, their capacity for suffering and their evident interest in their own survival? These are questions that Berry tackles directly in 'For the Hog Killing' (1979) in which he dwells explicitly on the visceral realities of the smallholder's animal relationships and not just on the contribution animal agriculture makes to a wider rural culture. If the focus on a pig's death here creates a different point of emphasis from that of 'A Vision', tellingly, the two poems are part of the same agricultural ethos in a way that helps to clarify the contours of a vegan critique of Berry's regen-ag aesthetics.

'For the Hog Killing' is framed as both a direct address to the pig and as a ritualistic invocation of the ecological politics of slaughter which emerges through the representation of a visual encounter between farmer and animal. Berry begins with the imperative for the pig to 'stand still for the bullet, and stare the shooter in the eye', hoping that they die 'while the sound of shot is in the air'.[37] This opening could be taken as a manifesto point for animal welfare as a distinctive ethical position that legitimates the killing of animals by insisting on an awareness of their capacity for suffering supported by compassionate practices of rearing and slaughter. Berry, accordingly, wants the hog to die with minimal pain. By attending to the gaze of the pig in this fatal moment, the poem insists on the smallholder's ethical responsibility for the killing and refuses the objectification of animals that structures industrial animal agriculture. While industrial animal agriculture relies on the impossibility of the consumers' gaze reaching the meat's material processes (which is why slaughterhouses *don't* have glass walls), here as the 'jugular blood' springs 'hot to the knife', the poem creates an unflinching experience of the pig's death.[38] But the moral of the moment pivots on a characteristic movement away from the pig to a larger frame, once again via the image of the world. It is through the killing and eating of the pig that, for Berry in the poem's conclusion, 'we celebrate again our lives' wedding with the world'.[39] The pig's death in this sense consummates the entanglement – via the figure of the wedding – of humans and nature that underpinned the ecological aesthetics of 'A Vision'.

A brief tour of the motif of marriage in Berry's writing elucidates the 'wedding with the world' the dying pig embodies. In expounding his agricultural–poetic method, Berry notes that 'living in your subject' is like 'marrying your sweetheart';[40] to write about agriculture is a kind of union analogous to heterosexual intimacy. While in a broader context, 'marrying your sweetheart' need not be a specifically heterosexual act, in Berry's work the concept of marriage revolves around the conventional pairing of man and wife. In 'The Country of Marriage' (1973), Berry offers an extended ecological metaphor for his life with his wife Tanya:

> Sometimes our life reminds me
> of a forest in which there is a graceful clearing
> and in that opening a house,
> an orchard and garden,
> comfortable shades, and flowers
> red and yellow in the sun, a pattern
> made in the light for the light to return to.[41]

The image of married life as a clearing in a forest operates as more than figuration in the context of Berry's oeuvre. This is both what their marriage is like – a calm, flourishing and productive natural order – and the material socio-agricultural vision that much of his poetry aspires towards; think again of the family singing in the field in 'A Vision'. As Gifford phrases it in a discussion of pastoral in William Shakespeare's *As You Like It*, marriage serves as a 'motif for natural harmony'.[42] The pig's embodiment through its slaughter of the smallholders' 'wedding with the world' operates therefore as part of a wider imagining of a natural order that in the logic of Berry's carnopoetics transcends the animal's experience. It is notable in this context that despite the call for the pig to look their killer in the eye, the poem does not allow for any resistance to the impending bullet. Given the interest Berry shows elsewhere in agricultural soundscapes, the pig strikingly remains silent; the 'sound of the shot' is the only aural element of the hog killing. Consequently, the depiction of the pig is something like the inverse of the livestock in 'A Vision'. While the 'stock bells in noon shade' imagine animals as sound not body, the pig of 'For the Hog Killing' is body not sound. In each poem, the animal presence is incomplete. Ultimately, when figured as part of the landscape, an animal may 'speak'; when witnessed in the desperate singularity of the moment of slaughter, the animal must remain silent.

There are reasons for this which are integral to the ethics of the scene. 'For the Hog Killing' was first published in a short book alongside an essay by Berry on 'The Neighborly Art of Hog Killing' and a series of photographs by his wife Tanya Amyx Berry documenting their lives, as Wendell puts it, within the 'hog-and-pork culture' of 'Henry County, Kentucky'.[43] He goes on to explain that the 'first rule of hog killing was, and ought always to be, "Don't make 'em squeal"' because 'none of them should be frightened or hurt'.[44] In the scene that the poem and photographs recount, the slaughter was conducted in exemplary style by a neighbour called Marvin Ford. Another literary pig death provides a telling point of comparison. In Thomas Hardy's *Jude the Obscure* (1895), the famous botched slaughter scene portrays the pig as anything but quiet. As Jude struggles to dispatch the animal, the novel registers the pig's 'cry of despair; long-drawn, slow and hopeless' before a 'final shriek of agony'.[45] As with Berry's poem, the visual encounter between human and animal is given a central place. As the pig's 'glazing' eyes 'rivet' themselves onto Jude's lover Arabella, Hardy registers the 'eloquently keen reproach of a creature recognizing at last the treachery of those who had seemed his only friends'.[46]

Hardy's agonized and agonizing depiction of the creature's death is a recurrent theme of his writing, in contrast with which Berry's pig appears almost complicit with its own demise: faced with death it has nothing to say for itself. A caveat might be located in the distinction between Jude's amateur slaughter technique (this is the first time he has killed a pig and he is reluctant to do so) and the idealized end Berry imagines in 'For the Hog Killing'. The whole point of Berry's poem is that this is how, in his ecocarnist vision, a pig's death *should* be. Reading these two scenes against one another presents a clear welfarist moral: when it comes to killing pigs, be more like Marvin and less like Jude.

Even so, the aspiration that the pig should 'stand still for the bullet' demands passivity as an integral characteristic of the model victim the poem depicts. Berry's ecocarnist aesthetics is premised on the imaginative construction of a biddable animal subjectivity that informs the 'natural' order he espouses. A key element of carnopoetics, therefore, is not just a recognition of the way that the multiple agencies of meat production are manifest in textual form but also an understanding of certain forms of animal agency as a phantasmagoric projection of poetic-agricultural strategies. Evidently, the pig's compliance is coerced in a way that intersects with animal studies scholarship on the killability of animals as a manifestation of biopolitics. Matthew Cole's application of Foucault's conception of pastoral power to the conception of 'happy meat' is particularly pertinent here. For Cole, happy farm animals must be understood to evince a 'submission' with 'the character of a self-willed obedience'.[47] The function of animal welfare, as expressed in Berry's hog-and-pork culture, is to engineer submissive, killable subjects.

By this point, it is clear that Berry's ecocarnist vision maps neatly onto the existing contours of a vegan literary studies critique. A vegan reading of Berry's meat politics might unfold in these five connected stages. First, and to begin in general terms, critical attention to Berry enacts Stewart Cole's summary (developed from Adams's *The Sexual Politics of Meat*) of 'a vegan mode of reading poetry' as a practice that attends 'not only to "vegan words" but also to "texts of meat"'. For Cole, 'vegan critics of poetry ... should find themselves taking up not only texts that embody alternative, anti-anthropocentric frameworks but also those that espouse the very attitudes that veganism finds its origins in opposing'.[48] Berry's carnopoetics provides a case study in how literature creates the imaginative terrain of carnism. Second, and as a more specific extension of Cole's point, vegan literary studies operates, in Sune Borkfelt's words, as a 'de-objectifying discourse' that insists on the lived materiality of animal experience in the face of modes of representation that seek – in various ways – to reduce animals to ciphers, commodities or neutral elements of a text's mise-en-scène.[49] The conclusion on Berry's regen-ag aesthetics that this perspective facilitates might run like this: the promise of ecological holism relies on the conscription of animals into a vision of 'world' to which their own being is subordinated. Vegan reading insists on animals' meaningfulness by, for example, careful critical attention to the life of the pig in 'For the Hog Killing'. Third, since the idea of holism is closely linked to the idea of meat's naturalness, this context evokes Robert McKay's coinage of 'carniveracity' (a combination of the linguistic roots of 'meat' and 'truth') to illustrate the carnist position that 'meat-eating goes without saying: it is natural, normal, fundamental, necessary, real, truthful, authentic',[50] just as the context of meat does not need to be explicitly stated in the image of the 'stock bells in noon shade' in 'Work Song'. Meat is central to the rural scene without any need to labour the point by spelling out the future prospects of the beasts the bells locate. In this way, a key element of ecocarnism (and the pastoral more broadly) is an undercoding of meat: the scene is understood to rely on a natural carnist order written into the landscape. It is the task of vegan literary history to draw out these implications.

Fourth, when it comes to the death of the pig in 'For the Hog Killing' another line of McKay's argument comes into view. 'For the Hog Killing' provides a literary example of a point McKay makes about John Berger's widely quoted observation: 'A peasant becomes fond of his pig and is glad to salt away its pork.'[51] The crux of Berger's argument is that to the ecologically alienated urbanite it is difficult to understand that 'the two statements … are connected by an *and* and not by a *but*'.[52] In other words, in the context of most consumers' distance from the productive origins of meat, it is hard to appreciate that a relationship with an animal might include both affection and slaughter. Berry's evocation of the smallholder's relationship to their animals is precisely the position Berger sets out. For McKay, 'in the pastoral world of the peasant, slaughter for meat-eating commands utter authenticity – being *un-estranged*, happy, homely, and true' (original emphasis). The 'effect' is to '*naturalise* one reality of killing (small-scale rural slaughter) in the act of demystifying the inauthenticity of another (industrial-scale urban slaughter)'.[53] McKay's aim is to contest a 'carnivorous story of meat in which edibility *just is* animals' fundamental reality'.[54] Ecological holism is a key part of this carnist narrative direction as an idea by which animals become food. The fifth and final point emerges from vegan studies' alliance with ecofeminism which facilitates scrutiny of the way in which the construction of meat's naturalness is produced via cultural machinations which also involve the construction of other expressions of a supposedly 'natural order'. The 'wedding with the world' the pig's death enacts in 'For the Hog Killing' can be understood as part of the intersecting network of patriarchal and speciesist domination. While Berry noted that 'there is an historical parallel, in white American history, between the treatment of land and the treatment of women',[55] his intersectional approach to gender evidently stops short of engaging with the kind of animal-centred trajectory vegan studies has drawn from ecofeminism. Marriage could be understood in this context as a carnivorous institution (think of the traditional formulation of 'animal husbandry') that provides a moral framework for animal killing.

What this means for the relationship between veganism and ecocarnism is on one level familiar: it remains difficult to reconcile an ecological interest in 'world' as the basis of ethical concern with a pro-animal recognition of the ethical demands individual animal sentience creates. From a vegan perspective, the ecocarnist world represents a form of false consciousness that functions through the assertion of a 'natural' order of species hierarchy. Kimberly K. Smith's summary of the ethical force of Berry's agrarian politics that 'we simply need to be more *human*' (original emphasis) reveals the inextricable link between ecocarnism and the hegemonic conceptions of human–animal relations that animal studies complicates.[56] Conversely, from an ecocarnist perspective, regenerative agriculture represents the sustainable salvation of meat and the positive imbrication of the human in the land, while veganism may, by extension, be read as a state of ecological alienation.[57] The centre of this ecocarnist vision is the convergence of aesthetics, labour and tradition that regenerative agriculture embodies. If attention to the lives of individual creatures remains a limitation of ecocarnism, there also remains a question to be answered about what forms a vegan landscape aesthetics might take and how this might engage with the imagining of labour outside capital that Berry's agrarian ethos encourages, which might in turn help vegan studies to hold onto a radical position against the prospect of 'plant-based capitalism'.

To frame this trajectory another way, what happens to the countryside if no one eats meat? For sure, vegans have heard this line of enquiry before as part of the perennial vegan 'gotcha': a question asked to 'check for moral consistency', as Giraud phrases it.[58] A fuller discussion of vegan landscape aesthetics will emerge at the end of the next chapter: the issues of landscape and habitat after animal agriculture – what we might call a post-meat environmental aesthetics – also provide a telling perspective on the representation of cultured meat (CM). While much of the vast and growing discourse around CM focuses on the substance itself – its status in Neil Stephens's much-quoted phrase as an 'as yet undefined ontological object' – its long history in fictional imaginings of the future is equally concerned with the depiction of agricultural and post-agricultural space in a way that contrasts notably with Berry's world-view.[59]

Notes

1 Angela Hume and Gillian Osborne, 'Ecopoetics as Expanded Critical Practice'. In *Ecopoetics: Essays in the Field*. Edited by Angela Hume and Gillian Osborne, 1–16, 4 (Iowa City: University of Iowa Press: 2018).
2 Berry, 'The Unsettling of America', in *The World-Ending Fire* (London: Penguin, 2018), 19–132, 126–7.
3 Berry, 'In Distrust of Movements', in *The World-Ending Fire*, 286–95, 287.
4 Berry, 'Why I Am Not Going to Buy a Computer', in *What Are People For?* (Berkeley, CA, Counterpoint, 2010), 170–7, 175.
5 Berry, 'In Distrust of Movements', 287.
6 Berry, 'Why I Am Not Going to Buy a Computer', 175.
7 Bill McKibben, 'Prophet in Kentucky', *New York Review of Books*, 14 June 1990, https://www.nybooks.com/articles/1990/06/14/prophet-in-kentucky/.
8 Berry, 'Why I Am Not Going to Buy a Computer', 170.

9 Berry, 'Two Minds', in *The World-Ending Fire*, 178–201, 189.
10 Berry, 'A Native Hill', in *The World-Ending Fire*, 1–36, 24.
11 Berry, 'The Pleasures of Eating', 150.
12 Berry, 'The Pleasures of Eating', 151.
13 Berry, 'The Making of a Marginal Farm', in *The World-Ending Fire*, 37–47, 44.
14 Scott Knickerbocker, *Ecopoetics: The Language of Nature, the Nature of Language* (Amherst: University of Massachusetts Press, 2012), 9.
15 Frederike Middelhoff and Sebastian Schönback, 'Coming to Terms: The Poetics of More-Than-human Worlds'. In *Texts, Animals, Environments: Zoopoetics and Ecopoetics*. Edited by Frederike Middelhoff, Sebastian Schönback, Roland Borgards and Catrin Gersdorf, 15 (Baden Baden: Rombach Wissenschaft, 2019).
16 Middelhoff and Schönback, 'Coming to Terms', 18.
17 Middelhoff and Schönback, 'Coming to Terms', 17.
18 Aaron Moe, *Zoopoetics: Animals and the Making of Poetry* (Lanham, MD: Lexington Books, 2014), 5.
19 Virgil, *The Georgics: A Poem of the Land*, translated by Kimberley Johnson (London: Penguin, 2009), 5.
20 Garrard, *Ecocriticism*, 33.
21 Garrard, *Ecocriticism*, 43.
22 Paul Alpers, *What Is Pastoral?* (Chicago, IL: Chicago University Press, 1996), 27.
23 Wendell Berry, 'Aldo Leopold: A Reader's Testimony', in Curt Meine, *Aldo Leopold: His Life and Work* (Madison: University of Wisconsin Press, 2010), xi–xvi, xiv.
24 Aldo Leopold, *A Sand County Almanac, with Essays on Conservation from Round River* (New York: Ballantine Books, 1966), 199.
25 Wendell Berry, 'Work Song', in *Wendell Berry: Collected Poems, 1957–1982* (New York: North Point Press, 1987), 187–9, 187, 188.
26 Berry, 'Work Song', 188.
27 Berry, 'Work Song', 188.
28 Wendell Berry, *The Farm* (Berkeley, CA: Counterpoint, 1995), 17–18.
29 Berry, *The Farm*, 21.
30 Berry, *The Farm*, 8.
31 Berry, 'Aldo Leopold', xii.
32 J. Baird Callicott, 'Animal Liberation: A Triangular Affair', *Environmental Ethics* 2.4 (1980), 311–38, 323.
33 Callicott, 'Animal Liberation', 337.

34 Val Plumwood, 'Animals and Ecology: Towards a Better Integration', https://openresearch-repository.anu.edu.au/bitstream/1885/41767/3/Vegpap6.pdf, 2, accessed 2 May 2025.
35 Plumwood, 'Animals and Ecology', 1.
36 Plumwood, 'Animals and Ecology', 2.
37 Berry, 'For the Hog Killing', in *Collected Poems*, 200.
38 Berry, 'For the Hog Killing', 200.
39 Berry, 'For the Hog Killing', 200.
40 Berry, 'The Making of a Marginal Farm', 44.
41 Berry, 'The Country of Marriage', in *Collected Poems*, 147.
42 Gifford, *Pastoral*, 87.
43 Tanya Amyx Berry, *For the Hog Killing* (Lexington: University of Kentucky Press, 2019), 5–6.
44 Amyx Berry, *For the Hog Killing*, 7.
45 Thomas Hardy, *Jude the Obscure* (London: Penguin, 1978 [1896]), 110.
46 Hardy, *Jude*, 110.
47 Matthew Cole, 'From "Animal Machines" to "Happy Meat"? Foucault's Ideas of Disciplinary and Pastoral Power Applied to "Animal-Centred" Welfare Discourse', *Animals* 1.1 (2011), 83–101.
48 Stewart Cole, 'Poetry'. In *The Edinburgh Companion to Vegan Studies*. Edited by Laura Wright and Emilia Quinn, 193–202, 195 (Edinburgh: Edinburgh University Press, 2022).
49 Sune Borkfelt, 'Veganism and Animals', in *Edinburgh Companion to Vegan Studies*, 93–106, 94.
50 Robert McKay, 'Read Meat'. In *Animal Remains*. Edited by Sarah Bezan and Robert McKay, 129–57, 133 (London: Routledge, 2022).
51 Cited in McKay, 'Read Meat', 147.
52 McKay, 'Read Meat', 147.
53 McKay, 'Read Meat', 148.
54 McKay, 'Read Meat', 151.
55 Wendell Berry, *A Continuous Harmony* (San Diego, CA: Harcourt Brace, 1972), 162. For a fuller discussion of this quotation see Kimberley A. Smith, *Wendell Berry and the Agrarian Tradition: A Common Grace* (Lawrence: University Press of Kansas, 2003), 139.
56 Smith, *Wendell Berry and the Agrarian Tradition*, 214.
57 See Jovian Parry, Speculative Fiction', in *Edinburgh Companion to Vegan Studies*, 287–300.
58 Giraud, *Veganism*, 57.
59 Neil Stephens, 'In Vitro Meat: Zombies on the Menu?', *SCRIPTed: A Journal of Law, Technology & Society* 7.2 (2010), 394–401, 400.

CHAPTER 3

Cultured meat landscapes

Despite its apparent novelty, cultured meat (CM), or something very like it, has been present *avant la lettre* in fiction at least since 1881 when Mary Bradley Lane's novel of a feminist utopia, *Mizora: A Prophecy*, raised the possibility of a 'chemically prepared meat' that liberates humanity from famine, poverty and patriarchy.[1] *Mizora* exemplifies an upbeat sense of the radical possibilities of technology characteristic of both its time and genre. The 1880s were heady days for utopian imaginings, with over one hundred utopian novels published in the United States in the period 1886–96, motivated, as Warren Belasco summarizes, by 'faith in progress'.[2] Although Lane is a little-known figure, an Ohio schoolmistress who wrote only two books (the other *Escanaba* from 1895 is lost), she can claim a certain literary historical significance. *Mizora* was among the earliest texts of the fin de siècle utopia boom; more specifically, the novel is, as Jean Pfaelzer claims, the first 'all-female utopia written in the United States'.[3] The narrative follows the travels of a Russian noblewoman Vera Zarovitch who, sentenced to exile in Siberia for her revolutionary views, 'attempts a journey no other of my sex has ever attempted' (8), escaping from her captors across the Arctic Ocean towards the North Pole, where rowing alone over the 'undulating waters' (13) she is swept into a whirlpool. She fears the worst but finds herself with 'bewildered delight' transported to 'a land of enchantment' (14). This is Mizora, a secret world in which 'not a man nor the suggestion of one, was to be seen' (16) and in which an egalitarian, secular, feminist society flourishes.

Since Lane's novel, CM has continued to function as a staple ingredient of utopian and dystopian imaginings. Initially, its representation was largely positive (though there are caveats to add in due course). The German sci-fi pioneer Kurd Lasswitz's 1897 *Two Planets* (which includes possibly the second literary depiction of cultured flesh) echoes the utopian elements of Lane's fiction. A Martian invasion brings humans into contact with the 'automat sausage' as a sign of the alien race's superior technological and cultural achievement.[4] If the (at times dubious) benefits of Martian civilization in *Two Planets* are contested by the beleaguered earthlings, Lasswitz emphasizes simulated meat's role in a cornucopian strand of thought that contrasts with downbeat Malthusian views of food futures with their presumption of impending ecological exhaustion.[5] As the British statesman Frederick Edward Smith, Earl of Birkenhead, would comment in his 1930 prophecy *The World in 2030*, 'Synthetic foods and the production of animal tissues *in vitro* will finally set at rest those timid minds which prophecy a day when the earth's resources will not feed her children.'[6] In this context, technology, in the form of CM, represents the transcendence of ecological and ideological limits as part of an expression of a progressive politics that was a prominent part of the utopian imagination from the late nineteenth century into the first decades of the twentieth.[7]

As science fiction developed as a form of mass entertainment from the 1940s onwards, CM became established as a recurrent sf novum. Among the steady stream of literary allusions to cultured flesh, there are, for example, brief references to butcher plants in Clifford D Simak's *Time Is the Simplest Thing* (1961), carniculture vats in H. Beam Piper's *Space Viking* (1961) and *Four-Day Planet* (1963) and beef trees in John Varley's *The Ophiuchi Hotline* (1977). Stories such as Arthur C. Clarke's 'Food of the Gods' (1964) and Larry Niven's 'Assimilating Our Culture, That's What They're Doing!' (1978) address CM in a more extended fashion and foreground one of its most recurrent and disturbing possibilities: the in vitro cultivation of human flesh for consumption by other humans in Clarke's story and by the alien race the Glig in Niven's. In contrast to CM's first, ostensibly uplifting appearances in Lane's and Lasswitz's fiction, what these texts have in common is a far more despondent sense of the future during a 'New Dark Age' of dystopian thought marked, as Belasco explains, by 'radical critique of consumer capitalism, technocratic efficiency, and corporate globalization [... and] a strongly Malthusian fear of overpopulation, congestion and crowding'.[8]

The most notable representation of CM in this context is Frederik Pohl and Cyril Kornbluth's 1952 novel *The Space Merchants*, which contains one of CM's most detailed literary representations. In figuring cultured flesh as a flourishing but corrupt future industry, *The Space Merchants* provides a stinging condemnation of post-war programmes of agricultural intensification as it nostalgically valorizes a lost pastoral world of purportedly authentic human–animal relations (the kind of place where Wendell Berry would feel at home).[9] The despondent literary depiction of CM reaches its highest profile realization in 2003 with Margaret Atwood's *Oryx and Crake*, by which time cultured flesh was becoming more than an sf fantasy with NASA beginning its first experiments in meat cultivation in 2001. Atwood's CM fantasy focuses on the disturbing image of ChickieNobs: 'bulblike objects' with 'a mouth opening at the top' but no 'eyes or beak' which are paradoxically 'liberated' by the environmentalist group, the God's Gardeners.[10] Since then, the literary and cinematic allure of CM has continued to grow, as in, for example, Brandon Cronenberg's 2012 horror movie *Antiviral* which introduces the theme of culturing meat from the cells of celebrities.

CM's literary history has much to reveal about the imagining of incipient shifts in animal agriculture and their links with biotechnology and the wider project of capitalist speculation. In this way, CM's connection with animal studies and vegan studies is self-evident; for Kate O' Riordan it heralds no less than 'the deconstruction of species', an effect which illustrates its profound implications for the future of human–animal relations via its adjustment of the meanings of meat and ideas of edibility.[11] One of the most prominent themes in the critical and cultural analysis of CM is thus the representation and interpretation of its substance or body. As Benjamin Wurgaft summarizes: 'This meat's utter weirdness cannot be overstated',[12] an observation that encapsulates a quandary for manufacturers and marketers faced with the challenge of generating a public appetite for the meat of the future. CM's literary depiction contributes not just to cultural understandings of its uncanny ontology, however, but also provides a portal into the wider ecological promises that are central to its rationale. If the defence for meat in Berry's poetry is an ethos and aesthetics of 'world' as a synonym for ecological holism, then assessment of CM as a theme in food futures that cuts across animal and ecological ethics must also involve analysis of the imagination of the kind of 'world' it entails. In what imagined landscapes does CM emerge, and what wider conditions for animal life does it produce beyond the confines of the laboratory? Its first, utopian depiction in *Mizora* allows for a case study of the interplay between ontology and ecology – between uncanny flesh and the coming *world* of cellular agriculture – that reveals landscape as a crucial factor in CM's dual signification of animal and environmental futures, which, in turn, provides some coordinates for a vegan studies perspective on this emerging form of carnism.

CM's utopian allure in *Mizora* derives initially from the idealized connection between diet, health and social equality that it facilitates. Not long after her arrival in 'this wonderful land', Vera discovers that

> agriculture ... was a lost art. No one that I questioned had any knowledge of it. It had vanished in the dim past of their barbarism. With the exception of vegetables and fruit, which were raised in luscious perfection, their food came from the elements. A famine among such enlightened people was impossible, and scarcity was unknown. Food for the body and food for the mind were without price. It was owing to this that poverty was unknown to them, as well as disease. The absolute purity of all that they ate preserved an activity of vital power long exceeding our span of life. (26)

The Mizoran promise of food's 'absolute purity' evokes widespread concerns about food adulteration at the fin de siècle and broader anxieties about physical and cultural degeneration, while also suggesting a more general achievement of social and bodily perfection that is key to Lane's vision of an apparently egalitarian, post-capitalist society (and in this sense *Mizora* answers Dutkiewicz's call for socialized lab meat). How this purity is realized is imagined in some detail by Lane. The Mizorans

> took certain chemicals and converted them into milk, and cream, and cheese, and butter, and every variety of meat, in a vessel that admitted neither air nor light. They claimed that the elements of

> air and light exercised a material influence upon the chemical production of foods, that they could not be made successfully by artificial processes when exposed to those two agents. Their earliest efforts had been unsuccessful of exact imitation, and a perfect result had only been obtained by closely counterfeiting the processes of nature.
>
> The cream prepared artificially that I had tasted in London, was the same color and consistency as natural cream, but it lacked its relish. The cream manufactured in Mizora was a perfect imitation of the finest dairy product.
>
> It was the same with meats; they combined the elements, and the article produced possessed no detrimental flavor. It was a more economical way of obtaining meat than by fattening animals. (56)

Evidently, there are some notable points of difference between Mizoran biotechnology and the development of CM in the twenty-first century. Rather than beginning with animal cells, Mizorans begin the process in the chemical constituents of life; perhaps the most straightforward technical gloss would be to think of Mizorans synthesizing meat and dairy products from amino acids.[13] Because of this, there is significantly less doubt about the vegan credentials of Mizoran CM than there is about our own version. No animal is needed in Mizora, and yet this is no plant-based substitute of the Quorn or Tofurkey variety but a 'perfect imitation' of the material substance of meat and dairy products. Today, CM entrepreneurs tend to avoid the language of imitation, preferring to emphasize that it is essentially the same substance as conventional animal protein: 'real meat' notwithstanding its avant-garde technological production. Nonetheless, *Mizora* includes reiterated claims for the authenticity of a form of protein created by 'closely counterfeiting the processes of nature'.

The link between biotechnology and nature is a key element of Lane's vision of a utopian food future. In Mizora, the whole of society 'might be called a great school of Nature, whose pupils studied her every phase, and pried into her secrets with persistent activity, and obeyed her instructions as an imperative duty' (64). Lane's language here contains an upbeat echo of the Urtext of literary biotech, Mary Shelley's *Frankenstein*. While Victor Frankenstein's 'fervent longing to penetrate the secrets of nature' is the basis for one of literature's most enduring cautionary tales, for Lane, the trope of the secret allows for technology to appear not as the violation of some natural law but as a fulfilment or expression of the deep structures of nature which unsettles the conventional opposition between the natural and the artificial.[14] It is the same philosophy of science that underpins one of the novel's other great technological advances: the development of a form of in vitro fertilization that enables the extinction of males and which is likewise based on the ability to 'control Nature's processes of development' (104). The Mizorans harness instead of violating nature. If *Frankenstein* pivots on the creature's violent revenge on the overreaching scientist who created him, *Mizora* is all about harmony, a point emphasized through the luxuriant feast that greets Vera on her first arrival.

After enjoying a 'chemically prepared' beefsteak 'of a very fine quality', Vera is presented with a cup 'that looked like the half of a soap bubble with all its iridescent beauty sparkling and glancing in the light' (18). The beverage it contains resembles a chocolate 'whose flavor could not have been surpassed by the fabled nectar of the gods' (18). Such purple prose adds a conventionally Romantic ambience to Mizora that, crucially, extends to the depiction of landscape with its 'languorous atmosphere, the beauty of the heavens, the inviting shores', veiled 'behind a haze of purple and gold' (14). Landscape aesthetics plays a significant role in the novel's depiction of its post-animal bioeconomy. With livestock farming taking up 30 per cent of the planet's land surface today, part of the enticement of CM is the possibility that it will free up a vast amount of land for other uses. What those uses might be is integral to the speculative territory surrounding CM. On one hand, Buxton's defence of regenerative agriculture and condemnation of CM is based on the anticipation of 'massive land grabs by property developers and industrialists' that would take hold of vacant farms.[15] On the other hand, as the Good Food Institute speculates, the prospect of freeing up land 'for rewilding or carbon sequestration' adds significantly to CM's possible ecological benefits.[16] Either way, CM could potentially open up a huge area.

Certainly, in Mizora there is plenty of space. Although Lane never makes the connection explicitly, Mizora's remarkable synthetic food production is part of what makes an idealized landscape imaginatively tenable. Released from the burden of productivity, the land becomes a place of leisure rather than labour, informed by the Mizorans' 'love of splendor' (28). Each family enjoys ground that is 'ornamented like a private park' with 'cascades, fountains, rustic arbors, rockeries, aquariums, tiny lakes, and every variety of landscape ornamenting' (41). This utopian geography is a theme that runs through CM's speculative prehistory. Winston Churchill notes in his often referred to (though seldom quoted) reflection on CM futures in 'Fifty Years Hence' (1931) how 'synthetic' food production will produce a new landscape in which 'parks and gardens will cover our pastures and ploughed fields'.[17] In this dream, ecological necessity and landscape aesthetics are brought into conjunction as part of the imagining of what we would now call a sustainable future. Accordingly, alongside the perfection of food biotechnology and urban planning, Mizora's 'wonderful students of Nature' have also developed an entirely clean form of renewable power based on hydrogen and oxygen extracted from water (59). Sustainable transport, meanwhile, is provided by airships (79). CM's utopian appeal in Lane's novel exists, then, as part of a network of technological improvements that prioritize social justice, physical health and the minimization of environmental impacts.

For all this, the appeal of Lane's prophecy to today's pro-animal scholars and activists is limited. *Mizora* is no zootopia, and its landscapes appear to be entirely anthropocentric in conception. When Vera first arrives in Mizora, her impression that she has chanced upon a 'land of enchantment' is based in part on her apprehension of the wildlife:

> I entered a broad river, whose current was from the sea, and let myself drift along its banks … The sky appeared bluer, and the air balmier than even that of Italy's favored clime. The turf that covered the banks was smooth and fine, like a carpet of rich green velvet. The fragrance of tempting fruit was wafted by the zephyrs from numerous orchards. Birds of bright plumage flitted among the branches, anon breaking forth into wild and exultant melody, as if they rejoiced to be in so favored a clime. (14)

The scene Vera describes creates a close relationship between animals and landscape aesthetics with the exultance of the birds' melody and the brightness of their plumage enhancing the effect of the velvet turf and balmy climate. To return to this passage from the vantage of a fuller appreciation of Mizoran culture, the birds function metonymically as signs of the social harmony that Vera will shortly discover. Animal aesthetics appears as an index of Mizora's political achievement in abolishing poverty, famine and disease.

The first hint that Mizora is no haven for animals comes shortly afterwards, as Vera is 'impressed by a weird stillness'. Scanning the 'enchanted country', she notes, 'No animals were visible, nor sound of any. No hum of life. All nature lay asleep in voluptuous beauty, veiled in a glorious atmosphere' (15). In due course, Vera discovers the cause: 'Animals and domestic fowls had long been extinct in Mizora ... Invention had superceded the usefulness of animals in all departments' (54). While this vision might appeal to vegan abolitionists opposed to all forms of animal exploitation, whether of their bodies or labour, this is not the ethos of Mizora. It is not respect for animals that is behind their absence from the landscape. Later, she learns from her guide Wauna that in Mizora it is believed that the 'association of animals is degrading' (113). Specifically, animals offend Mizoran conceptions of hygiene. Vera notes, 'Cities, towns, and villages were provided with paved streets, which the public authorities kept in a condition of perfect cleanliness. The absence of all kinds of animals rendered this comparatively easy' (113). The birds that Vera enjoys evidently do not compromise this agenda as they appear purely as aesthetic effects, characterized by their beauty, distance and fleeting appearance. Any more intimate form of engagement with animals connotes a 'state of barbarism' (113). Although the Mizoran diet involves no harm to animals, evidently this is not a culture that seeks multispecies flourishing but only a certain kind of human order.

The extinction of the majority of animals is not the only uncomfortable element of Lane's utopia. Mizoran society is underpinned by a policy of eugenics which has resulted in the production of complete racial homogeneity. When Vera is shown a portrait gallery including many historical paintings, she notes casually that while all the Mizorans she has met have blonde hair, many of the pictures represent people of 'dark complexions' (92). After questioning one of the Mizoran matriarchs, Vera learns that these people have been 'eliminated' (92). Vera experiences some unease at the discovery but moves on quickly, and the novel does little to question the racist agenda at the heart of Mizoran culture (indeed, when Vera leaves Mizora to return to her own world, the novel also contains some starkly racist assessments of the Arctic Indigenous people she meets). Elimination, moreover, is a term that recurs throughout the text. The Mizorans 'have eliminated hereditary diseases, and developed into a healthy and moral people' (108). The same language underpins Mizora's food revolution too: 'To eliminate from our food the deleterious earthy matter is our constant aim' (45). The novel's gender politics draws on the same language: 'The coarser nature of men was eliminated from the present race' (104). There is a telling point of comparison here to Berry's deployment of marriage as an image of the ecocarnist entanglement of smallholder and livestock. In a world where meat is produced artificially, the idea of marriage has disappeared; humans have become disentangled (or one might say divorced) from the land. The extinction of animals and the production of beastless meat are part of a network of eliminations in which undesirable bodies are cleared out to make way for a world of sterile perfection. CM is not so much utopian protein as eugenic protein; its 'absolute purity' testifies to an authoritarian biopolitics that is the ultimate consequence of the Mizorans' ability to reach into the secrets of nature. In *Mizora*, CM represents the materialization of a fascist principle of hygiene. It is worth recalling in this context the designation of CM as 'clean meat', a term premised on the claim that 'cultured meat provides a cleaner alternative to slaughtered meat, both in terms of sanitation and environmental impact'.[18] This materialist framing – the desire to address the hygienic failures of mass animal slaughter expressed in environmental pollution and public health concerns – is unavoidably linked in *Mizora* with an exclusionary ideology of purity that conjoins nationalism, racism and speciesism.

The 'world' of *Mizora* is one in which the perfection of food technology and the production of harmonious landscapes exist, then, through various forms of political violence; the possibility of life, for humans or animals, is based on the techno-ideological manoeuvres of a genteel but merciless elite. CM facilitates an aesthetic perfection of bodies and landscapes so that the blight of ugliness, work, slaughter and mess can be removed from life in the service of an idealized culture. Given Mizora's uncomfortable ideological grounding, it is possible to imagine a carnist reading of *Mizora* that posits a return to conventional meat as the antidote to the bleak purity of Lane's utopia, as something like a renewal of the vows of Wendell Berry's 'wedding with the world'. Certainly, this fits with a strand in the literary history of CM in which its representation is closely tied to a sentimental hankering after traditional forms of animal agriculture. In Pohl and Kornbluth's *The Space Merchants*, for example, 'regenerated-protein merchandise' (which is to say CM products) are viewed as inferior to authentic animal flesh known in the novel as 'new protein'.[19] Environmental activism in *The Space Merchants* draws energy from the opposition between CM as a sign of a denatured culture and 'roast beef' as a sign of the 'old days' of authentically meaningful connections between people and the land, a framing that recalls the promise of regenerative agriculture.[20] So, while CM and regen-ag appear in many ways in opposition (future/past; technology/nature; simulation/authenticity) each – in deconstructive terms – carries the trace of the other. The movement towards the hygienic future of cultured flesh constructs the contrasting desire to return to livestock and the land which, in turn, becomes meaningful through its opposition to biotechnological simulations. The distinction between the future of meat and its past in this sense is eroded. In more straightforward terms, and to loop back to the argument of Clean Meat Hoax and others from Chapter 1, CM functions not as a way out of meat culture but a diversification of it: a construction of the biopolitics of Berry's smallholding that runs to a deeper and more far-reaching extent. Recall how Berry's regen-ag ethos is structured around the exclusion of wild species from the biopolitical regime that in Mizora includes a range of other species too. Lane's and Berry's utopias are both, ultimately, premised on animal death, whether the quiet eliminations behind Mizora's lush landscapes or the deliberate sacrifices of Berry's ecological holism. Neither of these agricultural – or post-agricultural – visions extends ethical consideration to the experience of creatures outside the wider ethics of 'world'.

If this solidifies a sense of the opposition between veganism and ecocarnism, it may also provide an encouragement to think about what a vegan 'world' – understood as a synthesis of labour, aesthetics and species justice – might entail. The rapid evolution of vegan studies as a critical field in close dialogue with activist praxis, including campaigns for climate justice, has made it harder to give credence to what Jovian Parry describes (with particular reference to Haraway) as the 'straw figure of the ecologically alienated vegan' as the basis for a retrenchment of carnist ethics and politics.[21] Take, for example, the Vegan Land Movement (VLM), a campaigning group that aims to 'acquire land ... previously used for animal agriculture and to repurpose it for the benefit of local ecosystems and its inhabitants', creating 'vibrant, biodiverse landscapes – effectively giving the land back to the Earth'. Evidently, ecological concerns are central to the VLM's mission: 'We believe that transforming the land is a powerful response to many of our urgent crises: climate change; biodiversity loss; disconnection from nature and animal exploitation.' This green agenda includes 'veganic farming, such as community orchards, as well as compassionate conservation and rewilding'.[22] Arguments and counter-arguments between advocates for regenerative farming and vegan agriculture will doubtless continue, based partly on the vexed question of whether manure (and hence livestock) is needed to regenerate depleted soils. Nonetheless, it is possible to imagine a partial convergence of the VLM's vision of vegan agriculture with Berry's vision of regenerative agriculture through the emphasis on connection (or at least the mitigation of 'disconnection') with nature and the encouragement of human and more-than-human communities. The VLM could certainly be taken as an antidote to what Berry bemoans in 'Think Little' as a 'state of total consumerism' in which 'we have forgotten how to provide for ourselves' so that 'all meaningful contact between ourselves and the earth is broken'.[23] Moreover, an emphasis on a vegan landscape aesthetics as a discourse of labour and multispecies flourishing provides a bulwark against the repackaging of veganism as the plastic-wrapped, ultra-processed lifestyle choice of plant-based capitalism. In this way, a vegan land politics that draws on, while continuing to critique, the ecocarnist tradition of Leopold and Berry represents an important point of resistance to the disappearance of agriculture into neoliberal and corporate discourses of sustainable transition.

Evidently, without the rearing and killing of animals, the imbrication of vegan labour and reclaimed land could not constitute – to return again to Berry's terms – a 'wedding with the world', as he understands it. A vegan landscape aesthetics would necessarily represent a reformulation or escape from pastoral tradition as it is expressed in landscapes and literature formed by centuries of human and more-than-human labour with all the constructions of gender and class this cultural and material history entails. If Berry's imagery emerges from a long-standing, culturally embedded linkage between agricultural and literary historical discourses of the pastoral, the project of 'veganic farming' requires its own literary-historical-agricultural aesthetic: a vegan form of pastoral or a broader vegan poetics that establishes new visions and versions of the connection between landscape and non- (or minimally) violent human–animal relations. There is already a precedent for this approach in Anat Pick's formulation of a 'creaturely poetics' as a way of reading that is interested in 'contexts beyond an anthropocentric perspective' that express 'something *in*human' (original emphasis).[24] While Pick's poetics is structured around questions of embodiment and vulnerability, a wider vegan poetics necessitates greater emphasis on questions of landscape, habitat and labour that nonetheless hold onto the attention to the life-worlds of other beings.

On one level, the relationship between ecocarnism and vegan studies remains – inevitably – stuck to the question of animal killing. Behind this – on a more subtle but connected level – are intractable debates around the meaning and the status of the human. Berry's poetry and Lane's novel anchor both their ecocarnist ethos with a discourse of human self-realization. When Vera leaves Mizora, the 'voice of [her] heart' offers the parting cry: 'Farewell, sweet ideal land of my Soul, of Humanity, farewell!' (141) Ultimately, it is the realization of human potential that ultimately structures the appeal of Lane's prophecy. For Berry, it is the collective humanity expressed in '*our* lives' wedding with the world' (emphasis added) that underpins his idealized regen-ag community. These visions are differently entangled with the more-than-human world so that the aesthetic of each is distinct. In *Mizora*, the human links with the world through at the genetic level through the simulation of 'Nature'; for Berry it is the day-to-day practice of farming that constitutes the imbrication of the human in the land. But the human remains the ultimate point of reference.

Any movement towards the formation of a radical food politics in and against the Anthropocene needs to grapple with these carnist ontologies. Vegan studies (and many aspects of a wider animal studies) has long been embroiled in this task through the critique of the apparent taken-for-grantedness of the idea of the human which emerges in these versions of ecocarnism at the intersection between self and world. Robert McKay, for instance, posits a 'vegan form of life' as something like the antidote to the 'normative humanity' that structures carnism.[25] While food choice remains important in McKay's argument, it is a wider identification with animals that informs his claim that 'I no longer take it as a matter of course that I am human' but rather forms part of a 'community of species difference'.[26] Although McKay's argument does not engage directly with ecological, or ecocarnist, discourses, there is a telling resonance to his parting hope that 'vegan forms of life [will] continue ... to take shape in the *world* ... as complex lives rather than as realizations of a clearly articulated position' (emphasis added).[27] McKay's language here foregrounds a worldliness of vegan practice that opens up the possibility of a flow between pro-animal, vegan and ecological positions that offers a meaningful contribution to a diverse environmental humanities, as well as to animal studies, based on a refusal of compulsory humanity. To adapt a quotation from Plumwood from the previous chapter, the question of landscape aesthetics could be taken as part of a process of 'situating [vegan] life in ecological terms' as a way of adjusting the link between ontology and ecology.

It is not just in the context of meat that compulsory humanity comes to the fore; it is also an element of a compulsory automobility that structures the link between ecological and animal agendas in the next three chapters and illustrates the pervasion of carnist discourses beyond their immediate application to the question of meat.

Notes

1 Mary Bradley Lane, *Mizora: A Prophecy* (New York: Syracuse University Press, 2007 [1881]), 18.
2 Jean Pfaelzer, *The Utopian Novel in America, 1886–1896: The Politics of Form* (Pittsburgh, PA: University of Pittsburgh Press, 1985), 3; Warren Belasco, *Meals to Come: A History of the Future of Food* (Oakland: University of California Press, 2006), 206, 101.
3 Jean Pfaelzer, 'Introduction', in *Mizora: A Prophecy* (New York: Syracuse University Press, 2007), xi.
4 Kurd Lasswitz, *Two Planets* (Carbondale: Southern Illinois University Press, 1971 [1895]), 49.
5 See Belasco, *Meals to Come*, 86, on the historical tension between the cornucopian and the Malthusians views of food futures.

6 F. E. Smith, *The World in 2030* (London: Hodder and Stoughton, 1930), 20.
7 For a detailed account of the history of utopian food thinking see Belasco, *Meals to Come*, 95–118.
8 Belasco, *Meals to Come*, 126–7.
9 For a detailed account of the significance of cultured meat in Pohl and Kornbluth's novel, see John Miller, 'The Literary Invention of *In Vitro* Meat: Ontology, Nostalgia and Debt in Pohl and Kornbluth's *The Space Merchants*. In *Literature and Meat since 1900*. Edited by Seán McCorry and John Miller, 91–110 (London: Palgrave, 2019).
10 Margaret Atwood, *Oryx and Crake* (London: Virago, 2004), 237–8.
11 Kate O' Riordan, *Unreal Objects: Digital Materialities, Technoscientific Projects and Political Realities* (London: Pluton Press, 2017), 101.
12 Ben Wurgaft, *Meat Planet: Artificial Flesh and the Future of Food* (Berkeley: University of California Press, 2020), 1.
13 I am grateful to Mark Post for this interpretation of Mizoran biotech.
14 Mary Shelley, *Frankenstein* (London: Colburn and Bentley, 1831), 38.
15 Buxton, *Plant-Based Con*, 317.
16 Good Food Institute, 'Cultivated Meat', https://gfieurope.org/cultivated-meat, accessed 1 September 2024.
17 Winston Churchill, 'Fifty Years Hence', *Popular Mechanics* 57.3 (1932), 393.
18 FAIRR, 'ESG Risks and Opportunities of Clean Meat', https://www.fairr.org/resources/knowledge-hub/key-terms/clean-meat, accessed 1 September 2024.
19 Frederik Pohl and Cyril Kornbluth, *The Space Merchants* (London: Penguin, 1984 [1952]), 29.
20 Pohl and Kornbluth. *The Space Merchants*, 89.
21 Jovian Parry, 'Speculative Fiction'. In *The Edinburgh Companion to Vegan Studies*. Edited by Laura Wright and Emilia Quinn, 288 (Edinburgh: Edinburgh University Press, 2022).
22 Vegan Land Movement, 'Vegan Agriculture Land Buyout 8', https://veganlandmovement.com/animal-agriculture-land-buyout/, accessed 1 September 2024.
23 Berry, 'Think Little', in *World-Ending Fire*, 52.
24 Anat Pick, *Creaturely Poetics* (New York: Columbia University Press, 2011), 5.
25 Robert McKay, 'A Vegan Form of Life'. In *Thinking Veganism in Literature and Culture: Towards a Vegan Theory*. Edited by Emilia Quinn and Benjamin Westwood, 251 (London: Palgrave, 2018).
26 McKay, 'A Vegan Form of Life', 265.
27 McKay, 'A Vegan Form of Life', 266.

PART TWO

Automobility: Animals, oil and the energy humanities

CHAPTER 4

Carnism and motonormativity

The electric vehicle (EV) is the cultured meat (CM) of transport. Both promise to address complex ecological and ethical challenges while projecting problematic socio-economic practices and ideological assumptions indefinitely into the future. Just as CM emerges from and reinforces the assumption that carnism is an inevitable manifestation of human being in the world, so the EV emerges from and reinforces the assumption that the mass private ownership of automobiles is a non-negotiable condition of human cultures. In reinforcing the operation of driving and meat-eating as social norms, EVs and CM reassert the marginality of alternative social visions. Instead of formulating expensive meat simulacra, the cheaper and greener alternative to the problem of meat would be to eat plants; in similar terms, the most obvious response to the problems of automobility is to turn to public and/or active transportation, practices that Matthew Calarco refers to as 'altermobilities'.[1] Neither of these solutions comes easily. Just as mass or even universal veganism seems unlikely given the power of carnism's hold, so altermobilities are stymied by the structural role of car culture in the organization of urban spaces, the inadequacy of public transport and the depth of cultural attachments to automobility.

The appeal of both EVs and CM is that they represent forms of 'sustainability' that leave the status quo untroubled, which is to say they are premised on their integration with the hegemonic politics of consumerism and techno-capitalist speculation. For all its aura of post-modernity, CM's appeal, as Fassler notes, is 'all about nostalgia, a way to pretend that things will go on as they always have, that nothing really needs to change'.[2] Likewise, the EV fantasises the endless continuation of mass car ownership without the need to reckon fully with the consequences or to imagine new paradigms and geographies of mobility. The logic here, as Heather Rogers explains, is simply that 'global warming can be stopped by swapping out dirty products for green ones'.[3] While food and transport are distinct issues that raise specific questions, there are, as this first chapter of Part 2 sets out, close discursive and material relationships between them that deepen the analogy between CM and EVs as transitional artefacts that facilitate the ever-deeper entrenchment of neoliberal ideology in the age of climate breakdown.

As with meat, the detriments of automobility are profound, urgent and involve interlinked public health, environmental and species justice concerns. The World Health Organization (WHO) notes that 'almost all of the global population (99%) breathe air that exceeds WHO guideline limits' for pollution.[4] Automobility is not the only reason for this, but it is the most significant.[5] The human cost of the damage caused by automobility – directly and indirectly – is staggering. In an inventory of forms of what they call 'car harm', Patrick Miner et al. cite the statistic that 'approximately 246,000 annual deaths are attributable to traffic-related air pollution'.[6] In total, '1 in 34 deaths are caused by cars and automobility with 1,670,000 deaths per year'. 'Cars and automobility have killed 60–80 million people since their invention';[7] globally, 'traffic crashes are the leading cause of death for children over 4'.[8] There is, as Robert Braun and Richard Randell summarize, 'no other area of social or political life where such a constant, routine, violent attrition of human life … is considered normal and acceptable'.[9] To this grim picture can be added the ecological damage created by car use. Of the 23 per cent of global greenhouse gas emissions contributed by transport, 70 per cent come from 'road vehicles'.[10] Car culture, moreover, involves intensive resource extraction, necessary not just for the massive fuel load (automobility is responsible for 'around half of total oil consumption') but also for the manufacture and disposal of vehicles and their components.[11] Tyres are especially damaging; along with road markings they 'account for an estimated

35%' of 'primary microplastics (particles released directly rather than from the breakdown of larger plastics)' that enter the ocean.[12]

Evidently, there are pressing reasons to move away from the dominant culture of mobility. It is in this context that the decarbonization of cars has become a widespread imperative in mainstream party politics. Under the UK government's 'zero emissions vehicle (ZEV) mandate', for example, 80 per cent of cars sold must be fully electric by 2030 and 100 percent by 2035.[13] Much optimism has become attached to vehicles that comprise, in the words of the advocacy group EVA England ('The Voice for EV Drivers'), an 'environmentally friendly alternative to petrol or diesel cars' with 'a lower carbon footprint' and 'zero tailpipe emissions of CO_2, NOx and particulates'.[14] EVs thus function, as Gordon Sayre summarizes, 'as a conscientious objection against fossil fuels'.[15] Evidently, to think about cars is necessarily to think about oil. To think about oil is to enter the most intractable and urgent question of the twenty-first century's global crisis. Oil is not only integral to the development of democracy, prosperity and medicine but also inseparable from injustice, violence and the collapse of the biosphere. As Hannes Bergthaller notes, oil functions like Derrida's *pharmakon*: 'Flickering between remedy and poison ... it is both that which makes liberty possible, and, at the same time, poisons it at the root.'[16] Automobility constitutes a perspective – though for sure it is not the only one – from which to explore the ambivalences of the wider petroculture and its centrality to the current world system. If, as Christophe Bonneuil and Jean-Baptiste Fressoz argue, 'the automobile created the oil industry' and, in Imre Szeman's terms, 'oil and capital are linked inextricably', the EV at least signals some reconfiguration of fossil capital, even if it remains tightly bound to the status quo in other ways.[17] But, in another echo of CM, there remain extensive questions about the ethical credentials of EVs that dampen any sense of they might herald a radical future beyond petrocapitalism.

For all the positive spin, Hans A. Baer calculates that it will take '230 years to replace the world's current car fleet with EVs'.[18] Even if technological innovations allow for a more rapid transition, the manufacture of a new generation of vehicles will produce a considerable carbon footprint. Once an EV is on the road, its promised attainment of carbon neutrality depends on the source of the electricity it uses. The assumption that EVs will utilize an expanded provision of renewable energy sources is not straightforward. By creating a substantial additional demand for electricity, EVs appear likely to impact negatively the chances of nations being able to move entirely to sustainable sources of generation. Then there are questions about the supply of the minerals necessary for the batteries of EVs – principally cobalt, copper, lithium and manganese – and the rare earth materials (neodymium, praseodymium, dysprosium and terbium) used in their motors. Enthusiastic targets set by governments for the transition to EVs rarely take account of concerns around these minerals' future availability.[19] Moreover, the extraction of many of these elements carries alarming ethical implications. As Siddharth Kara notes in his heartrending exposé of conditions in the Democratic Republic of Congo (DRC) where 75 per cent of the global supply of cobalt originates, the 'scale of destruction caused by cobalt mining in the name of renewable energy is without contemporary parallel' with widespread use of child labour and devastating ecological consequences. Kara's conclusion is stark: 'Our daily lives are powered by a human and environmental catastrophe in the Congo.'[20] At the heart of this disaster is the explosion of the EV market since 2010. 'Meeting the ambitions of the Paris Agreement' signed in 2015 to limit global heating would require, Kara explains, 'at least 100 million total electric vehicles in use by 2030', which will inevitably 'push hundreds of thousands of Congolese women, men and children into hazardous pits and tunnels to help meet demand'.[21] Neither is this the first time that the Congo has been ravaged by the global automobile industry. The horrors of Belgian colonial rule in the late nineteenth and early twentieth centuries under King Leopold II were motivated to a significant degree by the 'millions of square kilometres of rubber trees' necessary for the tyres that drove 'the first automobile revolution'.[22]

If resource extraction to service the EV revolution in places like the DRC is deeply problematic, this begs the question, as Thomas Peacock puts it, whether we can 'do a better job in the ocean than we do on land'.[23] At any rate, the metals used in EV batteries (and in other forms of digital and green technology) are, as Lisa Yin Han notes, 'found in greater quantities at the ocean bottom than on land'.[24] The ethical credentials of deep-sea mining as the next frontier for resource extraction do not look encouraging, however. Current ocean mining practices are so intensive that, as the marine biologist Douglas McCauley notes, 'anything that's living in that habitat will be destroyed'.[25] The rise of EVs may thus require the decimation of large areas of the sea floor. It is here that pro-animal politics comes into view alongside environmental discourses as a perspective from which to interrogate the promise of sustainable automobility via the emergence of EVs. The possible colonization of the sea floor by extractive capitalism threatens a dramatic increase in the scope of animal harm in the name of car culture. From its beginnings, mass automobility has produced mass animal death. Statistics on the precise extent of this are hard to garner, but it has been estimated that 'roadkill might be responsible for more than one million animal deaths *per day* in the United States alone' (original emphasis).[26] Because they are characteristically quieter than conventional cars, it is possible that EVs will entail greater animal mortality on the roads to add to the potentially vast scale of the death of marine life in deep-sea mining (and indeed of terrestrial species in mining operations in the DRC and elsewhere).

If the transition to EVs is not a magic bullet in terms of ecological or animal ethics, neither does it absolve automobility from its links to public health detriments, despite the evident benefits of a reduction of street-level emissions of particulate matter and other pollutants. A possible increase in roadkill implies a potential increase of deaths of human pedestrians in road traffic accidents.[27] EVs will do nothing to address the link between car culture and health risks created by physical inactivity.[28] As Miner et al. conclude, the 'political prioritisation of electric vehicles is unlikely to result in large reductions in deaths, injuries, injustices, or the environmental damage caused by automobility'.[29] Many of the overarching problems with automobility stem from the simple fact that cars run on roads (and on tyres) and will continue to do so at least until the next, often-cited speculative transition to flying cars. The history of cars is marked, in Braun and Randell's terms, by a 'process of massive land appropriation' that the electrification of automobility is unlikely to assuage.[30] Roads will remain places of harm. Along with collisions between cars and other beings – animal and human – roads (and other forms of automobile-related hard standing) are dead zones that increase the risk of flooding, exacerbate the urban heat island effect and contribute to the erosion of animal habitats by facilitating illegal logging and other forms of unsanctioned resource extraction. Cars will remain a problem whether they are powered by electricity or fossil fuels, and the sense of a straightforward binary between electric and petrol-fuelled vehicles is in any case misleading as long as some electricity is still generated by fossil fuels.

Automobility thus represents a pivotal, and as yet unresolved, topic in debates about sustainability. The transition to sustainable transport might be taken as an opportunity to embrace more radical ideological and economic possibilities beyond the triumvirate of oil, automobility and capital. But to reach any such point, a deeper and more widespread critique of automobility, not just of oil, needs to take hold. To that end, in the remainder of this chapter, and the subsequent chapters in Part 2, I explore both pro-animal and ecological approaches to the question of automobility as an instantiation of petrocapitalism.

The lines between animal and ecological ethics are less clearly drawn in the context of automobility, and with reference to the larger question of petroculture, than they are in relation to debates around meat. Evidently, the link between the environmental humanities and petroculture is conceptually intimate. There can be no meaningful analysis of climate crisis without a discussion of oil. Despite this, the analysis of oil was largely absent from foundational work in ecocriticism. Pollution was a key conceptual focus, as in the opening chapter of Garrard's *Ecocriticism* (2004), but there is little explicit engagement with oil as a feature of ecological emergency that merits extended analysis on its own terms and not just as part of the general background to climate crisis. Texts like Cheryl Glotfelty and Harold Fromm's *The Ecocriticism Reader* (1996) and Richard Kerridge and Neil Sammells's edited volume *Writing the Environment: Ecocriticism and Literature* (1998) yield nothing of sustained petrocultural interest. There are brief references to oil in Lawrence Buell's *Writing for an Endangered World: Literature, Culture, and Environment in the U.S. and Beyond* (2001) but then less in *The Future of Environmental Criticism* (2005). Even more recent state-of-the-field volumes like *The Cambridge Companion to Literature and the Environment* and *The Oxford Handbook of Ecocriticism* (both published in 2014) contain minimal direct references to oil. Ecocriticism's scant engagement with oil can be taken as evidence of Szeman's claim that fossil fuels are 'hiding in plain sight' from 'critical scholarship' and the 'literature and culture of modernity', even in those fields that would seem most closely linked to them.[31]

Despite ecocriticism's belatedness in tackling oil head-on, the beginnings of petroculture as a topic in critical inquiry were already taking shape in the early 1990s. Amitav Ghosh's 1992 essay 'Petrofiction: The Oil Encounter and the Novel', a review of Abdelrahman Munif's *Cities of Salt* (1984), is widely taken as an inaugural moment in the cultural analysis of oil that begins from the observation that despite oil's absolute centrality in the modern world, it has 'produced scarcely a single [literary] work of note'.[32] Ghosh's hypothesis that there are very few books about oil gave rise to the countervailing claim that, in an era structured around the supply and consumption of oil, all books are involved to some extent with it; as Graeme Macdonald argues, 'Modern writing is premised on both the promise and the hidden costs and benefits of hydrocarbon culture.'[33] Even when oil is not explicitly represented, its effects and manifestations can be traced everywhere in the texts of what came to be known as petromodernity. The critical analysis of the role of oil 'in shaping culture and society', as Szeman phrases it, was formalized in 2011 with the foundation of the Petrocultures Research Group.[34] An ever-expanding lexicon has accompanying this task: from petrocriticism, to petrosexuality, to petromelancholia and much more. Not long afterwards, in 2013, the energy humanities was added to the roster as a form of enquiry closely linked to petroculture, though with a broader remit to investigate other forms of energy before, beyond or after oil while retaining a focus on petromodernity as the key context for this agenda.[35]

The task of understanding energy was from the outset connected – how could it not be? – to ecological questions. As Szeman and Dominic Boyer note in the 'Introduction' to *Energy Humanities: An Anthology*, a landmark publication in the emerging field, a focus on energy provides a 'new vantage point on global warming and environmental crisis'.[36] Consequently, there is a strong link between petroculture and the energy humanities and the environmental humanities, which, formalized around 2010, is part of the same intellectual moment. So, for Bergthaller, 'understanding the ways in which energy systems condition the life-worlds people inhabit, their sense of agency, horizon of expectations, and modes of communication, will therefore have to rank among the principal tasks of the environmental humanities'.[37] If this attitude informs the consistent inclusion of questions of oil and energy in state-of-the-field handbooks and companions to the environmental humanities (in contrast to their absence from similar ecocritical volumes), this does not mean that the link between the energy and environmental humanities has been entirely clear. Despite being premised on ecological concerns, much work in the energy humanities is not conceptualized directly as part of the environmental humanities. Szeman and Boyer's 'Introduction' prefers the looser term 'environmental studies' to the environmental humanities when glossing wider endeavours in ecological thinking. Moreover, they insist that the energy humanities should be seen as 'more than just a specialist field of study – a subset of environmental studies'.[38] While there are continual points of exchange and influence between the energy and environmental humanities to the extent that it is not easy to demarcate between them, they do not map completely onto each other. Given the insistence that the energy humanities is a distinctive enterprise, it would perhaps be more accurate to see it as a perspective that has been partially absorbed into the environmental humanities rather than one that has radiated out from it.

Neither is the more specific question of automobility straightforwardly located in the history of green cultural thought. It is hardly surprising that ecocriticism's first wave had little to say about cars given its reticence on oil. Nor, conversely, is it surprising that automobility played a decisive role in the formation of what might be called a petrocritical methodology, which is to say a determination to trace the presence of oil in texts from which it might easily be thought to be absent. So, for example, in an editorial on the nascent energy humanities in 2011, Patricia Yaeger uses Jack Kerouac's *On the Road* (1957) to illustrate how it might be possible to 'think systematically about how … texts relate to energy sources across time and space'. For Yaeger, Kerouac's characters are 'gasaholics', moving through a world created by 'oil dependency' even if the substance of oil is not immediately visible in the narrative. Is there, Yaeger asks, 'an energy unconscious at work' in the text?[39] In this way, analysis of literary and cultural representations of cars is integral to how 'we understand, respond to, and engage with our oil ontologies', to quote Szeman's summary of the task of petroculture and the energy humanities.[40]

There are close links – again unsurprisingly – between this turn in the humanities and the multidisciplinary field of automobility studies which is anchored largely in the social sciences and which found its origins in the 2000s (though with some notable antecedents). Despite this network of scholarly work around cars, there has been little engagement with automobility in work explicitly conceptualized as part of the environmental humanities, as distinct from the energy humanities. There remains a tendency to see cars, as Harilaos Stecopoulos argues in an essay on *The Great Gatsby* as petrofiction, as only an 'indirect' form of the representation of oil that does 'little more than testify to the ubiquity of the resource'.[41] The claim that the relationship between oil and automobility can be characterized as indirect ignores their intimate material links (recall that automobility accounts for 'around half of global oil consumption') as well as underplaying the decisive role of automobility in the ideology and experience of petrocapitalism. It is through analysis of the material manifestations of oil that its ubiquitous but routinely repressed cultural meanings can be traced. Cars are part of the bedrock of our oil ontologies.

To date, ecological approaches to oil have been significantly more developed than pro-animal approaches. To put this another way, there are more fully realized links between the environmental humanities and the energy humanities than there are between the energy humanities and animal studies, though that picture is starting to change. Josephine Taylor's work, for example, is premised on an intention to 'awaken a consciousness of the nonhuman suffering at the centre of energy production'.[42] There is particularly significant work emerging at the confluence of animal studies and automobility studies that draws on extensive historical and thematic connections between cars and animals, beyond the analogy between CM and EVs, and which may have a crucial role to play in stimulating critical ecological approaches to the promises of green transport, which in turn refract back on to the wider questions of petroculture and sustainable transition.

One direction into the connections between animals and automobility is to develop a comparative analysis of the ways in which opposition to cars and meat has been configured. Grappling with the persistence of automobility requires reflection on the extraordinary lack of coherent opposition to the mass private ownership of cars. The lingering spectre of car harm suggests that there might be an ethical imperative to avoid travelling in any automobiles, including EVs. (Buses and other forms of public road transport are also linked with car harm but constitute a lesser violence because of the economy of scale of a single vehicle transporting multiple passengers against the often-solitary transit of the privately own car.) Yet, despite the ample evidence that can be marshalled in support of a post-car politics, the refusal of automobility as a matter of conscience remains a significantly more marginal position than veganism. Vegan activism and scholarship provide a direct and concerted challenge to carnism's dominant status, but there is no word in common usage for someone who refuses automobility. The conception of a 'car-free movement', encompassing the long history of road protests, advocacy for investment in public transport and campaigns to improve infrastructure for cyclists, pedestrians and wheelchair users, remains informal and largely manifested in local actions, even if it is strongly connected to more concerted international efforts to move away from fossil fuels (though these movements, as in the case of Just Stop Oil, tend to focus on fossil fuels in a way that appears to grant relative immunity to EVs). 'Anti-car' is in common usage as an often-pejorative description of an aversion to or refusal of automobility but frames such a position only as a negation. There is currently no widely used positive descriptor of post-automobile ethics in the way that veganism might be characterized not just as the refusal of animal products but also as a distinguishing (if certainly not unitary) ideological orientation that results in an identity category that is not just defined oppositionally; to think of veganism as being just 'anti-meat' would be to miss the wider implications of vegan practices and politics. The terms 'cyclist' or 'pedestrian' may each carry the force of an affirmative ethics ('bike activism', moreover, is a long-standing social movement) but without capturing the overarching position of a resistance to car culture. It is possible to be both a cyclist and a motorist, while it is not possible to be vegan and to consume animal products. The most encouraging term for car refusers is Calarco's coinage of 'altermobility' as a way of expressing a multifaceted commitment to forms of movement beyond the car, though at the time of writing the idea has yet to gain wider traction. Cynically, one explanation of the relative incoherence of anti-car activism compared to veganism is that it is easier to commodify plant-based diets that it is to commodify pedestrianism. (Walking in this sense might be a surprisingly radical act.) Or it might simply be the case that the love of cars runs deeper than the taste for meat.

The reason for the lack of a concerted movement against automobility is that, as Miner et al. conclude, 'car harm has grown to be so ubiquitous that it is socially constructed as normal ... or inevitable'.[43] As car harm increases, so ironically has car use so that, according to Peter Freund and George Martin, since the 1970s the world has been in the grip of 'hyperautomobility', characterized by a continuing expansion of car ownership.[44] This historical trend is neither innocent nor accidental. As Calarco notes, the 'capitalist class and others invested in hyperautomobility do whatever they can to persuade us that the future is and must be ever-more hypermobile'.[45] Given automobility's cultural, political and economic centrality, it is evident that society is structured, to follow the argument of Walker et al., on an 'inability to think objectively about cars'.[46] The enduring hegemony of automobility is not based on empirical evidence of its utility and social necessity but rests rather, for Walker et al., on far more complex 'psycho-socio-cultural' factors by which the self-evident violence of car culture is emptied of ethical and political significance.[47] Cars are widely seen, as Baer argues, as 'an extension of the self' with an intimate connection to questions of identity and a function as an index of social and personal success.[48] Margaret Thatcher insisted, 'If a man finds himself on a bus having attained the age of 26, he can count himself a failure.'[49] The car is the exemplary neoliberal artefact through which the psyche and commodity are brought into alignment. As Christian Schwägerl puts it, 'We merge with [cars] as if in some kind of personal union:' '"I'm parked over there."'[50] Again links to food readily suggest themselves: 'You are what you drive' has emerged, for example, as a play on the old adage 'you are what you eat'. Integral to the intimate connection of mind and vehicle is the way in which, as Heathcote Williams frames it in his documentary poem *Autogeddon*, the car appears to

> satisfy a compendious spectrum of desires:
> Sexual,
> Social,
> Economic
> And religious,
> Gratifying am A to Z of unbridled cravings
> In the guise of getting from A to B.[51]

Automobility is never just about transport (just as meat is never just about food).

Automobility's cultural centrality is highlighted by debates around the introduction of low emissions zones in urban areas. When the former British prime minister Rishi Sunak described efforts to increase the regulation of traffic as against 'the right values of the British people', his declaration mobilized the long-standing involvement of cars with identity politics.[52] Such populist soundbites are not a mode of discourse that encourages critical analysis, though it is precisely the assumption of self-evidence in such rhetoric that demands attention. As Braun and Randell argue, 'Automobility is a hegemonic ontology because it has been constructed as an imaginary that appears not as an imaginary but as real.'[53] Sunak's comments provide a portal into automobile ideology masquerading as common sense. For Sunak, any restrictions on car use – 'hare-brained schemes' like 'Low Traffic Neighbourhoods' or 'blanket 20mph speed limits' – represent a 'war on motorists'.[54] 'British values' inhere, therefore, in the reassertion of motorists' rights. How exactly we should understand British values in relation to automobility remains underdetermined, though again it is precisely the sense of taken for grantedness that underlines the force of automobility. The car and the open road are among the most potent emblems of individual liberty; the interpretation of traffic regulation as an attack on 'people's freedoms' is structured on the mythic imaginary behind mass automobility. Given the extent of car harm, however, the alignment of motoring and British values encourages a bleak satire. Since cars are a significant factor in child mortality, should we conclude that an integral part of British values is allowing children to die? That the issue of child death – an essential part of the rationale for reducing speed limits and controlling traffic in residential areas – does not register in Sunak's defence of the car provides further evidence of the extent to which automobility's violence is repressed. In fact, so deep is the imbrication of automobility in capitalist culture that Walker et al. conclude that even 'minority non-drivers have internalised the mindset of the majority drivers'.[55] Their argument runs that if you do not drive a car, you are still likely to evince a broad acceptance of the damage wreaked by automobility, including forms of harm generated by so-called green transport. The car from this vantage appears indivisible from human existence under capitalism, a phenomenon Ian Walker et al. characterize as 'motonormativity': the widespread social assumption that privately owned cars will remain the default and non-negotiable mode of transportation.[56]

These 'compulsory forms of mobility', as Calarco calls them, encourage deeper reflection on the links between motonormativity and carnism, or carnonormativity, as it is framed by some scholars.[57] In this way, the methods of the energy humanities mirror those of vegan studies; each field is interested in locating the symptoms and expressions of occluded forms of violence. As Taylor asks, with reference to Carol J. Adams's influential work, 'What if we were to extend [the] notion of the absent referent to think about how the oil industry likewise moves through systematic and structural effacement and elision, therefore bringing meat and oil culture into dialogue?'[58] One way to advance such a dialogue would be to transpose Melanie Joy's three ns of carnism – the social construction of meat as 'normal', 'natural' and 'necessary' – to automobility, a task which can be completed with surprising precision. The assumption that cars are *necessary* is the most straightforwardly applicable of the three terms. Sunak's attack on emergent forms of traffic regulation was supported, for example, by his claim that the 'vast majority of people in the country ... are dependent on cars'.[59] That automobility is widely considered *normal* is evidenced by the characteristic designation of active or shared modes of transportation as 'alternative', even though walking evidently predates automobility by millennia.[60] Just as vegans might be considered 'weird' from a normative standpoint, so the refusal of automobility as a matter of conscience announces a distance from the structures of social acceptability.

A more counter-intuitive link between automobility and Joy's three ns appears in the idea that cars might be considered *natural*, a claim that on the face of it seems preposterous. For John Urry, automobility is so central to twentieth- and twenty-first-century industry and economics that the car can be considered the 'quintessential *manufactured object*' (original emphasis).[61] Carnism may derive ideological energy from the imagining of primeval humans eating animal flesh as evidence of a biological orientation towards meat, but it is evidently much harder to imagine the car as an expression of a natural or authentic human selfhood. Nonetheless, the semiotics of automobility is intimately involved with the imagining of nature. Car advertising makes frequent usage of wilderness landscapes, a trope that emerges most recurrently with reference to SUVs (one of the most carbon-intensive forms of automobility, even in their electric incarnations). As Shane Guster summarizes, 'Speeding through deserts and jungles, fording raging rivers, and even scaling the heights of Mt. Everest, the SUV is routinely depicted in the most spectacular and remote natural locations.'[62] Rather than an ecologically damaging intrusion into the natural world, the car appears as part of the wilderness. The widespread connection of car marketing to animality via the names of cars (think of the Jaguar or Mustang) and in advertising slogans ('put a tiger in your tank', as an old Esso campaign incited) emphasizes the generation of the meanings of automobile through the iconography of the natural. Cars, as Nicole Shukin's influential argument points out, 'symbolically occupy the place of animal life' at the same time that 'car culture materially displaces animals ... through the infrastructure of roads and highways that transect animal habitats'.[63] The idea that cars are natural reinforces the ironic structure at play in the counterpoint between the semiotic and the material dimensions of automobility: as automobility, in the terms of Steffen Böhm et al., unsettles 'taken-for-granted boundaries separating ... nature from artifice', the situation arises in which the erosion of the natural is facilitated by the iconography of the natural.[64] The reasons to think about meat and animals together with car culture gain further emphasis from the origination of the mass production of cars following Henry Ford's visit to a Chicago slaughterhouse. As Shukin explains, Ford's vision of the factory assembly line contains a 'crucial mimetic twist: his automated lines sped the assembly of a machinic body rather than the disassembly of an animal body'.[65] To follow history forward from that moment, the more cars that have been assembled, the more animal bodies (as we have seen) have been disassembled. Automobility might thus be the vegan 'gotcha' par excellence. Given the multiple forms of harm integral to automobility, should vegans drive?

The links between automobility and animal ethics are elucidated in an intriguing way by ongoing debates around the relationship between veganism and roadkill. One of the central reference points here is Donald W. Bruckner's use of the example of roadkill to form the argument that 'strict vegetarianism is immoral'.[66] For Bruckner, while eating meat from factory farms is wrong because it supports an industry that causes 'extensive harm to animals', eating roadkill by contrast 'completely avoids supporting practices that cause harm to animals':[67] because 'road-killed animals are already dead ..., they are not harmed by picking them up'.[68] It may even be 'morally obligatory' to eat roadkill.[69] Bruckner's argument has gained some support among vegan thinkers. Josh Milburn sees Bruckner's position as possibly the 'best argument ... against veganism' and an element of a wider conclusion Milburn draws that 'the food system of an animal-rights-respecting state might not be vegan'.[70] What is most significant in the context of automobility about Bruckner's argument, and the vegan response to it, is not so much the direct question of whether vegans should eat roadkill – or should participate in a wider freeganism that includes animal-based foods – but rather the way in which car harm is naturalized. Remarkably, automobility remains largely invisible in these debates.

While Milburn offers the caveat that 'we should probably be doing much more to prevent roadkill', the central claim in Bruckner's discussion that roadkill 'completely avoids supporting practices that cause harm to animals' requires more reflection than it receives.[71] Bruckner goes into some detail about the relative harmlessness of eating roadkill. On the topic of pollution, he notes that 'the collection of roadkill increases petroleum consumption only by the tiniest amount of additional fuel one uses transporting the additional weight' of the dead animal.[72] Moreover, overlooking the structural centrality of the road network, he suggests that 'no ... land need to be devoted to producing roadkill' (as opposed to the land needed to grow crops, for example).[73] In short, the multifarious harms of automobility are evaded in order to construct a position in which animal bodies killed by automobility can be considered ethically 'free' (and hence part of or analogous to freeganism). The more radical pro-animal position is to see roadkill, in Calarco's terms, as part of a discourse of mobility 'in which both animal and human lives are rendered sacrificable and subject to being killed with impunity'.[74] The key point is not how much carrying a dead deer in the boot of a car increases fuel expenditure, as Bruckner would have it, but that the normalization of automobility (of which Bruckner's position is an example) comes at an enormous ethical cost. Calarco's argument aims to make visible the wider network of harm that constitutes automobility; these forms of violence are not, for Calarco, 'accidents of the system but are fundamental to its design'.[75]

The analysis of roadkill provides an invitation to bring vegan studies – and the broader field of animal studies – much more fully into the critical discussions of automobility. Calarco suggests that in animal justice movements 'little has been said or done to challenge the horrific effects of dominant modes of mobility', though his work is a notable step in that direction.[76] Accordingly, the following two chapters address this lack by exploring automobility as a multispecies phenomenon that deepens the investigation of cars in environmental thought on either side of the sustainable transition from petrol to EVs. At the heart of this enterprise is an affirmative view of the possibility that literature might, as Calarco claims, help 'to expand our future imaginary and to denaturalize the present system' through attention to both the suffering of non-human creatures in car culture and the violence inherent in the landscapes of automobility.[77]

Notes

1 Matthew Calarco, *Reflections on Roadkill between Mobility Studies and Animal Studies: Altermobilities* (London: Palgrave, 2023), 268.
2 Fassler, 'The Revolution That Died on Its Way to Dinner', *New York Times*, 9 February 2024, https://www.nytimes.com/2024/02/09/opinion/eat-just-upside-foods-cultivated-meat.html, accessed 24 June 2024.
3 Heather Rogers, *Green Gone Wrong: Dispatches from the Front Line of Eco-Capitalism* (London: Verso, 2010), 2.
4 World Health Organisation, 'Air Pollution', https://www.who.int/health-topics/air-pollution#tab=tab_3, accessed 6 November 2024.
5 Ioannis Manisalidis, Elisavet Stavropoulou, Agathangelos Stavropoulos and Eugenia Bezirtzoglou, 'Environmental and Health Impacts of Air Pollution: A Review', *Frontiers in Public Health* 8 (2020), 14, 1–13, 2.
6 Patrick Miner Elisavet Stavropoulou, Agathangelos Stavropoulos and Eugenia Bezirtzoglou, 'Car Harm: A Global Review of Automobility's Harm to People and the Environment', *Journal of Transport Geography* 115 (2024), 103817, 1–17, 6.
7 Miner et al., 'Car Harm', 3.
8 Miner et al., 'Car Harm', 4.
9 Robert Braun and Richard Randell, *Post-Automobility Futures: Technology, Power and Imaginaries* (Lanham, MD: Rowman and Littlefield, 2022), 85–6.

10 Miner et al. 'Car Harm', 10.
11 Miner et al. 'Car Harm', 5.
12 Miner et al. 'Car Harm', 11.
13 Jasper Jolly, 'Most New Cars Sold in UK Will Have to Be Fully Electric by 2030', *The Guardian*, https://www.theguardian.com/environment/2023/sep/28/majority-of-newscars-sold-in-uk-will-have-to-be-fully-electric-by-2030-government-confirms, accessed 6 November 2024.
14 EVA England, 'Benefits of EVs', https://www.evaengland.org.uk/about-electric-vehicles/benefits-of-evs/, accessed 6 November 2024.
15 Gordon Sayre, 'Automobile'. In *Fueling Culture: 101 Words for Energy and Environment*. Edited by Imre Szeman, Jennifer Wenzel and Patricia Yaeger, 54–6, 56 (New York: Fordham University Press, 2017).
16 Hannes Bergthaller, 'Fossil Freedoms: The Politics of Emancipation and the End of Oil'. In *The Routledge Companion to the Environmental Humanities*. Edited by Ursula Heise, Jon Christensen and Michelle Niemann, 424–32, 426 (London: Routledge, 2017).
17 Christophe Bonneuil and Jean-Baptiste Fressoz, *The Shock of the Anthropocene: The Earth, History and Us* (London: Verso Books, 2016), 100; Imre Szeman, *On Petrocultures: Globalization, Energy and Culture* (Morgantown: West Virginia University Press, 2019), 94.
18 Hans A. Baer, *Motor Vehicles, the Environment and the Human Condition* (Lanham, MD: Lexington Press, 2019), 177.
19 See Benjamin Ballinger, Martin Stringer, Diego R. Schmeda-Lopez, Benjamin Kefford, Brett Parkinson, Chris Greig, and Simon Smart, 'The Vulnerability of Electric Vehicle Deployment to Critical Mineral Supply', *Applied Energy* 255 (2019), 113844.
20 Siddharth Kara, *Cobalt Red: How the Blood of the Congo Powers Our Lives* (London: St Martin's Press, 2023), 5.
21 Kara, *Cobalt Red*, 27.
22 Kara, *Cobalt Red*, 27.
23 Cited in Lisa Yin Han, *Deepwater Alchemy: Extractive Mediation and the Taming of the Seafloor* (Minneapolis: University of Minnesota Press, 2024), 105.
24 Yin Han, *Deepwater Alchemy*, 92.
25 Kiley Price, 'Will the Drive for EVs Destroy Earth's Last Ecosystem', *Live Science*, https://www.livescience.com/planet-earth/climate-change/mining-crystals-locked-in-the-deep-sea-could-help-fight-climate-change-it-may-also-destroy-earths-last-untouched-ecosystem, accessed 6 November 2024.
26 Calarco, *Roadkill*, 270.

27 Lero, 'Electric Cars More Likely to Cause Accidents, Research Shows', *Sci Tech Daily*, https://scitechdaily.com/electric-car-drivers-more-likely-to-cause-accidents-research-shows/, accessed 6 November 2024.
28 Ian Walker et al., 'Motonormativity: How Social Norms Hide a Major Public Health Hazard', *International Journal of Environment and Health* 11.1 (2023), 21–33.
29 Miner et al., 'Car Harm', 12.
30 Braun and Randell, *Post-Automobility Futures*, 99.
31 Szeman, *On Petrocultures*, 6.
32 Amitav Ghosh, 'Petrofiction: The Oil Encounter and the Novel', *The New Republic*, vol. 2, 2 March 1992, 29–33.
33 Graeme Macdonald, 'Oil and World Literature', *American Book Review* 33.3 (March–April 2012), 7–31, 7, 31.
34 Imre Szeman, 'On the Energy Humanities; or, What Can Philosophy Tell Us about Oil?', *European Union Centre of Excellence Papers*, no. 1 (2015), 4–23, 7.
35 See Imre Szeman and Dominic Boyer, 'Acknowledgments'. In *Energy Humanities: An Anthology*. Edited by Szeman and Boyer, vii–viii (Baltimore, MD: John Hopkins University Press, 2017).
36 Szeman and Boyer, 'Introduction', in *Energy Humanities*, 1–14, 2.
37 Bergthaller, 'Fossil Freedoms', 82.
38 Szeman and Boyer, 'Introduction', 4.
39 Patricia Yaeger, 'Literature in the Ages of Wood, Tallow, Coal, Whale Oil, Gasoline, Atomic Power, and Other Energy Sources', *PMLA* 126.2 (2011), 305–26, 306.
40 Imre Szeman, 'Introduction to Focus: Petrofictions', *American Book Review* 33.3 (2012), 3.
41 Harilaos Stecopoulos, 'The Heat of Modernity: The Great Gatsby as Petrofiction', in *The Cambridge Companion to American Literature and the Environment* (Cambridge: Cambridge University Press, 2022), 81–92, 81.
42 Josephine Taylor, *The Nonhuman Narratives of Energy: Multispecies Encounters in Extraction Zones* (London: Palgrave, 2025), 7.
43 Miner et al., 'Car Harm', 3.
44 Peter Freund and George Martin, 'Hypermobility, the Social Organisation of Space and Health', *Mobilities* 2.1 (2007), 37–49.
45 Calarco, *Roadkill*, 88.
46 Walker et al., 'Motonormativity', 3.
47 Walker et al., 'Motonormativity', 12.
48 Baer, *Motor Vehicles*, 48.
49 Cited in James McLelland, 'Why the Left Loves Trains (and Hates Cars)', *Challenge Magazine*, 29 January 2023, https://

challenge-magazine.org/2023/01/29/why-the-left-loves-trains-and-hates-cars/, accessed 29 April 2025.
50 Christian Schwägerl, *The Anthropocene: The Human Era and How It Shapes the Planet* (London: Synergetic Press, 2014), 128.
51 Heathcote Williams, *Autogeddon* (London: Jonathan Cape, 1991), 10–12.
52 Carlton Reid, '20mph Zones "Against British Values" Rishi Sunak Says Prior to Unveiling Pro-Motorist Policies', *Forbes*, https://www.forbes.com/sites/carltonreid/2023/09/29/20mph-zones-against-british-values-rishi-sunak-says-prior-to-unveiling-pro-motorist-policies/, accessed 6 November 2024.
53 Braun and Randell, *Post-Automobility Futures*, 28.
54 Graeme Baker, 'Sunak Vows to Stop 20mph Zones', *BBC News*, https://www.bbc.co.uk/news/uk-politics-66965714, accessed 6 November, 2024.
55 Walker et al., 'Motonormativity', 12.
56 Walker et al., 'Motonormativity', 11.
57 Calarco, *Roadkill*, 81; for a sample use of the term 'carnonormativity' see C. P. Freeman, 'Lisa and Phoebe, Lone Vegetarian Icons: At Odds with Television's Carnonormativity'. In *How Television Shapes Our Worldview: Media Representations of Social Trends and Change*. Edited by Deborah A. Macey et al., 193–212 (Lanham, MD: Lexington Books, 2014).
58 Taylor, *The Nonhuman Narratives of Energy*, 57.
59 Oliver Slow, 'Sunak Orders Review of Low Traffic Neighbourhoods in Pro-Motorist Message', *BBC News*, https://www.bbc.co.uk/news/uk-politics-66351785, accessed 6 November 2024.
60 See Miner et al., 'Car Harm', 1.
61 John Urry, 'The System of Automobility', *Theory, Culture & Society* 21.4–5 (2004), 25–39, 25.
62 Shane Gunster, '"You Belong Outside": Advertising, Nature, and the SUV', *Ethics and the Environment* 9.2 (2004), 4–32, 4.
63 Nicole Shukin, *Animal Capital: Rendering Life in Biopolitical Times* (Minneapolis: University of Minnesota Press, 2009), 126.
64 Steffen Böhm, Campbell Jones, Chris Land and Mat Paterson, 'Introduction: Impossibilities of Automobility'. In *Against Automobility*. Edited by Steffen Böhm, Campbell Jones, Chris Land and Matthew Patterson, 3–16, 3 (Oxford: Blackwell, 2006).
65 Shukin, *Animal Capital*, 87.
66 Donald A. Bruckner, 'Strict Vegetarianism Is Immoral'. In *The Moral Complexities of Eating Meat*. Edited by B. Bramble and B. Fisher, 30 (Oxford: Oxford University Press, 2015).
67 Bruckner, 'Strict Vegetarianism Is Immoral', 32, 33.

68 Bruckner, 'Strict Vegetarianism Is Immoral', 37.
69 Bruckner, 'Strict Vegetarianism Is Immoral', 36.
70 Josh Milburn, 'The Best Argument against Veganism', *ShARC Blog*, https://sharc.sites.sheffield.ac.uk/blog/the-best-argument-against-veganism, accessed 6 November 2024.
71 Milburn, 'The Best Argument against Veganism'.
72 Bruckner, 'Strict Vegetarianism Is Immoral', 39.
73 Bruckner, 'Strict Vegetarianism Is Immoral', 40.
74 Matthew Calarco, 'Animals, Mobility and the Future of Meat'. In *The Future of Meat without Animals*. Edited by Brianne Donaldson and Brian Carter, 270 (Lanham, MD: Rowman and Littlefield, 2016).
75 Calarco, *Roadkill*, 41.
76 Calarco, 'Animals, Mobility and the Future of Meat', 268.
77 Calarco, *Roadkill*, 83.

CHAPTER 5

Roadkill in J. G. Ballard's autoscapes

Initial critical assessments of J. G. Ballard's contribution to ecological thought tended to be skewed towards his suite of early apocalyptic, and post-apocalyptic, fictions in which the Earth is subjected to what have become (for the most part) familiar scenarios of emerging and future catastrophe. In *The Wind from Nowhere* (1961) – Ballard's often overlooked first novel – the planet is devastated by a 'meteorological phenomenon of unprecedented magnitude': 350 mph gales initiated, it is speculated, by 'unusually high levels of cosmic radiation' following a solar eclipse.[1] His second novel *The Drowned World* (1962) depicts a superheated planet deluged with water from the melted icecaps following a series of solar storms. *The Drought* (1964, first published as *The Burning World*) conversely imagines an Earth parched after 'vast quantities of industrial wastes discharged into the ocean basins' have prevented 'almost all evaporation of surface water into the air space above'.[2] The last novel in this phase is *The Crystal World* (1966) in which a West African jungle crystallizes in a rapidly progressing emergency that threatens to encompass the whole planet. This disaster is caused, mysteriously, by 'random discharges ... set off by the creation of anti-galaxies in space' depleting 'the time-store available to the materials of our own solar system'.[3]

It is hardly surprising that the 'disaster quartet' as it has been described should have attracted the attention of ecocritics.[4] If the aetiology of these successive catastrophes does not map consistently on to the situation of our own environmental crisis, Ballard's apocalyptic mood in the 1960s nonetheless exemplifies one of environmentalism's most prominent rhetorical strategies. For Lawrence Buell, the apocalypse is 'the single most powerful master metaphor that the contemporary environmental imagination has at its disposal'. In this tradition, 'the fate of the world hinges on the arousal of the imagination to a sense of crisis'.[5] The attention to the 'world' directed by three of the titles (until *The Burning World* was relabelled *The Drought*) gives explicit emphasis to the perception of a planet in peril that structures this strand of environmental thought. At the same time, Ballard's interest in extreme weather in the first three of these texts fosters readings that foreground the specific ecological anxieties of the late twentieth and early twenty-first centuries. Although the term 'cli-fi' was not coined until 2008, there is a recurrent claim in environmental criticism that Ballard was already writing it, nearly half a century before the term entered critical discourse.[6] As Adrian Tait observes, Ballard's early work 'is "cli-fi" before climate change was itself understood'.[7] Yet, despite the evident promise of the disaster quartet for ecocriticism, there are also some significant caveats to add to the greening of J. G. Ballard.

Evidently, as Tait's comments attest, chronology presents a problem to Ballard's status as a pioneer of cli-fi. Having successfully predicted in 1967 that Ronald Reagan would become US president (an eventuality which came to pass in 1981), Ballard is often regarded as a prophetic writer. Climatological readings of the disaster quartet could take encouragement from this reputation, though other forms of impending global catastrophe – the prospect of nuclear war most conspicuously – provide a more immediately relevant historical context for Ballard to which environmental concerns are still central. But if the ecological ramifications of the disaster quartet seem clear one way or another, there remains a notable distance between the apparent ecological force of Ballard's fiction and his commentaries on his writing in interviews. As Robert Macfarlane suggests, 'Ballard is not always to be trusted as his own best interpreter', but, even so, his sometimes scathing remarks on environmentalism present a challenge to ecocritical analysis.[8] *Rushing to Paradise* (1994), for example, depicts attempts to save an endangered species of albatross on a remote Pacific island, 'loosely based' on Greenpeace's campaigns against nuclear testing in the 1980s. Reflecting on the novel's politics, Ballard identifies green activism as part of a network of 'extremist cults' that he fears might coalesce into a 'very sinister movement'.[9] From this vantage, the causation of the disaster quartet's apocalypses appears significant. It is only in *The Drought* that humanity is unequivocally to blame; in the other three texts in the sequence the origins of the catastrophes are cosmic rather than anthropogenic. The disaster quartet may carry ecological ramifications, but Ballard does not see these as cautionary tales in the conventional manner of the eco-apocalypse. In another interview, Ballard gave his own, seemingly left-field, interpretation of the meaning of the apocalyptic forces at work in these texts, suggesting that the 'geophysical changes that take place ... are all positive and good ... so they are not disaster stories at all'.[10] For all its appeal for an ecocriticism closely tied to apocalyptic imaginaries, therefore, Ballard's early work has an ambivalent relationship with green politics.

There is good reason, then, to agree with Jim Clarke's assessment of ecocritical readings of the early novels as a form of 'co-option' that risks creating a 'critical lacuna' around the characteristic 'psychological and ontological' elements of Ballard's work.[11] But rather than pointing away from ecological questions, Ballard's interest in the psychological dimensions of disaster is an integral part of his significance for the more-than-humanities. At the core of Ballard's fiction – in the disaster quartet and beyond – is an interplay between his characters' inner worlds and the outer worlds, construed variously and interrelatedly through depictions of environment, landscape, architecture and technology. So, in a moment that is exemplary of this trajectory, Sanders, the doctor at the centre of *The Crystal World*, looks out over the 'distant forest' of Cameroon and closes his eyes slightly 'as if he were deliberately merging the view in front of him with some inner landscape within his mind'.[12] Ballard's (post-)apocalyptic environments facilitate both the novels' interrogation of psychosocial experience and deal with catastrophe as an expression of human psychological orientations. Psychology and ecology in Ballard's work are necessarily conjoined. Consequently, another critical anachronism has emerged to sit alongside Ballard's designation as a cli-fi pioneer. For Thomas Knowles, again drawing on the critical tradition of Ballard as prophet, his fiction stands as something like a guidebook to the Anthropocene: 'a tentative aesthetic and critical means of finding our way in this new geological epoch' characterized by an instability between the inner world of 'man' and the outer world of 'nature'.[13] A consistent element of this process of destabilization in the disaster quartet is a reconfiguration of species politics that embodies the increasing marginality of humankind in their rapidly evolving environments.

As the Earths of the disaster quartet change, so do the forms and geographies of human–animal relations. In *The Drowned World*, for example, London's Ritz Hotel, from which the scientist Robert Kerans surveys the biota of the new environment, is characterized by a 'crocodile-skin desk' and 'ivory-handled squash rackets' that function as reverberations from the lost civilization before the flood.[14] Later, sailing through London's deluged streets, Kerans encounters creatures that contrast markedly with these commodified and objectified animal bodies: giant iguanas 'perched in the windows of the office blocks and department stores'.[15] Animals are no longer the victims of human depredations but have, in the case of the iguanas, 'taken over the city'.[16] A similar pattern unfolds in *The Drought*. A swan 'suffocating in the oil' left by the desiccating environment emphasizes the familiar role of animals as metonymic embodiments of the unfolding catastrophe, but the release of the local zoo animals contrastingly figures the resurgence of animals in the landscape. As the novel's human survivors eke out a meagre living in what remains of the parched city, they are surrounded by a community of white lions 'baying among the dunes'.[17] This disruption of human spaces by animals exemplifies a trend in Ballard's fiction, as Frida Beckman notes, to refuse 'existing structures and patterns of an anthropocentric liberal humanism'.[18] If this makes Ballard's fiction promising ground for an animal studies structured on the contestation of species hierarchies (though there have been far fewer animal-focused readings that there have been ecological approaches), it is again necessary to add caveats. Ballard included animal rights movements in his list of ideologies in danger of coalescing with environmentalism into a sinister cult.

Ballard's situation, then, in a broad more-than-humanities involves an ambiguous relationship to the anachronistic critical terms cli-fi and the Anthropocene, which articulate the environmental humanities' orientation towards the idea of the world. In ecological terms, Ballard is, perhaps above all, an author of the end of nature (to appropriate Bill McKibben's influential phrasing), an orientation that pivots on the intermeshing of the inner and outer worlds and, connectedly, a disruption of conventional human–animal relations.[19] These critical coordinates provide a telling lens on the sterile post-natural terrain of automobility that comes to the fore in what is sometimes described as Ballard's 'urban disaster trilogy': *Crash* (1973), *The Concrete Island* (1974) and *High Rise* (1975).[20] While the disaster quartet links clearly to ecological questions, the environmental implications of this body of work took longer to establish. As Knowles notes, 'Ecocriticism seems to wither and fall away at the prospect of Ballard's concrete wastelands of the 1970s.'[21] If the alliance of the environmental humanities with petroculture and the energy humanities provides a critical context for thinking about this suite of novels as integrally and radically connected to the project of ecological analysis, it is striking how prominent violence against animals is in Ballard's urban disasters, particularly through the representation of roadkill.

Set within Greater London and its immediate surrounds, *Crash*, *The Concrete Island* and *High Rise* provide a forensic interrogation of the intimate human imbrication in petromodernity through the ubiquitous attachment to the automobile. If the disaster quartet seems notable for its anticipation of later environmental discourses and scenarios of the future, these novels have a close relationship to their historical moment. Conflict in the Middle East and an oil embargo imposed by the Organization of Arab Petroleum Exporting Countries (OAPEC) resulted in dramatic increases in the price of fuel and a decrease in its supply as the question of energy entered painfully into public consciousness in the 1970s. But Ballard is not explicitly concerned with the geopolitical machinations of global petroculture; rather, his interest focuses on the psychosocial experience of oil dependency. In this context, it might be more fitting to think of these novels as Ballard's oil trilogy. *Crash* – as Ballard put it 'the first pornographic novel based on technology' – explores the psychopathology of automobility through the depiction of an obsessive sexual interest in traffic accidents.[22] The second novel in the trilogy, *The Concrete Island*, provides a petrocultural revision of the Robinson Crusoe story that narrates the experience of spatial and psychological entrapment in the landscapes of hyperautomobility. After an accident leaves the architect Robert Maitland stranded in an inaccessible patch of land between motorways, the myth of automobility as a promise of infinite freedom collapses into a narrative of incarceration. The last of the trilogy *High Rise* is the least directly focused on cars as a study of violent unrest in a luxury apartment block. If the characters of *High Rise* spend less time on and around roads than those of *Crash* and *The Concrete Island*, the novel is nonetheless underpinned by an understanding of automobility as, to quote John M. Myer, 'a coercive practice' that 'structures patterns of living, working and playing'.[23] In this way the apartment block in which the novel's crisis unfolds exemplifies the spatial and architectural structures of automobility as an integral element of the car harm depicted across the three novels.

Although the settings and scenarios of the oil trilogy are markedly different from those of the disaster quartet, there is a striking continuity between the two sequences, constituted through Ballard's enduring interest in catastrophe. Ballard's 'Introduction' is clear that *Crash* should be read as disaster fiction, though this is no 'imaginary disaster' but a 'pandemic cataclysm that kills hundreds of thousands of people each year'.[24] Maitland battles against an inhospitable environment in *The Concrete Island* just as Ballard's protagonists do in his (post-)apocalyptic worlds. The internecine conflict that the residents of the apartments of *High Rise* fall into is another version of the strife produced by societal collapse in the quartet. In this way, hyperautomobility in the oil novels appears as an apocalypse of the everyday that diagnoses the manifold violence of car culture. In what should be by now a familiar pattern for Ballard, however, the apparent criticism of car culture does not extend to an explicit political position. In the same interview in which he lambasted animal rights and environmental activists, Ballard noted that 'there's another group of weirdoes that are anti-car'.[25] Ballard's characteristic ambivalence towards his topic in the oil trilogy precisely encapsulates social attitudes towards automobility: while creating scenarios in which the relationship between cars and violence is unequivocal, he also remains attached to the overarching system that produces such widespread suffering. It would be oversimplified to think of Ballard's fiction as espousing a straightforward ethical position on automobility.

The naming of the narrator of *Crash* as 'Ballard' brings this point home. Just as Maitland is stuck inside the road network in *The Concrete Island*, the author situates himself inside the system the novels seemingly critique. There is no outside to escape to or from which to denounce automobility. Such stuckness – again characteristically of Ballard, and of car culture more widely – is both psychological and spatial as cultural and personal attachments to cars exist in an intimate relation with landscapes constructed for automobility. Ballard blends psychology, automobility and urban space in 'endless landscapes of concrete' as he phrases it in *Crash* (48). In this way the spaces of the oil trilogy stand as 'autoscapes': thanatological terrains of 'habituated practices' (to quote Braun and Randell) that express the dark implications of motonormativity's status as the unavoidable ground of human, and more-than-human, life.[26] While the novels are resolutely local in their setting in Greater London, the sterility they depict is extrapolated onto a global scale. Vaughan, the obsessive moto-fetishist at the centre of *Crash*, dreams of 'the *whole world* dying in a simultaneous automobile disaster' (16, emphasis added). Similarly, the narrator 'Ballard', after experiencing his own road crash (the means of his introduction to Vaughan), looks to the motorway traffic for 'the first signs of this *end of the world* by automobile for which the accident had been my own private rehearsal' (50, emphasis added). All of this points towards cohesion between the disaster quartet and the oil trilogy, though there are some telling differences in the status of animals across the two sequences, particularly with reference to *Crash*.

In marked contrast to the relatively biodiverse settings of the disaster quartet in which creatures are integral to the representation of the changing world (even in the parched landscape of *The Drought)*, animals are few and far between in *Crash*; this is not an environment conducive to any kind of organic life. The only living elements of the novel's autoscapes are a 'tree-lined avenue' on which cars are parked nose to tail (52), the 'rhododendron-screened lawn of a convalescent institution' where a woman recovers from a road accident (99) and an 'ornamental flower-bed' in the 'courtyard of a filling station' (113). The more-than-human world endures only as a tawdry adornment of hyperautomobility. Yet there are a number of subtle but pivotal animal interactions in *Crash*, specifically the killing of dogs, and a broader and more sustained engagement with animal lives and deaths in *High Rise* that corroborates Calarco's argument that animals, and roadkill in particular, represent 'a uniquely important site from which to understand and contest the dominant social order' expressed in automobility.[27] Perhaps surprisingly, there is a notable echo between Ballard's figuring of animal death in *Crash* and Wendell Berry's ecocarnist rationale for killing animals on his smallholding. In Berry's 'For the Hog Killing', the pig's death articulates the farmer's 'wedding with the world': the participation of farmer and pig in a tradition of sustainable agriculture as a form of place-making to which meat is structurally central. Similarly, in *Crash* killing dogs connects with a motif of marriage that runs through the oil trilogy; roadkill is integral to automobility's function as a form of place-making that materializes the marriage of human and machine.

Marriage is a concern of all three of Ballard's oil novels. The plot of each revolves to some extent around extra-marital affairs, which in the case of *Crash* and *High Rise* unfold through a violent and promiscuous erotics. In *The Concrete Island*, meanwhile, it is Maitland's division of his time between his wife and mistress that means that no one notices his absence or seeks to rescue him after his accident. The breakdown of the traditional social institution of marriage goes hand in hand with the disappearance of human subjectivity into the realm of the automobile. While for Berry the idea of marriage is part of an ostensibly harmonious dwelling in the natural world which is both metaphor and lived reality, for Ballard images of or narrative scenarios concerning marriage signal the unravelling of these exhausted ideologies of social order.

The car, of course, is the key artefact through which the union of sex and technology is enacted. So, after Vaughan picks up two 'airport whores' (139) in his car, 'Ballard' drunk-drives them towards the city as they smoke hash and continue to drink. Vaughan touches the women 'as if taking part in a dance of severely stylized postures that celebrated the design and electronics, speed and direction of an advanced kind of automobile' (142). Moments later this '*marriage* of sex and technology reached its climax as the traffic divided at the airport overpass' (142, emphasis added). The car is not just the location of the sex act but a partner in it; the inner world of sexual desire merges with the outer world of car culture. In another of the novel's obsessively reiterated scenarios of automobile sex, Vaughan and 'Ballard' discover a site where a 'middled-aged woman dentist had skidded through the railings' (169). Vaughan gets into the ruined vehicle, performing a sex act *with* the 'instrument panel', 'celebrating the *marriage* of his own genitalia and the skull-shattered dashboard binnacle against which this middle-aged woman dentist had died' (169, emphasis added). Significantly, this necrotizing marriage of human and car is central to how the novel integrates roadkill into its vision of petromodernity.

Although animals appear marginal in *Crash*'s fixated delineation of the psychosexual seductions of car harm, the novel contains three episodes in which dogs are killed. In the first a 'large mongrel dog' is deliberately run over by Vaughan swerving off the road and accelerating away after 'the animal was carried over the roof'.[28] As a routine expression of hyperautomobility, animal death carries minimal ethical weight, though it is precisely the dog's insignificance that draws the narrative attention as 'Ballard' offers a gnomic reflection on the life Vaughan takes so flippantly. Pondering the incident shortly afterwards, 'Ballard' notes how 'the long triangular grooves on the car had been formed within the death of an unknown creature, its vanished identity abstracted in terms of the geometry of this vehicle' (13). What remains of the animal is the mark on the car that functions as something like its memorial on the vehicle's altering form, but it is a memorial that operates through a doubled anonymity: the 'vanished identity' of an 'unknown creature'. In this way, the dog's indentation on the vehicle encapsulates Jean Baudrillard's reading of *Crash* as 'bodies and technology fused, seduced, inextricable one from the other'.[29] There is no dog, just the mark of the dog on a car. The dog's meaning exists in its complete disappearance into the global system of hyperautomobility.

The second and third depictions of killing dogs come together towards the end of the novel in a scene that raises the possibility of acknowledging, if not quite grieving, animal death before absorbing it once again into the sexual politics of automobility. 'Ballard' is waiting by Vaughan's car with his wife Catherine at the site of an accident – a three-way collision on a flyover – when he observes a 'black gelatinous material smeared [across] the fender and wheel housing, marking the muddied disc of the whitewall tyre' (157). Touching the 'gummy residues', he notes a 'heavy dent' in the car as 'the same deformation' that had been produced two years previously when he 'had been hit by a German shepherd dog running blindly across a street'. He recalls the image of 'two schoolgirls vomiting into their hands over the dying dog' (157), before turning to a more immediately pressing matter presented by the current roadkill: how to clean the animal's body off the car so their hunt for traffic accidents does not draw the attention of the police. Vaughan suggests they drive to an 'all-night carwash in the airport service area' and sits next to Catherine in the back seat, rubbing his 'groin absent-mindedly' as 'Ballard' drives (158). In what follows 'Ballard' watches Vaughan and Catherine engage in a bout of increasingly rough sex as the dog's remains are washed away.

At the heart of the scene is Ballard's characteristic merging of sex, violence and automobility:

> The distant headlamps, refracted through the soap solution jetting across the windows, covered their bodies with a luminescent glow, like two semi-metallic human beings of the distant future making love in a chromium bower ... As the rollers drummed against the roof and doors, Vaughan began to drive his pelvis upwards, almost lifting his buttocks off the seat ... In the mounting roar of the rollers around us she and Vaughan rocked together, Vaughan holding her breasts with his palms as if trying to force them into a single globe. At his orgasm Catherine's gasps were drowned by the roar of the carwash. (161–2)

By this point of the novel, the key elements of the scenario are familiar. Vaughan's motion as he begins to '*drive* his pelvis upward' utilizes the language of automobility to describe human sexual activity; in similar terms, Catherine is depicted shortly afterwards '*steering* her nipples into Vaughan's mouth' (162, emphasis added). In this way, sex is enclosed in automobility not only spatially (in the literal sense that cars are the location for most of the novel's sexual activity) but also in a deeper ontological sense. In figuring the body's movements as driving and steering Ballard presents the discourses, practices and fantasies of automobility as inextricable from the subjective experience of sex. The dog that brought them to the carwash merits no further mention in the scene though the dent of its body remains part of the car that contains and defines the occasion. Moreover, the process by which the dog's remains are cleaned away is an active part of Vaughan and Catherine's sex through the 'luminescent glow' of the headlamps that covers their bodies, 'refracted through the soap solution', and 'the mounting roar of the rollers' that provides the scene's soundtrack. An episode that begins with the 'black gelatinous material smeared [across] the fender' ends with 'an immense pool of white bubbles subsided into the wet concrete' (164). As the psychosexual adventures accelerate, the traces of the dog are unobtrusively disappeared.

The relationship between the sex act in the carwash and the dog's death that leads up to it is thus indirect; it is not that Vaughan and Catherine are turned on by roadkill as such. Rather, the pattern that unfolds in the scene foregrounds the erasure of the animal central to what 'Ballard' again identifies as 'the *marriage* of [Vaughan and Catherine's] bodies with this benign technology' (162, emphasis added). To join with the machine is to negate the animal. That the machine is identified as 'benign' just after it has killed a dog emphasizes the animal's insignificance. The novel's technofetishistic prose corroborates the point. Ballard's preference for clinical terms throughout these erotic encounters over prurient or emotional language removes any sense of the animalistic from this sexuality. For a novel that is so notoriously oversexed, it is remarkable that *Crash* contains so little swearing; there is, for example, only a single occurrence of 'fuck' compared to twelve uses of the word 'binnacle'. As Baudrillard notes, 'All the erotic vocabulary is technical.'[30] *Crash*'s style enacts the containment of the mind within automobile culture through its obsessive reiteration of car parts, as if the novel is a psychic circular road with no exits. In *Crash* Ballard could be said to be forming a 'motopoetics' as a counterpart to Berry's carnopoetics: a form of imaginative creation premised on the agency of the automobile. As Mark Thomas argues, the 'human occupants of vehicles serve only as a means to technology's ends'; the human 'becomes an extension of technology-as-agent'.[31] And behind the dominion of the machine is the dominion of capital; as Ballard reflects in the 'Introduction' to *Crash*, experience is 'ruled' by 'mass-merchandizing, advertising, politics conducted as a branch of advertising' (4). The dog has always already disappeared into this realm.

The meaning of dogs in a pathological hypermobile culture moves from the narrative margins in *Crash* to the thematic centre of *High Rise*. While the dead dog is washed away in *Crash*, in *High Rise* dogs are held onto, primarily, as food. The novel begins with the recently divorced doctor Robert Laing sitting on the balcony of his 'studio apartment on the 25th floor' of a 'huge apartment building' eating the 'roast hind quarter' of a white Alsatian which, by the end of the novel, is revealed as the pet of Anthony Royal, the building's designer who lives in luxury with his wife on the top floor.[32] The novel's opening image initiates a sequence of dog – and other animal – killings that mark the violent unrest that overtakes the apartment block. After a power outage, Laing discovers two children watching an accountant at work with a skimmer in the building's swimming pool: 'Floating in the ... centre was the drowned body of an Afghan hound' (22). The dog's death is initially a mystery; Laing reflects that the 'blackout had lasted little more than fifteen minutes, and a dog of this size was powerful enough to swim for hours' (24). Later the novel fills in the back story behind this macabre discovery in a way that provides the key to the meaning of the novel's numerous canine presences.

The Afghan – the companion of a television actress (58) – was killed by Richard Wilder, a rugby league professional turned documentary filmmaker who is at the heart of the tower block's disturbances. Waking at night from an 'uneasy dream' (62) Wilder interrogates his own somewhat obscure motivations:

> He was sure that he had drowned the Afghan, not because he disliked the dog particularly or wanted to upset its owner, but to revenge himself on the upper storeys of the building. He had seized the dog in the darkness when it blundered into the pool. Giving into a cruel but powerful impulse, he had pulled it below the water. As he held its galvanized and thrashing body under the surface, in a strange way he had been struggling with the building itself. (63)

The crucial point in Wilder's summation of his reasons is the role played by the building in the Afghan's demise. On the one hand, it is his desire for revenge against the 'upper storeys' that drives his actions. A central element of the violence that engulfs the high rise is its spatial materialization of social stratifications. In this 'vertical city' (65), the rich live at the top of the building, the less well-off residents live closer to the ground. Because the television actress lives, with her Afghan, on the thirty-seventh floor and Wilder's lowly home is on the second floor, the killing of the dog strikes a blow against the privilege of the higher echelons. In this sense the Afghan is merely collateral damage in the war between the levels created by the hierarchy the building manifests. But, on the other hand, the 'cruel but powerful impulse' Wilder gives in to indicates that more than paramilitary strategy is at play here. The building's effect on its residents is to remove 'the need to repress every kind of anti-social behaviour, and left them free to explore any deviant or wayward impulses'. Consequently, the high rise is a 'model of all that technology had done to make possible the expression of a truly "free" psychopathology' (44–5). As Wilder holds the dog's 'galvanized and thrashing body under the surface', the narrative emphasizes the subjective psychological experience of killing in a way that recalls the psychosexual dynamics of *Crash*.

The fate of a cat later in the novel provides a more extended illustration of the novel's interest in sadistic violence against animals. During a night of collective drunken rampages, Laing discovers that the orthodontic surgeon Steele has 'cornered a small cat' and 'whirled the terrified creature into the bathroom'. Steele asks Laing to stay for the coup de grâce with a voice 'infused with a strange cold gaiety, like an erotic machine's' (155):

> Laing watched Steele manipulate the cat under the curtain. By some ugly logic the dentist's pleasure in tormenting the creature was doubled by the presence of a squeamish but fascinated witness. Laing stood in the bathroom doorway, hoping despite himself that the lights would not fail again. He waited as Steele calmly smothered the cat, destroying it under the curtain as if carrying out a complex resuscitation under a hospital blanket. (156)

The orthodontist's machinic voice strengthens the sense that the erotics of *High Rise* continue those of *Crash* but the difference in the role of animals is clear. Rather than being subsumed into a technological landscape, in *High Rise* animals are forced agonisingly and chaotically into the narrative foreground. What matters to Steele is that the cat feels his cruelty, just as Wilder's assault on the dog is energized by his apprehension of the animal's body in his grip. That both Steele and the passive Laing are medical professionals (note too the simile of the 'complex resuscitation under a hospital blanket') accentuates the sense that the novel's violence emerges from within the social and economic success the building materializes.

Animal suffering, then, is an integral element of the violence created by the novel's socio-economic and architectural structures. In marked contrast to the absence of animals in *Crash*, animals are everywhere in *High Rise* and carry multiple meanings. As well as objects of cruelty, they are signs of power and a source of companionship. Royal assembles the surviving array of 'retrievers, poodles and dachshunds' into 'his personal hunting pack' and realizes that he feels 'most at home' while among them and the birds that gather ominously around his rooftop apartment (198). The architect's name and status demonstrate a temporal regression that structures the representation of animals; Royal, with his pack of dogs, becomes the novel's feudal overlord. Food is a key element of this nostalgic pattern and connects with an interest in unusual meats that appears consistently in Ballard's depictions of disaster. In *Concrete Island*, Maitland discovers that a central part of the diet of Proctor, the tramp he is stranded with, is rats.[33] Meanwhile, in *Rushing to Paradise*, the starving conservationists end up eating many of the creatures they had hoped to protect. Meat in *High Rise* is grotesque, surreal and constructs humans not just as savage predators turning on their pets but also as food themselves. Eleanor Powell (a film critic) allows a cat to 'dine off her flesh', gnawing on her 'bloodied wrist' (216). By the end of the novel the swimming pool has become a 'bone-pit' covered with the corpses of 'residents who had died of old age or disease and then attacked by wild dogs' (243). There are even indications that 'some of the residents had reverted to cannibalism' (244). Frida Beckman sees the strange carnivoracity Ballard's characters resort to as a sign that they are 'devouring the framework of meaning into which they have been inscribed'.[34] Eating dogs in particular recalls Ballard's central theme of marriage and the family. As the social order of the high-rise collapses, pets escape from the signification of the bourgeois family and become instead the emblem of a primal ecology of mutual predation: the embodiment of a dog-eat-dog world.

All of this seems distant from *Crash* and the erotics of automobility, but the events of *High Rise* are intimately, if subtly, connected with cars. Surrounded by ranks of automobiles in parking lots (6) and the wider 'concrete landscape' (28), the building is part of Ballard's engagement with the automobility imaginary, conceived by Braun and Randell as pertaining not just to cars but also to infrastructure and the 'myriad images, visions, accounts, representations and descriptions' through which automobility structures modernity.[35] To be a resident of the high-rise is to be a motorist; there is no other option. Hence, in this architecture, automobility is coerced.

If the building – and what it represents – is the ultimate cause of the violence, then car culture is also necessarily implicated. Accordingly, as the unrest develops, cars are recurrently brought into the narrative. The building's first fatality is, in a manner of speaking, killed by a car. Residents are alerted by the sound of someone falling from a balcony; peering down over the railings Laing notices that 'embedded in the crushed roof of a car in the front rank, was the body of a man in evening dress' (52). This might be an idiosyncratic form of car harm but the description of the sound – as 'of a harsh metallic collision, almost as if a car had crashed' (51) – makes the connection between events in the high-rise and the automobile culture that encompasses the building. But if car culture is woven into the nature of the crisis, as the residents abandon themselves to the deviant attractions of the unfolding furore, they ironically pay less and less attention to their vehicles. By the time the disaster is in full swing, the cars in the parking lots 'had not been moved for weeks' (104). Left where they stand, they are 'spattered with broken eggs, wine and melted ice-cream', their windscreens 'knocked out by falling bottles' (42). By the end of the novel, when Royal watches from above a car turning 'into the parking-lot and thread[ing] its way through the maze of access lanes', he concludes that 'this unknown man was probably the last resident to leave the building and set off for his office' (194). The abandonment of car culture encapsulates the end of social order; it is seeing the cars around the high-rise 'spattered with debris, their once-bright bodywork streaked and stained' that for Wilder causes the 'illusion of normalcy … to give way' (55). *High Rise* depicts the implosion of motonormativity.

In this context, as petrofiction the novel works as something like the inverse of *Crash*. As automobility consumes the world in *Crash*, animals are repressed: killed and then absented from the narrative. In *High Rise*, as automobility is suspended, the repressed returns through the novel's proliferating canine presences, dead and alive. Consequently, *High Rise* is much closer to the animal aesthetics of the earlier disaster quartet. Indeed, the primal carnist energy that engulfs the building echoes an interest in prehistoric animals that occurs in *The Drowned World*, for example, with its oversized iguanas looming like dinosaurs. Central to the oil trilogy is thus a paradoxical temporality, a merging of the glittering technologized future with the dark energies of the unconscious, a pattern that returns us to the central question of Ballard's intermeshing of inner and outer worlds. As Ballard asks in the 'Introduction' to *Crash*, 'Will modern technology provide us with hitherto undreamed-of means for tapping our own psychopathologies?' (6) Roadkill provides an exemplary manifestation of this dynamic, a form of violence that brings the aesthetic allure of technology into alignment with the carnist satisfactions of a world set free from the restrictions of social propriety. Although *High Rise* foregrounds animal pain, it never registers eating dogs as problematic. Ballard's work, as we have seen, does not cohere into such straightforward ethical allegiances.

Yet, despite the moral ambivalence of Ballard's automobility imaginary, there is a striking, if perhaps ironic resonance between his representation of animals in the oil trilogy and Calarco's radical vegan perspective on roadkill. Calarco advocates for a ritualized response to animals killed by cars: 'To pause and sit with roadkill, to remove it from the road, to consider its life and death and relations' in order to 'engender a subjective conversion and reconstitution'. In such rituals Calarco locates the possibility of 'apprehending the entire arc of the life and death of roadkill, the broader systems of power that override this arc, and the need for a genuine alternative to current systems of mobility'.[36] For Calarco, the 'problem of roadkill demands of us that we become something other than who we are, born again, in response to an event that calls us to a different way of life'.[37] Although Ballard's violent moto-erotics is miles apart from Calarco's idealistic framing of the recognition of roadkill as a moment of transformative ethical potential, the remaking of the self in relation to animal death is part of the narrative drama and political force of *High Rise*. By the end of the novel Laing's transformation is profound. Living in a curious ménage with his sister Alice and Eleanor (who is still feeding the cat from the wound on her wrist), he plans to introduce them to morphine as a way to 'increase their dependence on him'. As Laing ponders this 'intimate family circle, the first he had known since childhood' (246), Ballard ironically resolves the novel's marriage plot. From a somewhat lost and lonely divorcee at the start, Laing has found his place in the world, relishing the 'ample freedom to explore himself' created by the complete social collapse of the high-rise (246).

It is particularly telling that *High Rise* returns in its final scene to the image it begins with. Feeling that for 'the moment, at least, everything was highly satisfactory' (241), Laing embarks on the 'major culinary effort' (242) of cooking Royal's Alsatian for Alice and Eleanor. Keen to make a good impression, he consults 'an advanced cookery book' preparatory to 'skinning and disembowelling this huge animal' (241), while listening to the sound of the dog's 'nervous whimperings' as it begins to sense what is happening. This perverse mirroring of the carnist ritual of the Sunday roast leads to Laing gazing out towards a neighbouring high-rise in which a blackout suggests the spread of the crisis into the wider city. The novel's closing sentence has Laing watching 'them contentedly, ready to welcome them to their new world' (248). Again, as with Berry, we have a carnist linkage between the animal's death and the world it embodies, in this case the world of the automobile apocalypse. It is worth thinking back here from Royal's Alsatian to the German Shepherd 'Ballard' kills in *Crash*. The connection between the species – Alsatian and German Shepherd are synonymous in British English – encourages the altermobile provocation that all the dead dogs in *High Rise* are ultimately roadkill because it is the architecture of automobility that drives the crisis. Indeed, all of the deaths that occur in the novel – of whatever species – are in a sense roadkill. Laing in his own way is 'born again' to a 'different way of life' by roadkill, though evidently not quite in the way that Calarco imagines.

It is possible to offer a reading of the text as cautionary tale that brings ecological and pro-animal readings into alignment. Petroculture has reshaped the world and human subjectivities into violently denatured forms that demand the sacrifice of our most familiar animal companions. If dogs in this reading function metonymically as signs of the ecological violence of automobility, they also provide an opportunity to attend to the lived realities of animals under hyperautomobility. In this way a reading between the environmental humanities and literary animal studies could provide a critical manifestation of Calarco's injunction to 'pause and sit with roadkill' and to understand through this process the operation of 'broader systems of power' under petromodernity with a view to shaping an altermobile future.

This critical act becomes more striking if we recall that any reading of Ballard's disaster fiction purely as a cautionary tale misses the studied ambivalence of these texts: the sense that, as Brian Baker notes of *Crash*, it is possible to see the oil trilogy, perversely, as 'celebratory rather than cautionary'.[38] When 'Ballard' makes the casual remark on a visit to a ministry research project on road traffic accidents (RTAs) that 'they're trying to reduce the number of accidents here, not increase it', Vaughan responds dismissively: 'I suppose that's a point of view' (124). The force of Vaughan's remark is to hint that the ministry is not in fact interested in reducing accidents. Evidently, the claim is counter-intuitive and coloured by Vaughan's fetish, but there is nonetheless a striking similarity to Calarco's view that incidents of car harm are not 'accidents of the system but are fundamental to its design'.[39] Roadkill is never really an accident in the sense that it is an unanticipated and avoidable event; killing animals, and indeed humans, is integral to the structure of automobility.

Nor is it, in Ballard's fictional world, much to be lamented, though this is precisely the point for animal studies and the environmental humanities. The automobility imaginary, to return to Braun and Randell's terms, is a realm in which 'death and climate change … are not imagined';[40] the popular cultural and mainstream political representation of cars comprises an extraordinary case study in the laundering of an extraordinary violence. Critical attention to Ballard's dogs reinstalls the multispecies violence repressed in motonormativity and encourages reflection on its construction by the environments of automobility which in turn demands a wider ecological consciousness of the ideological and material world that produces this. The force of Ballard's writing is that it is possible to follow this chain of reasoning and to remain ethically untroubled. If the oil trilogy performs something like Braun and Randell's demand for 'the deconstruction and collapse of the automobility imaginary' in the service of 'a post-automobility future', it does so as the fulfilment of the psychic allure of violence.[41] The post-automobile world intimated at the end of *High Rise* is not a progressive and flourishing future but merely the unfolding of the car crash that is petromodernity: not so much the end of automobility as its bleak climax. Ballard's fiction might be taken – on the surface at least – as an illustration of the necessity of sustainable transition as a means of sanitizing automobility from the dark energies he depicts, but that view would be to miss the wider attachments to technology and commodity culture he insists on. The EV is the evolution not the abnegation of motonormativity. The following chapter provides at least a more upbeat view of the future of transportation, though if the significance of Ballard's trilogy inheres in its exposure of car harm, Nnedi Okorafor's fiction – for all its post-oil energy – illustrates the obfuscation of violence in the utopian form of the EV.

Notes

1 J. B. Ballard, *The Wind from Nowhere* (London: Penguin, 1967 [1962]), 55.
2 J. G. Ballard, *The Drought* (London: Flamingo, 2001 [1965]), 36.
3 J. G. Ballard, *The Crystal World* (London: Fourth Estate, 2014 [1966]), 85.
4 See Adrian Tait, 'Nature Reclaims Her Own: J. G. Ballard's *The Drowned World*, *Australian Humanities Review* 57 (2014), 25–40.
5 Lawrence Buell, *The Environmental Imagination* (Princeton, NJ: Princeton University Press, 1995), 285.
6 See, for example, Adam Trexler and Adeline Johns-Putra, 'Climate Change in Literature and Literary Criticism', *Wiley Interdisciplinary Reviews: Climate Change* 2.2 (March/April 2011), 185–200.
7 Tait, 'Nature Reclaims Her Own'.
8 Robert Macfarlane, 'Introduction', in *The Crystal World* (London: Fourth Estate, 2014 [1966]), 3–7, 3.
9 J. G. Ballard Interviews, 'Don't Crash: The J. G. Ballard Interview', https://jgballard.ca/media/1995_kjb.html, accessed 14 February 2025.
10 Cited in Jim Clarke, 'Reading Climate Change in J. G. Ballard', *Critical Survey* 25.2 (2013), 7–21, 9.
11 Jim Clarke, 'Reading Climate Change in J. G. Ballard', *Critical Survey* 25.2 (2013), 7–21, 7, 9.
12 Ballard, *The Crystal World*, 16.
13 Thomas Knowles, 'J. G. Ballard and the "Natural" World', *Green Letters* 22.4 (2018), 341–53, 352, 350.
14 Ballard, *The Drowned World*, 10.
15 Ballard, *The Drowned World*, 18.
16 Ballard, *The Drowned World*, 18.
17 Ballard, *The Drought*, 218.
18 Frida Beckman, 'J. G. Ballard's Dark Ecologies: Unsettling Nature, Animals and Literary Tropes'. In *Animalities: Literary and Cultural Studies beyond the Human*. Edited by Michael Lundblad, 60–79, 64 (Edinburgh: Edinburgh University Press, 2017).
19 Bill McKibben, *The End of Nature* (New York: Random House, 1989).
20 For a discussion of Ballard's 1970s novels as a trilogy see Rachele Dini, '"Things Playing a More Important Part Than People": Waste in J. G. Ballard's Urban Disaster Trilogy', *Deep Ends* (2016), 113–29.

21 Knowles, 'J. G. Ballard and the "Natural" World', 350.
22 J. G. Ballard, 'Introduction', in *Crash* (London: Vintage, 2004 [1973]), 6.
23 Cited in Baer, *Motor Vehicles*, 2.
24 Ballard, 'Introduction', 6.
25 J. G. Ballard Interviews, 'Don't Crash'.
26 On the use and origins of the idea of the 'autoscape', see Braun and Randell, *Post-Automobility Futures*, 26, 73–4.
27 Calarco, *Roadkill*, 2.
28 J. G. Ballard, *Crash* (London: Vintage, 2004 [1973]), 12; subsequent references in parenthesis.
29 Jean Baudrillard, 'Ballard's *Crash*', *Science Fiction Studies* 18.3 (1991), 313–20, 315.
30 Baudrillard, 'Ballard's *Crash*', 316.
31 Mark Thomas, 'The Rules of Autogeddon: Sex, Death and Law in JG Ballard's Crash', *Griffith Law Review* 20.2 (2011), 333–61, 350–1.
32 J. G. Ballard, *High Rise* (London: Fourth Estate, 2014 [1975]), 2; subsequent references in parenthesis.
33 J. G. Ballard, *The Concrete Island* (London: Fourth Estate, 2011 [1974]), 126.
34 Beckman, 'Ballard's Dark Ecologies', 74.
35 Braun and Randell, *Post-Automobility Futures*, 16.
36 Calarco, *Roadkill*, 68.
37 Calarco, *Roadkill*, 69.
38 Brian Baker, 'The Resurrection of Desire: J. G. Ballard's *Crash* as a Transgressive Text', *Foundation* 29.80 (2000), 84–96, 88.
39 Calarco, *Roadkill*, 41.
40 Braun and Randell, *Post-Automobility Futures*, 24.
41 Braun and Randell, *Post-Automobility Futures*, 145.

CHAPTER 6

Multispecies automobilities in Nnedi Okorafor's Africanfuturism

Nnedi Okorafor's speculative, multispecies mobilities provide a significantly more upbeat take on the future than Ballard's necrotizing oil ontologies. Against Ballard's sterile autoscapes, Okorafor's writing unfolds complex post-oil ontologies which are structured – though not without ethical tensions – around inclusive depictions of animal and ecological flourishing. At the heart of Okorafor's fiction is the imaginative disruption and reconfiguration of petrocapitalist energy regimes as part of a creative ethos she describes as Africanfuturist, a term she coins in 2019 to distinguish her work from the longer-established Afrofuturism. By Okorafor's definition, 'Africanfuturism is concerned with visions of the future, is interested in technology, leaves the earth, skews optimistic, is centered on and predominantly written by people of African descent'.[1] Afrofuturism, by contrast, in its initial 1993 definition by Mark Dery, 'positioned African American themes and concerns at the ... center'. As Jenna N. Hanchey explains, such 'Black diasporic visions of the future are often disconnected from African material realities, geopolitical contexts, and life experiences'.[2] In response, Okorafor's Africanfuturism 'is rooted first and foremost in Africa' rather than in the Diaspora (though Okorafor also insists that Africanfuturism 'branches out to embrace all blacks').[3] Evidently, the two forms have significant links, not just in their focus on Black cultural perspectives on futurity and by extension their imbrication in science fiction (though both forms exceed literary and cinematic cultures) but also through a prominent emphasis on history. For Okorafor, Africanfuturism 'acknowledges, grapples with and carries "what has been"'; similarly, in Dery's thought, Afrofuturism affirmatively answers the question, 'Can a community whose past has been deliberately rubbed out ..., imagine possible futures?'[4] It is the projection of the history of Africa and the Diaspora into the future that structures both Afro- and Africanfuturism's engagement with the question of energy politics.

The theme of history in Okorafor's work – the grappling with 'what has been' – circulates in many of her novels and stories around oil as a decisive context for understandings of the political and socio-economic dynamics of contemporary Nigeria. Nigeria is Africa's second largest producer of oil, with the majority of production concentrated in the Niger Delta, the world's third largest wetland, Africa's largest river delta and mangrove ecosystem and the area with the 'richest biodiversity in Nigeria'.[5] The damage wreaked on the Niger Delta by oil spills has had devastating consequences for the environment, public health and for livelihoods centred on fishing and agriculture. Amnesty International has identified the Niger Delta as 'one of the most polluted places on Earth'.[6] Attempts to compel Royal Dutch Shell to clean up the damage and to compensate affected communities remain ongoing at the time of writing.[7] Oil politics have played a significant role in Okorafor's family history. Her parents immigrated from Nigeria to the United States as a result of the Biafran War (or Nigerian Civil War) of 1967–70, a conflict Okorafor identifies as 'one of the world's first wars over oil'. Nigeria's oil wealth has been, she summarizes, 'more like a curse than a blessing'.[8]

The problem of pollution often comes to the fore in Okorafor's fiction. In 'Spider the Artist' (2013), a short story focused on a community living alongside a pipeline in the Niger Delta, the narrator Eme describes the devastation in her village: 'The fish, shrimps and crayfish in the creeks were dying. Drinking the water shrivelled women's wombs and eventually made men urinate blood ... Cassava and yam farms yielded less and less each year.'[9] The same issue provides the premise for *Lagoon* (a novel which will come more fully into view shortly), when the alien visitor Ayodele declares to the Nigerian people that 'YOUR LAND IS FULL OF A FUEL THAT IS TEARING YOU APART'.[10] Her announcement that 'WE COME TO BRING YOU TOGETHER AND REFUEL YOUR FUTURE' (113) could stand as the key manifesto point in Okorafor's engagement with energy, expressed in the imaginings of green technologies that move through her fiction.

On one level, as Josephine Taylor contends, the upbeat approach to technology that infuses Okorafor's Africanfuturism might seem to risk reinvigorating what Imre Szeman calls 'techno-utopianism', a discourse with a strong connection with climate change inertia when 'employed as mere political rhetoric to defer difficult decisions with negative economic impacts to some distant future'.[11] There is no need to worry (a techno-utopian argument might run): some coming, as yet unmade invention will save the planet. As Szeman exemplifies, the aspiration – perhaps even the assumption – of techno-optimism is that 'technological innovation will create entirely new forms of energy, such as hydrogen fuel cells for space-age automobiles' (an objective which like cultured meat indicates a strong link between hegemonic environmentalisms and sf).[12] Against such formulations, however, Okorafor's fiction foregrounds technology as a site of ideological contestation that resists any glib assumption of the redemptive power of corporate innovation.

The action of *Noor* (2021), for example, pits its protagonists AO (a mechanic with extensive medical prostheses) and the nomadic herdsman DNA against the authoritarian power of Ultimate Corps, a shadowy global corporation which utilizes clean energy to deepen its hold over a future Africa and the wider world. No one 'knows where Ultimate Corp is actually based', and 'tracking its activities is tricky', but its influence is pervasive.[13] At the heart of the corporation's business plan is a never-ending, artificially generated sandstorm which enables it to harvest '*clean energy from one of the world's worst environmental disasters*'. As AO encounters one of Ultimate Corp's '*enormous turbines*', her assessment is blunt: the '*evil things generated energy for the evil corporation*' (original emphasis).[14] The novel 'stands out' in Ossana's summary, for its 'strongly ideological depiction of a globalized milieu that explicitly criticizes capitalist private autocratic exertions concerning the misuse of clean energies'.[15] As AO and DNA, encouraged by the wizard Baba Sola, fight back against Ultimate Corp, corporate digital networks and their hardware (drones in particular) become a battleground in which the mystical rubs shoulders with the technological and the ancient (in the traditional form of the nomad DNA) with the emergent (in the form of the cyborg AO). This pattern is elucidated by another coinage of Okorafor's: Africanjujuism, a term that describes a 'subcategory of fantasy that respectfully acknowledges the seamless blend of true existing African spiritualities and cosmologies with the imaginative'.[16] Technology is never reducible in Okorafor's worlds to corporate power but forms part of the more complex ontologies and political investments her fiction produces. As she summarizes in an interview, 'We know that technology is not an evil thing in itself; it's the minds behind it and how we use it ... We have technology solving problems and creating problems.'[17]

Behind the involvement of technology with ideological struggle in Okorafor's writing is a long-standing engagement with the question of energy in African- and Afrofuturism which pivots on a telling double meaning of power as both the possibility of political emancipation and the physical basis of petrocapitalist energy regimes. As Graeme Macdonald argues, 'sf's subgenres provide various manifestations of energy consciousness' – think of the fabled warp drive of the *Star Trek* franchise, for example.[18] While in many sf texts fuel remains in the narrative background, the task of the energy humanities is to bring it into the critical foreground by piecing together its meaning and significance. The energy humanist is drawn, Macdonald suggests, to what may seem the overly literal questions that haunt the spectacular aesthetics of the sf energy sublime: 'What is powering those spaceships? What heats those megacities? How are its inputs extracted and refined and commodities made and distributed?'[19] For Macdonald, the fantastic properties of sf materials can provide a 'starting jolt to think of alternatives to ... our carbon-driven system and the hegemonic energy ontologies it reproduces'.[20] In this way, sf may be 'the genre best placed to advance our understanding not only of present and future energy crises but also the manner in which we (fail to) envisage and conceive energy as a matter for culture'.[21] Afrofuturism provides an important context from which to develop and exemplify Macdonald's argument about the role and significance of energy in speculative futures. An extensive discussion of the intersections of Afrofuturism and the energy humanities is beyond the scope of this chapter, but a brief overview of energy's role in some of its foundational and most culturally prominent speculations provides some key coordinates for Okorafor's development of Africanfuturist – and Africanjujuist – mobilities.

Dery reads Ralph Ellison's 1952 *The Invisible Man* as constituting an initial 'glimpse' of Afrofuturism (though it is by no means the first), a claim that has been developed by other critics in relation to the novel's combination of sf tropes with its narrative explorations of the possibilities of Black futurities. For Linda Yaszek, *The Invisible Man* is 'one of the central texts of literary Afrofuturism';[22] W. Andrew Shephard sees it in similar terms as 'one of the seminal works of Afrofuturism'.[23] As Johnnie Wilcox notes, it is the unnamed narrator's 'encounters' with the 'forces of electricity' that allow him to discover 'increasingly effective strategies for opposing the dominant system of white, racist power'.[24] The novel's 'Prologue' situates the narrator in a basement in New York and initiates the novel's concerns with a surreal evocation of energy as he taps 'illegal juice from a line owned by the rapacious Monopolated Light & Power', as Dery phrases it.[25] As he explains the 'deeper reason' for his battle with the power company, Ellison's narrator introduces the dazzling lighting rig with which he has surrounded himself:

> In my hole in the basement there are exactly 1,369 lights. I've wired the entire ceiling, every inch of it. And not with fluorescent bulbs, but with the older, more-expensive-to-operate kind, the filament type. An act of sabotage, you know. I've already begun to wire the wall. A junk man I know, a man of vision, has supplied me with wire and sockets. Nothing, storm or flood, must get in the way of our need for light and ever more and brighter light. The truth is the light and light is the truth. When I finish all four walls, then I'll start on the floor.[26]

From the exaggerated illumination of his hole, the narrator derives a sense of 'vital aliveness' that counteracts the deadening effects of his marginalized existence.[27] If, as Shephard summarizes, the novel utilizes 'the metaphor of "invisibility" to highlight the estranging effect of being black in early twentieth-century America', the function of the narrator's wired-up basement is to bring him hyperbolically into visibility.[28] Energy here functions figuratively, but the appropriation of electricity from Monopolated – as a manifestation of white power in the text – also demonstrates that such figuration operates through an awareness of the material conditions of energy supply and their imbrication in a racist politics. The novel's intimations of alternative Black futures thus rely on a vision of energy that combines the material and the semiotic.

Part of the narrator's agenda in hacking electricity from Monopolated Light & Power is to enable him to listen to Louis Armstrong's melancholy evocation of racial marginalization 'What Did I Do to Be So Black and Blue' (1929); his aim is to have five radio phonographs so that he can hear five recordings of it 'all at the same time' as white infrastructure is redirected to Black culture.[29] Ellison's 'Prologue' consequently introduces music as a central element of Afrofuturism. The experimental jazz musician and poet Sun Ra (born in Alabama as Herman Poole Blount) is one of the most frequently cited contributors to Afrofuturism *avant la lettre*. At the heart of Ra's extensive oeuvre is a mythic relationship with outer space and a refusal to consider Earth his home: 'I'm not human', he claimed, 'I've never been part of the planet'.[30] Rather, according to his personal mythology, he was contacted by 'space men' who took him to Saturn and exposed him to a 'giant spotlight' that created an 'energy transformation'; here, his 'whole body changed into something else'. The aliens told Ra that he 'would speak, and the world would listen'.[31] In short, Ra's task was the redemption of planet Earth.

The figure of the extraterrestrial central to Ra's work holds a privileged position in the development of Afrofuturism that hinges on the polyvalence of the term alien as both a being from outer space and the alienated African American subject. As Paul Youngquist glosses, Ra 'was the original brother from another planet, dedicated to inventing a future for fellow aliens consigned to dark streets and dead-end dreams'.[32] Throughout his career, the names of Ra's backing band evolved to express various dimensions of the allure of outer space: the Astro Intergalactic Infinity Arkestra, the Intergalactic Splendors of Love Arkestra and dozens more.[33] As his own mythic transformation indicates, Ra's extensive speculations on outer space are closely connected with energy and mobility imaginaries, themes which come to the fore in the 1974 film *Space Is the Place*, developed out of a series of lectures Ra gave on the theme of 'The Black Man in the Cosmos' at Berkeley. The movie imagines a 'plan for the salvation of the black race' that unfolds through the migration of the Black population of Oakland,

California, to a space colony: 'See what they can do on a planet all of their own without any white people there', Ra explains in the opening sequence. Energy humanists preoccupied with the question of what is powering the spaceships are given some telling, if fantastic hints to work with: 'We'll bring them here through either isotrope teleportation, transmolecularization, or better still, teleport the whole planet here by music.'[34] A key plot point is the plan by white NASA scientists to kidnap Ra to discover these mysteries. As NASA interrogates him, they desperately ask, 'What is the source of your power?'; 'How do you convert your harmonic progressions to energy?' It is not just that NASA wants the secrets; it also wants Ra not to have them. A radio announcement that reports the arrival of Ra's spaceship reports with alarm: 'Today a party of Negroes claimed to know the secret of space travel, threatening to undermine both the economy and social structure of the strongest nation of Earth and destroy our way of life.'[35] The radical political potential of such technology remains necessarily beyond the apprehension of the panicked white establishment which tries to assassinate Ra during a concert. The attempt fails and the film ends with Ra and the Black travellers leaving planet Earth which explodes behind them. While Ellison envisages the Black appropriation of white (electric) power, Ra's mystical energy source is a distinctively Black form of locomotion that emerges from the sonic experimentation of free jazz and creates a liberatory response to the forced migration of slavery.

The restriction of access to sources of power is a crucial element of the most popular early-twenty-first century instantiation of Afrofuturism, the 2018 Marvel Studios film *Black Panther*, based on a Marvel Comics character who first appeared in 1966. From its inception, the series is concerned with energy and mobility. Notably, the first *Black Panther* comic opens with the superhero team the Fantastic Four in a 'sky-craft' (something between a spaceship and a flying car) gifted to them by 'an African chieftain'. As Mister Fantastic pilots the vehicle, he speculates on a mechanism that 'seems to be powered by some sort of magnetic waves'.[36] Speculative mobilities are integral to the Black Panther series.

Beginning in Oakland (the setting of much of *Space Is the Place* as a key site of Black resistance movements in the 1960s and 1970s), the 2018 film gives an oblique nod to Ra and, as it moves between the United States and the fictional African nation of Wakanda, connects with both Afro- and Africanfuturism. While the narrative remains on Earth, *Black Panther* retains a sense of cosmic consciousness central to Ra's mythic Afrofuturism. The magnetic waves that power the sky-craft are created by a utopian energy source that arrived from space in a meteorite tens of thousands of years ago. This is vibranium, a metal with extraordinary energetic properties, that underpins Wakanda's technological advancement. The Marvel Universe contains extensive lore around vibranium. According to the Marvel Database, if 'tempered properly through a mix of magic and science, vibranium can amplify mystical energies' to produce 'an energy flow on the quantum level that is virtually infinite'.[37] Although the early Marvel comics give an alternative source of vibranium in Antarctica (and the second *Black Panther* movie in 2022 also extends vibranium's range to the deep sea in a pertinent nod to the real-world direction of rare earth extraction), in the first *Black Panther* film it is unique to Wakanda, which has carefully nurtured its isolation from the rest of the world. Vibranium's potential for weapons technology makes it a coveted resource and much of the film's intrigue revolves around its acquisition for this purpose, but the depiction of the futuristic capital city of Wakanda, Birnin Zana, the Golden City, exemplifies its peaceful use. Vibranium, we learn, 'powers their city and their tech' as the material basis of community that has moved beyond fossil fuels.[38] Transportation in *Black Panther*'s Birnin Zana reprises the structure of the inaugural sky-craft through its 'mag-lev' (magnetic levitation) trains; there are no cars in a conventional sense, though there are 'flying ships' which, as Alessio Gerola notes, are 'biomimetic in design': technological plays on the form of 'dragonflies and birds'.[39] In a significant example of the interplay between sf imaginaries and real-world sustainable transitions, Birnin Zana has 'inspired grand visions about what a technologically-advanced African city could look like'.[40] In locations such as Senegal's Akon City, the construction of a 'real-life Wakanda' is already underway (though at the time of writing work has stalled).[41]

Okorafor has herself contributed to six comics in the *Black Panther* franchise, and her depiction of transitions beyond oil draws on several aspects of these earlier Afro- and Africanfuturist speculations around energy, particularly the role of outer space and alien life; the evocation of fantastic technologies; and the location of these strands within a radical political imaginary. In this context, how her characters move through space evokes the wider question of how Africa and Africans move into the future. Importantly, these themes, in Okorafor's writing, consistently involve a multispecies perspective that provides a case study of the way that the depiction of speculative post-oil cultures, and of sustainable automobility in particular, invites both ecological and animal critical perspectives.

The link of animals and petroculture is at the fore of Okorafor's upbeat reimagining of the alien invasion narrative in *Lagoon*. The novel begins with a swordfish 'on a mission' against those 'who brought the noise and made the world bleed black ooze that left poison rainbows on the water's surface' (3). In an incident based on a 2010 news report of a swordfish attack on an offshore oilfield in Angola,[42] Okorafor's marine eco-warrior spears a pipeline and 'swims away in triumph' as 'black blood spews in her face from the hole she's made' (4). It is at this moment that the aliens arrive. The swordfish observes a 'great shifting bar of glimmering sand' which gives off 'sweet clean water' she hopes will 'drown out the foul blackness of the dead snake she's pierced' (5). As the water becomes 'clean and clear', the swordfish apprehends 'something wilder and more alive than her lost paradise' (5), which comes not from 'the sea's greatest depths or the dry places' but from 'far, far away' (5). This is the start of *Lagoon*'s utopian, post-oil trajectory: with the arrival of the aliens, 'everything is changing' (6).

The ensuing imagination of something like sustainable transition is based to a significant degree on a collaboration between animals and aliens. After the oil leak, '*the ocean water just outside Lagos*' becomes '*so clean that a cup of its salty-sweet goodness will heal the worst human illnesses ... It is more alive than it has been in centuries and it is teeming with aliens and monsters*' (6, original emphasis). The sea's regeneration pivots here on a long-standing trope of the creatures of the deep as a terrestrial embodiment of the extraterrestrial, a motif Stacy Alaimo describes as the 'rhetoric of the "alien seas"'.[43] As the ocean teems '*with monsters and aliens*', the alien from out of space and the alien from below the seas are joined together in multispecies alliance against petrocapitalism. By the end of the novel, animal life is looking towards a new dawn as the damage wreaked on creatures by oil is reversed: 'Extinct creatures would return and new ones would appear' (279). There can be no place for oil in this future. The Nigerian president (recently healed by the aliens from a debilitating medical condition) is brought to the realization that 'oil could no longer be Nigeria's top commodity. It could no longer be a commodity at all' (273). The 'people of the water' (which is to say the 'aliens and monsters' of the deep) will not allow it. In oil's place the aliens have 'something better to give': 'Their technology' (273), which will enable them, as Ayodele (the novel's ET protagonist) declares, to '*NURTURE YOUR WORLD*' (128, original emphasis), even if various religious and political forces are initially, steadfastly opposed to their presumptuous green agenda.

The interplay between animals and extraterrestrials in *Lagoon* forms part of a wider blurring of categories of identity that unfolds in the struggle against Nigerian petroculture. Against the oil ontologies of capitalist modernity, *Lagoon* erodes the distinctions between human, animal, alien and spirit. Ayodele, the novel's lead alien, is a shapeshifter who moves between human and animal form, as well as inhabiting ambiguous states beyond this binary. For the most part Ayodele appears in the guise of a Nigerian woman, but also for a time, as a gesture of frustration at the aggressive response of humans to her arrival, she takes the form of a small monkey (though one that looks like a human): 'fuzzy, soft, brown [with a] pinched face like a sour elder' (152). Ayodele's movement between human and animal form involves a playful exploration of anthropocentrism. Arriving in the home of Adaora, a marine biologist and the novel's main human protagonist, Ayodele explains to Adaora's children why – of all the forms she might inhabit – she prefers to appear as a human: 'Human beings,' she observes, 'have a hard time relating to that which does not resemble them' (67). Kola (Adaora's daughter) readily understands and corroborates Ayodele's identification of a solipsistic anthropocentrism with the example of cartoons in which 'even the animals who could talk also had to *look* human' (67, original emphasis). In the logic of *Lagoon*, to move beyond oil is to move beyond a narrow hierarchical configuration of the human as that which opposes and dominates the animal.

A crucial part of this narrative patterning is Okorafor's Africanjujuism through which African cosmologies are integrated into the imagining of post-oil ontologies. The central figure in this regard is Mama Wata, a water spirit of West African tradition notable for her association with transformation and one of many mythic figures of African cosmology that take their place in the novel's interrogation of petroculture. When Ayodele emerges from the sea off the coast of Lagos, she appears 'like Mama Wata' (13).

Consequently, as Melody Jue describes, 'the arrival of the aliens does not mark a break with indigenous cosmologies and traditions, but rather a continuation of them'.[44] In this way, the unravelling of petroculture is expressed as a movement that comes from within African instead of appearing as the kind of transnational neo-colonial endeavour behind the renewables of *Noor*. To emphasize the point, Adaora is also reminiscent of Mama Wata. Born with 'webbed feet and hands' and 'legs joined together with flesh' which are 'surgically separated' (257), she is herself an amphibious shapeshifter of sorts who functions as the human equivalent of the alien Ayodele and retains a mystical attachment to the water that encourages her born-again Christian husband Chris's suspicions that she is a marine witch. Consequently, at the heart of *Lagoon*'s Africanfuturist version of sustainable transition is a complex mingling of human, animal, spirit, technology and alien that, as Brett Banks, Jethro Kayat and Jean Rossman argue, 'opens multiple possibilities for the destabilisation of rigid categories and provides a new (sustainable) model for survival'.[45] Moreover, if the aliens' intention to nurture the world encapsulates the central premise of the environmental humanities, the interrogation of human exceptionalism and an emphasis on animal agency evoke the central concerns of animal studies. The overarching narrative arc of *Lagoon* hints towards an idealized synthesis of ecological and pro-animal politics that may emerge in a world after petrocapital.

It is in this context that the question of car culture comes into view in *Lagoon*. The African spiritual energies of *Lagoon* form an integral part of the novel's depiction of automobility and its infrastructure, a theme which is prominent in Okorafor's animist reimagining of the Lagos–Benin expressway as a sentient 'Road Monster' known as the 'Bone Collector' for its malign intentions towards its users (202, 208), or to put it in more sober realist terms for its status as a hotspot for robberies and traffic accidents. As the chaos created by the aliens' arrival adds to Lagos's notorious congestion, the road seizes its opportunity, 'rising up in a huge snake-like slab of concrete', knocking 'cars off itself' and devouring drivers who succumb with 'shrieks of agony' (207). Significantly, one of the aliens – in the form of a 'Nollywood woman' – is able to intervene, asking the road to explain its conduct. The road replies simply, 'I collect bones ... I have always collected bones. I am the road.' In an act of self-sacrifice, the alien gives herself to the road with the words: 'Collect my bones and never collect again ... Take me and you will be free of your appetite' (208). After the road consumes her, it is satisfied, emitting the 'relieved sigh of millions of ghosts' (208). Miraculously, the gridlock immediately clears up and, for a time, at least no 'other people died on the Lagos–Benin Expressway' (209) as the problem of Lagos's traffic is added to the list of problems solved by the novel's extraterrestrials.

It is tempting the read the story of the Bone Collector allegorically as an anticipation of a movement from car harm into a sustainable world after oil. The road, in this reading, would function metonymically as an image of the rapacity of petroculture with its insatiable appetite for human victims. The shapeshifting alien, accordingly, is the image of liberation from the shackles of fossil capital. This view is too neat, however. Rather than straightforwardly a creation of petromodernity, the road is animated by a spirit entity that has 'been here since the roads were built, maybe even before then' (207). In this way, the novel moves away from a straightforward binaristic understanding of automobile infrastructure and the progressive network of alien, animal, spirit that heralds the death of the oil state. Ultimately, as the novel develops, it appears that if the aliens are keen to do away with oil, they are not so keen to do away with cars, at least not in their sustainable incarnation as EVs (which explains why alien intervention improves rather than moves beyond automobile infrastructure).

The electric car figures, significantly, at the novel's conclusion when the journalist Femi publishes an eyewitness account of the dying Ayodele, killed by soldiers horrified at her apparent witchcraft. Ayodele's final act of social transformation is to turn herself into a fog which when inhaled immediately creates a shift in perspective and memory and instigates widespread social change (287). Femi's story is 'the most honest piece of journalism he had ever produced' (288) and functions as further testimony to the positive future initiated by the aliens; dishonest reporters are a thing of the past. While the key plot point is ostensibly Femi's message to the world, the narrative lingers tellingly over his electric Honda Civic, as he locates his car charger from beneath the passenger seat, and reflects approvingly on the performance of the vehicle: 'He had bought a Honda for more than its plain unassuming look. Hondas *lasted*. Even on the roads of Nigeria' (286, original emphasis). Honda may not necessarily be pleased by the downbeat assessment of their product's aesthetics, but the durability Okorafor foregrounds is curiously reminiscent of advertising rhetoric. In a novel so invested in the exuberant unravelling of the logic of petromodernity, the representation of automobility here is curiously familiar. On climbing into his car, Femi notes that it 'smelled faintly like his girlfriend's perfume' (286) as if offering a reminder of the automobile's long-standing cultural significance in the depiction of heterosexual attachment. He has also customized the car with a 'secret hiding place' for his phone and laptop so that his vehicle is brought into an intimate relationship with his personal needs and sense of identity. This recapitulation of the terms of motonormativity becomes particularly significant when Femi plugs his phone into his car charger to enable him to share his story with the world. The good news of the coming sustainable transition is delivered from within an EV. For all the novel's interest in fluid ontologies and fantastic reimaginings of petrocapitalism, *Lagoon* also makes an apparently straightforward ideological investment in the EV. The novel's dissident perspectives with their multispecies ecological orientations remain attached to this exemplary artefact of neoliberal environmentalism. Given *Lagoon*'s focus on the ocean and its creatures, there is a subtle irony in the way the EV emerges into the foreground of the novel. If the pursuit of materials for batteries takes extractive capitalism to the sea floor, the redemption from petroculture imaged at the start with the swordfish's attack on the pipeline could only be a pyrrhic victory.

The motonormative allure of the EV is certainly not a universal element of Okorafor's Africanfuturist mobilities; elsewhere, sustainable transportation is stranger and more creaturely. *The Shadow Speaker* (first published in 2007 but revised and expanded in 2023) is a young adult novel that forms the first part of *The Desert Magician's* duology and contains Okorafor's most explicit engagement with automobility as a facet of both petroculture and post-oil imaginaries. The narrative sets out from Niger in 2074 and depicts a world after an apocalyptic event known as 'the great change'.[46] Some 'decades ago', the outbreak of nuclear war – initiated it seems by North Korea, though nobody really knows – had been counteracted by the use of 'peace bombs', the 'tool of an environmental group called the Grand Bois' (57), which had long set itself against the machinations of global capital in a way that draws on both ecological and animal ethics. The Grand Bois 'systematically blew up oil refineries, disabled and blew up equipment used to cut down trees in the rainforest, and set loose chickens, turkeys, ostriches, pigs and cows at slaughterhouses' (57). By 'crossing science and juju' (57), Dieuri, the Haitian leader of the Grand Bois, designed the peace bombs to 'create where nuclear bombs destroyed' and to 'cause so many "glorious" mutations amongst humans … that no one would want to fight each other' (57–8). Although the new world is far from utopia – violence remains widespread – business as usual has been exploded into a mystical state of ecological potentiality beyond what Dieuri had expected: 'All over the world, there were new forests and fields, lakes, oceans and mountains' (57); there are 'birds that fly backwards' and people who 'have turned into pink dolphins' (152). A segment of the population develops supernatural powers and becomes known as 'the Changed' (59). Among these is the novel's central protagonist, Ejii, who as a shadow speaker is able to tune into spirit voices and to communicate with animals.

An encounter between Ejii and a desert cat provides a gloss on the global situation that diagnoses the problems of late capital while revealing the transitional state of human–animal relations. '*You humans have made a mess of things*', the cat observes. Ejii concedes, '*My ancestors were arrogant*' but insists on her distance from the old regime: '*I can talk to you can't I? … And one night I put my hands to the Earth and could hear its heart beating … there was more than one rhythm.*' The cat replies, somewhat gnomically, '*Ah, the other places. They're close now*' (91). These other places are central to the novel's narrative intrigue. A key impact of the 'great change' is the destruction of the boundaries between parallel domains. In the universe of *The Shadow Speaker*, there are five worlds. Now, 'all the worlds have merged and something's going to happen' (208). Ejii's mission, along with her companion Dikéogu and his camel Onion, is to travel to the mystical ecocentric otherworld Ginen in order to prevent war with Earth being fomented by the irascible Red Queen Sarauniya Jaa, who beheaded Ejii's corrupt father before departing for a summit of the leaders of the worlds being held in Ginen. The ecological situation of *The Shadow Speaker* thus has two dimensions: Earth is undergoing its own geographical, social and ontological upheavals as the world is made anew after the 'great change'; meanwhile, the depiction of Ginen provides an external perspective on Earth's environmental condition as a version of the Afrofuturist trope of outer space.

The distinctions between Earth and Ginen are imagined to a significant extent through the depiction of petroculture and its speculative alternatives. As Ejii and Dikéogu are introduced to Ginen's culture by Buji, one of Jaa's two husbands, they are keen to get to grips with their new surroundings: '"What's the rest of Ginen like?" Dikéogu asked, "Are there airplanes? Cars?"' (210). Buji's evasive response draws out the implications of the differences from Earth; 'In Ginen, plants, trees and bushes rule, not humans', he explains (210). The point here is that terrestrial petroculture serves an anthropocentric regime that does not apply in Ginen. In fact, Ginen does have cars which, in tune with its botanical principles, are made from hemp. *The Shadow Speaker* makes consistent contrasts with terrestrial automobile technology. In Ginen, car 'engines produce the electricity they run on' (231); instead of exhaust they produce 'clean, flower-scented air' (232). When Ejii takes her first ride in one of Ginen's hemp cars, she giggles as 'tiny puffs of flowery-smelling mist came from near the windows and filled the car' (275). Crucially, Ginen is effectively allergic to oil-fuelled vehicles.

An early mission to Ginen involved 'Earth's finest' driving across the threshold between the worlds in 'large trucks' (268) with devastating consequences. Sunrise, a friend of Buji's, explains this tragic moment in Ginen's history. When

> those trucks crossed into Ginen, they began a path of destruction. The vehicles spewed smoke and fumes, poison to this land. If I were to take you over to the area ... you'd see how all the land was turned to ash. The soil can't grow even a fungus! There's no place in Ginen where a flower cannot grow! I've seen every inch of this planet and no such place exists! Until that envoy came. (268)

As 'a clean place', Ginen 'has no tolerance for that poison' (268). The concern among the people of Ginen is that if war between the two worlds transpires, Earth could effectively use petroculture 'as a weapon' (269): all the humans would need to do would be to drive right in and let the devastation unfold. Ginen thus exemplifies the outside of petroculture. As the evocation of a sustainable alternative, the people of Ginen take a similar role to the aliens of *Lagoon*.

As with Ayodele and her extraterrestrial kin, in Ginen 'technology is far superior' (293). At the end of the novel – with war averted for now – Ejii imagines a plan to 'send Ginen people to Earth to teach people about Ginen's machinery – *peacefully* cause the Earth vehicles to go extinct' (296, original emphasis). The merging of the worlds in this sense provides Earth with an unrivalled opportunity for sustainable transition.

If the key element of Ballard's autoscapes is the antipathy of automobile culture to any and all forms of life, the opposite holds true in Okorafor's Ginen. Along with hemp cars, residents of Ginen have another form of lively locomotion in the form of mutatos: 'large birds' with 'soft downy black hair' that function as 'public transportation'; they do not seem to mind being ridden but expect certain standards of their passengers (256). Even architecture here is alive in a green counterpoint to Ballard's necrotic urban space in *High Rise* and elsewhere. The Ooni Palace where the summit will be held is a living botanical structure maintained by a 'tribe of ants' (236); 'all sorts of wildlife' flourishes inside the building. To travel, and to live, in Ginen is to exist in an intimate symbiotic relationship with the more-than-human world. As Okorafor phrases it in an essay on 'Organic Fantasy' (in terms that emphasize the juxtaposition with Ballard and create an echo with Berry), Ginen represents 'a perfect marriage between the ancient and the modern, nature and technology'.[47] In *The Shadow Speaker* the apprehension of the interconnection between the human and the natural is arrived at not just geographically (through the journey to Ginen) but also mystically through Ejii's ability to communicate with the 'shadows': entities from a non-material plane. As the shadows speak to her, Ejii has an 'overwhelming' experience that she is 'part of something greater':

> With a surprising relief, she shed her individuality. And she was free. She joined the Whole, connecting with billions of other winds, waters, lands and spaces. The Whole was undying, young, old, ancient, constant. One great sigh of love, existence and purpose. (227)

Ejii's mystical realization of the underlying interconnection between all beings is part of the test that comes to all shadow speakers: a form of death, or at least ego death, that proves she is fit for the task.

Shortly afterwards, Ejii and her companions appear in Ginen as the mystical and geographical fade into one another. The transition between mystical and geographical worlds through the glimpse of the capitalized 'Whole' provides a precise echo of the terms of ecological holism as a foundational philosophical position for the environmental humanities. As Ejii returns to her own individual, human consciousness, the significance for this for understandings of the relationship between this environmental position and the question of the animal comes subtly into focus.

As Ejii comes back to herself, Buji is keen to keep her talking. The reason for this is that the transition from Earth to Ginen is marked by language: one minute you are speaking 'Hausa or Igbo' (two of the most commonly spoken Nigerian languages), then you find yourself speaking Ooni, the language of Ginen. So, the language the characters speak is a quick way of ascertaining which realm they are in. Casting around her mind for something to say, Ejii realizes how hungry she is and begins listing foods. The last thing she says before she enters Ginen is 'pepper soup with goat' (230). Okorafor's fiction consistently celebrates African cuisine; in 'Organic Fantasy', she notes that 'food is very important' to her.[48] That the last thing Ejii says before entering Ginen is a meat dish reverberates through the preceding evocation of her mystical apprehension of the Whole to make a clear ecocarnist point. Meat-eating is part of the Whole. If the biocentric automobility of Ginen reveals something of how technology might serve the idealized aim of a sustainable imbrication of the human in a multispecies world, then a pro-animal approach might find itself caught in uncomfortable territory. Even in Okorafor's fantastic multispecies mobilities, car culture remains wedded to carnism. Okorafor's vision of multispecies flourishing in this way is closer to an environmental humanities sensibility than the kind of position most intimate to animal studies, or at least to vegan studies with its commitment to interrogate the texts of meat by unravelling the multiple logics of carnism.

This is, admittedly, an awkward position for a vegan studies keen to complicate the carnist association of veganism with a white metropolitan liberal elite. For sure, there is some evidence of an emerging convergence between Afrofuturism and veganism. A blog post from Grainger Flint identifies the chef Bryant Terry's vegan reinvention of African American cooking in *Afro-Vegan* (2014) as an example of Afrofuturism which draws on the history of the

Diaspora to gesture towards a different future.[49] More precisely, for Aph Ko, 'black veganism is an Afrofuturistic praxis' in which people 'who have been oppressed and minoritized are actively challenging white supremacy by rearticulating their relationship to literal nonhuman animals'.[50] Black, or Afrofuturist (or Africanfuturist), veganism offers a specific perspective from which to rethink the questions of sustainability and human–animal relations as they pertain to projections of green automobility, though this is not a trajectory that exists within Okorafor's fiction. The liberation of animals from petroculture produced by *Lagoon*'s alien invasion and the other world of *The Shadow Speaker* is only partial and conditional on the continued availability of animals as food. Like *The Shadow Speaker*, *Lagoon* includes numerous asides on the satisfactions of meat in Nigerian cuisine.

Given the investment of Okorafor's fiction in EVs (and other sustainable vehicles), it is possible to see an animal studies perspective – inflected by vegan ethics – as the essential underpinning of what Calarco sees as the key task of progressive transportation: 'shrinking hyperautomobility in order to make room for human and more-than-human altermobilities'.[51] Bringing this animal-centred approach into dialogue with Okorafor's ecological holism allows for a more all-encompassing understanding of the networks of harm automobility exists within. This is not to say that there are not awkward questions to ask of Okorafor's depictions of automobile futures from an ecological vantage as well as from a pro-animal perspective. Where, to return to Macdonald's energy humanities agenda, does the cobalt in the battery of Femi's Honda Civic come from in *Lagoon*? (What, moreover, are the labour conditions of vibranium workers in Wakanda?) If, as Kara argues, the 'scramble for cobalt is reminiscent of King Leopold II's infamous plunder of the Congo's ivory and rubber' during the period of Belgium's colonial rule, then the politics of resource extraction are key to African futures and their imbrication within a neocolonial world order.[52] Okorafor is studiously attentive to the materiality of oil but, in a way that is reminiscent of the wider cultural investment in the techno-utopian promise of EVs, less concerned with the materiality of 'sustainable' transport. Okorafor's automobilities operate in this way through an ambivalent blending of radical post-oil politics and neoliberal complicities. At the heart of this is the aesthetic and narrative investment in the EV as one of green capitalism's most seductive fantasy objects, subtly woven into the redemptive logic of *Lagoon* and extrapolated out into the creaturely mobilities of *The Shadow Speaker*.

Both Ballard's petrocultural apocalypse and Okorafor's post-oil speculations provide significant perspectives on the meaning of automobility, the possibilities of sustainable transition and the intersections of these ideas with ecological and pro-animal critical priorities. At the broadest level, the reading of this suite of texts in these terms constitutes an act of attention that counteracts the normalization of car harm in mainstream discourses of automobility. More specifically, reading Ballard and Okorafor in dialogue with one another suggests the movement from oil to post-oil automobility can be understood in part through the depiction of animals. For Ballard, modernity's love affair with the automobile involves the violent erasure of animals in *Crash* and an obsessive attraction to animalistic violence in *High Rise* as car culture disintegrates in the implosion of petromodernity. Either way, animal death functions as an index of the violence of automobility that shows the value of an animal studies approach to the unravelling of the logic of the automobility imaginary. Here understanding of the ecological harms of automobility is facilitated by attention to the lives and deaths of Ballard's dogs.

In Okorafor's work, the countervailing sense that the movement away from oil towards a sustainable, multispecies automobility involves a release of animals from the violence of petrocapitalism is only partially true. Here the meaning of animals as meat creates a link between Ballard's roadkill and Okorafor's speculative mobilities. Meat, in these terms, is woven into the energy unconscious. Thinking these connections through manifests Braun and Randell's claim that 'technosocial visions need to be evaluated not against their future promises but their ontopolitical assumptions'.[53] What world-view do EVs embody? How do these world-views square with the underlying materiality? Any sense that the ecocarnist undercurrent comprises a reactionary component in Okorafor's work needs to be balanced, however, against the radical force of her explosion of categories of being in her Africanfuturist vision of sustainable transition, which is in turn intricately interwoven with the writing of African cuisine, though limited by the tendency to dematerialize sustainable transport through a fantasy of mobility beyond extraction. The task for both animal studies and the environmental humanities is to develop the critique of petrocapitalism into a critique of its renewal through EVs and other forms of sustainable transition that promulgate the neoliberal fantasy of a flight from harm. The EV can be taken as a point at which the radical green force of Okorafor's fiction partially unravels. It is perhaps above all the deconstruction of environmentalism that is the EV's most profound effect. In Part 3, the meanings of environmentalism come into focus from a different but interrelated perspective: the development of forms of natural capital economics that are increasingly taking centre stage in debates around the mitigation of biodiversity loss.

Notes

1 Nnedi Okorafor, 'Africanfuturism Defined', https://nnedi.blogspot.com/2019/10/africanfuturism-defined.html, accessed 3 March 2025.
2 Jenna N. Hanchey, 'Desire and the Politics of Africanfuturism', *Women's Studies in Communication* 43.2 (2020), 119–24, 119.
3 Okorafor, 'Africanfuturism Defined'.
4 Mark Dery, 'Black to the Future: Afro-Futurism 1.0'. In *Afro-Future Females: Black Writers Chart Science Fiction's Newest New-Wave Trajectory*. Edited by Marleen S. Barr, 6–13, 8 (Columbus: Ohio State University Press, 2008).
5 Olalekan Adekola and Gordon Mitchell, 'The Niger Delta Wetlands: Threats to Ecosystem Services, Their Importance to Dependent Communities and Possible Management Measures', *International Journal of Biodiversity Science, Ecosystem Services & Management*, 7.1 (March 2011), 50–68, 52.
6 Amnesty International, 'Niger Delta Negligence', 16 March 2018, https://www.amnesty.org/en/latest/news/2018/03/Niger-Delta-Oil-Spills-Decoders/, accessed 3 March 2025.
7 Amnesty International, 'Shell Must Clean Up Its "Toxic Mess" in Niger Delta', 13 February 2025, https://www.amnesty.org.uk/press-releases/london-shell-must-clean-its-toxic-mess-niger-delta, accessed 3 March 2025.
8 John Joseph Adams, 'Author Spotlight: Nnedi Okorafor', *Lightspeed*, March 2011, 10, https://www.lightspeedmagazine.com/nonfiction/author-spotlight-nnedi-okorafor/, accessed 3 March 2025.
9 Nnedi Okrafor, 'Spider the Artist', in *Kabu-Kabu* (Germantown, MD: Prime Books, 2013), 100–15, 101.
10 Nnedi Okorafor, *Lagoon* (London: Hodder and Stoughton, 2014), 113. Subsequent references in parenthesis.

11 Josephine Taylor, *The Nonhuman Narratives of Energy: Multispecies Encounters in Extraction Zones* (London: Palgrave, 2025), 68; Szeman, *On Petrocultures*, 101.
12 Szeman, *On Petrocultures*, 101.
13 Nnedi Okorafor, *Noor* (New York: Daw, 2021), 107.
14 Okorafor, *Noor*, 3.
15 Ossana, 'Decolonizing the Desert', 2.
16 Okorafor, 'Africanfuturism Defined'.
17 Karen Rignall and Nnedi Okorafor, 'Energy Politics and Africanfuturism – a Conversation with Nnedi Okorafor', *Middle East Research and Information Project* 311 (Summer 2024), https://merip.org/2024/07/energy-politics-and-african-futurism-a-conversation-with-nnedi-okorafor/, accessed 8 April 2025.
18 Graeme Macdonald, 'Improbability Drives: The Energy of Sf', *Paradoxa* 26 (2014), 111–44, 114.
19 Macdonald, 'Improbability Drives', 121.
20 Macdonald, 'Improbability Drives', 121.
21 Macdonald, 'Improbability Drives', 111.
22 Linda Yaszek, 'Afrofuturism, Science Fiction and the History of the Future', *Socialism and Democracy* 20.3 (2006), 41–60, 43.
23 W. Andrew Shepherd, 'Afrofuturism in the Nineteenth and Twentieth Centuries'. In *The Cambridge History of Science Fiction*. Edited by Gerry Canavan and Eric Carl Link, 101–9, 113 (Cambridge: Cambridge University Press, 2019).
24 Johnie Wilcox, 'Black Power: Minstrelsy and Electricity in Ralph Ellison's *Invisible Man*', *Callaloo* 30.4 (Fall 2007), 987–1009, 987.
25 Dery, 'Black to the Future', 9.
26 Ralph Ellison, *The Invisible Man* (London: Penguin, 1965 [1952]), 10.
27 Ellison, *The Invisible Man*, 10.
28 Shepherd, 'Afrofuturism', 113.
29 Ellison, *The Invisible Man*, 10.
30 Cited in Paul Youngquist. *A Pure Solar World: Sun Ra and the Birth of Afrofuturism* (Austin: University of Texas Press, 2016), 11.
31 Cited in John F. Szwed, *Space Is the Place: The Life and Times of Sun Ra* (New York: Da Capo Press, 1998), 29–30.
32 Youngquist, *A Pure Solar World*, 11.
33 For a full list of the Arkestra's continually morphing names, see Szwed, *Space Is the Place*, 94–5.
34 Sun Ra, *Space Is the Place*, directed John Coney, 1974.
35 Ra, *Space Is the Place*.
36 Don McGregor, Rich Buckler, Billy Graham, Stan Lee and Jack Kirby, *Black Panther* (London: Penguin, 2022), 4.

37 The Marvel Database, 'Vibranium', https://marvel.fandom.com/wiki/Vibranium#Wakandan_Vibranium, accessed 3 March 2025.

38 *Black Panther*. On fossil fuels see https://marvel.fandom.com/wiki/Wakanda#Technology, accessed 3 March 2025.

39 Alessia Gerola, 'Vibranium Dreams and Afrofuturist Visions: Technology, Nature and Culture'. In *Black Panther and Philosophy: What Can Wakanda Offer the World?*. Edited by Edwardo Pérez and Timothy E. Brown, 176–83, 181 (Hoboken, NJ: Wiley, 2022).

40 Blair Melsom, 'Is Wakanda a Real Place? Building Smart Cities Within Africa', https://www.bcs.org/articles-opinion-and-research/is-wakanda-a-real-place-building-smart-cities-within-africa/, accessed 3 March 2025.

41 Aisha Salaudeen, 'R & B Singer Akon Is Building a "Real-Life Wakanda" Worth $6billion in Senegal', *CNN News*, 2 September 2020, https://edition.cnn.com/travel/article/akon-city-senegal-wakanda-intl/index.html, accessed 3 March 2025.

42 Reuters, 'Swordfish Attack Angolan Pipeline', 2 February 2010, https://www.reuters.com/article/oukoe-uk-angola-crude-idAFTRE6113BU20100202/, accessed 3 March 2025.

43 Stacy Alaimo, 'The Anthropocene at Sea: Temporality, Paradox, Compression'. In *The Routledge Companion to the Environmental Humanities*. Edited by Ursula K. Heise, Jon Christensen and Michelle Niemann, 153–61, 155 (London: Routledge, 2021).

44 Melody Jue, 'Intimate Objectivity: On Nnedi Okorafor's Oceanic Afrofuturism', *Women's Studies Quarterly* 45.1 and 2 (2017), 171–88, 177.

45 Brett Banks, Jethro Kayat and Jean Rossman, 'Future Frontiers: Ontological Osmosis and Africanfuturist Cyborgs in Nnedi Okorafor's *Lagoon*', *Image and Text* 37 (2023), 1–20, 10.

46 Nnedi Okorafor, *The Shadow Speaker* (New York: Daw Books, 2023 [2007]), 48; subsequent references in parenthesis.

47 Nnedi Okorafor, 'Organic Fantasy', *African Identities* 7.2 (2009), 275–86, 281.

48 Okorafor, 'Organic Fantasy', 279.

49 Grainger Flint, 'Afrofuturism in Food', English @ SUNY Genesco, https://morrison.sunygeneseoenglish.org/2018/09/23/afrofuturism-in-food/, accessed 31 March 2025.

50 Aph Ko and Syl Ko, *Aphro-ism: Essays on Pop Culture, Feminism and Black Veganism from Two Sisters* (New York: Lantern Books, 2017), n.p.

51 Calarco, 'Animals, Mobility and the Future of Meat', 274.

52 Kara, *Cobalt Red*, 2.

53 Braun and Randell, *Post-Automobility Futures*, 132.

PART THREE

Conservation: Neoliberalism and extinction studies

CHAPTER 7

(Un)natural capital and endangered species

The term 'natural capital' has been in circulation since at least 1973, when it appeared in E. F. Schumacher's volume of essays *Small Is Beautiful: A Study of Economics As If People Mattered*. At the heart of Schumacher's argument was a diagnosis of 'man's attitude to nature' in which the 'illusion of unlimited powers' over the world created the tendency to 'treat as valueless everything which we have not made ourselves'.[1] The error of the prevailing economic system, for Schumacher, was a belief that 'natural capital' (the resources on which industrial production is based) is 'expendable' without consequence. Schumacher saw by contrast that if 'we squander our fossil fuels, we threaten civilisation'; even more significantly, 'if we squander the capital represented by living nature around us, we threaten life itself'.[2] The solution – or a step, at least, towards one – would be the recognition that 'the capital provided by nature' is both essential and limited and that 'we should do everything in our power to minimise their current rate of use'.[3] From this starting point could flow 'a new life-style, with new methods of production and new patterns of consumption' that allow for an environmentally sustainable culture.[4]

Unsurprisingly given Schumacher's subtitle ('Economics As If People Mattered'), his economic philosophy revolved not around questions of profit and prosperity but more around a wider interest in beauty, happiness and emotional fulfilment. Schumacher saw human well-being and ecological flourishing as necessarily conjoined and part of a wider theological vision. His overarching hope was that we 'learn to live peacefully, not only with our fellow men but also with Nature and, above all, with those Higher Powers which have made nature and have made us'.[5] In promulgating a pacifist, green politics, Schumacher found himself at odds with what remains one of the most intractable underlying principles of global capital: the ideology of economic growth with which – ironically given its origins in Schumacher's thought – the phrase 'natural capital' has come to be inextricably linked. In the first decades of the twenty-first century, natural capital has, in the words of the UK government, 'become a standard analytical approach to thinking about nature' that 'helps us to account for its contribution to the economy'.[6] The aim, ultimately, is 'to ensure nature and economic growth can work hand-in-hand'.[7] Schumacher's position – that 'infinite growth in a finite environment is an obvious impossibility' – makes him an awkward fit with this economically driven agenda. Indeed, Schumacher is a significant figure in the development of degrowth as an alternative economic model that refuses GDP as a measure of a nation's success and prioritizes instead welfare, justice and environmental equilibrium, ideas which are routinely part of the rhetoric of economic growth but which have been incorporated into it in real terms at best unreliably.[8]

Schumacher's writing is significant for my purposes in this chapter, then, not just for the inauguration of the term 'natural capital', a concept increasingly to the fore in the formulation of sustainable transition for its promise to reconceive key ecological problems like pollution and habitat degradation in economic terms, but because his philosophy highlights a central problem of green capitalism, which in turn provides another context for thinking through the relationship between pro-animal and ecological critical positions. When environmentalism proceeds through economic mechanisms, what are the implications for cultural, spiritual, ecocentric or other dissident or historically divergent conceptions of the value or meaning of life forms? What positions, connectedly, might a neoliberal environmentalism offer on the ethical weight of animal lives beyond their designation as commodities (if, indeed, there is anything beyond that)? Many of the thinkers involved, after Schumacher, in developing the idea of natural capital into workable practices and policies have stressed that innovations in environmental economics should be seen as part of a diverse portfolio of conceptions of value and not as a totalizing force that rules other forms of knowledge out of court by simply 'putting a price on Nature'.[9] As Dieter Helm, among the most influential proponents of natural capital, concedes (somewhat begrudgingly), 'The more radical arguments for nature should be respected' (though tellingly elsewhere in the same work he lambasts the opposition to natural capital as a 'an environmental fundamentalist position').[10]

Critics of natural capital economics, particularly those from within the humanities, have found Helm's gesture towards pluralism unconvincing. Schumacher himself noted a tendency in the process of 'pressing non-economic values into the framework of the economic calculus' to move 'from preconceived notions to foregone conclusions' as economics shows itself 'prone to usurp' other, non-material forms of value. In a culture fixated by the bottom line, 'even simple, non-economic values like beauty, health or cleanliness can survive only if they prove to be "economic"'.[11] For Schumacher, the exaltation of economy over ecology in this way represents a culture that is 'estranged from reality'.[12] By this reading, it is nature, as the physical basis of all economic and social activity, that represents the ultimate grounds of existence; the problems he outlines develop when economics does not acknowledge this primary fact, resulting in a predicament in which 'modern man does not experience himself as a part of nature'.[13] Relationships between nature and economy are, of course, massively complex. Nature, moreover, in the wake of Timothy Morton's *Ecology without Nature* in particular, has become a term that is widely avoided in the environmental humanities (and beyond) as a conduit towards unhelpful oversimplifications. In Morton's influential argument, 'Putting something called Nature on a pedestal and admiring it from afar does for the environment what patriarchy does for the figure of Woman.'[14] The problem, in Morton's analysis, is that 'Nature' has become a 'transcendental principle' that mitigates against an ethics and politics based on detailed understandings of the intricate relationships between human and more-than-human actors.[15]

Crucially, in the context of the evolution of discourses of natural capital after Schumacher, Morton's critique of Nature might, in part, be transposed to discourses of capital. Today it is capital that has become the transcendental principle, which is why, in the often-quoted phrase of Fredric Jameson, it is 'easier for us today to imagine the thoroughgoing deterioration of the earth and of nature than the breakdown of late capitalism'.[16] Or to offer Mark Fisher's summation, 'Capitalism seamlessly occupies the horizons of the thinkable' through a process of 'precorporation: the pre-emptive formatting and shaping of desires, aspirations and hopes by capitalist culture'.[17] Capital, for Fisher, even 'follows you when you dream'.[18] To see natural capital as a specific, and even in some framings relatively modest, contribution to the larger, diverse project of sustainable transition is to miss the extent of capital's hold and the imaginative paucity of a mainstream politics hooked on business as usual. Crucially, faith in market-based approaches to sustainability continues to deepen in mainstream politics, even though there is very little evidence of their success. As Adrienne Buller argues, natural capital has 'quickly fallen apart in confrontation with the realities of financialised global capitalism ... and, critically, with the profound complexity of our planet's natural systems'.[19] In the wider context of capitalism's seemingly incontestable hegemony, 'natural capital' might be taken as a particularly loaded and ambiguous phrase. On a surface level, it communicates the economic principle that in Helm's summary, 'Once nature is viewed as a set of assets it can be valued in economic calculations.'[20] But, grammatically, 'natural capital' does not simply integrate ecology into economics by insisting on its previously obfuscated value as Helm suggests. The phrase also subtly designates capital itself as 'natural': an originary social order that constitutes the unavoidable grounds of human existence and indeed all other forms of existence. Capital, in this way, is the planet's primary reality. This line of argument is not just cynical leftist wordplay; rather, it identifies a structurally integral characteristic of the social and political framework of natural capital.

The idea of natural capital has been marching steadily into the foreground of environmental debates since the 1980s as part of what Elia Apostolopoulou describes as the 'global mainstreaming' of economic valuation as a central pillar of sustainability discourses.[21] A key moment in this history came with the launch of the Brundtland Report, a landmark text in the formulation of sustainable development, which emerged out of the UN World Commission on Environment and Development in 1987. Published with the universalizing title *Our Common Future* (as if the manifold histories of the world might be compressed into a single world to come), the text leaves in no doubt the centrality of discourses of capital in the formation of global environmental politics, as it aspires towards a 'new era of economic growth ... that must be based on policies that sustain and expand the environmental resource base'.[22] The common future that is envisaged here is a future in which the language of finance moves ineluctably to the fore. In the 1990s, notable for the second phase of neoliberalism under the Clinton and Blair administrations, attempts to develop the concept of natural capital gathered pace. The 1992 Rio Earth Summit established the need for 'better measurement of the crucial role of the environment as a source of natural capital'.[23] The year 1993 saw the origins of the UN's System of Environmental-Economic Accounting (SEEA), 'a framework that integrates economic and environmental data to provide a more comprehensive and multipurpose view of the interrelationships between the economy and the environment'.[24] By the second decade of the twenty-first century, a spate of high-profile publications had solidified the conceptual framework of natural capital and allowed it to put it into practice more widely.

In the UK, the premise of an economically driven environmentalism was formalized in the 2011 *UK National Ecosystem Assessment* (*UK-NEA*), 'a comprehensive overview of the state of the natural environment in the UK and a new way of estimating our national wealth'.[25] Publicizing this groundbreaking document, the Secretary of State, Caroline Spelman, offered a telling metaphor for human–ecological interactions. 'We need to recognise,' she explained, 'that if we withdraw something from Mother Nature's bank, we've got to put something back in to ensure that the environment has a healthy balance and a secure future.'[26] The soundbite of nature as bank indicates an imaginative deepening of green capitalism that complements the emerging practices of natural capital accounting; indeed, by the time Spelman imagined Mother Nature's bank, the UK's Environment Bank had already been formed in 2006 with the aim of 'shaping nature policy in England' along natural capital lines.[27]

Shortly after the publication of the *UK-NEA*, the significance of natural capital in policy deliberations was formalized through the establishment of DEFRA's 'natural capital committee', set up in 2012 to 'help the Government better understand how the state of the natural environment affects the performance of the economy and individual well-being'.[28] This committee echoes the launch of 'the Natural Capital Declaration' at the UN Conference on Sustainable

Development in Rio, marking the twentieth anniversary of the Earth Summit.[29] The aim of the declaration was to 'maintain and enhance Natural Capital as a critical economic, ecological and social asset'.[30] It was 'signed by the CEOs of more than 40 financial institutions from around the world, formalising their commitment to the integration of natural capital considerations into financial sector reporting'.[31] As this potted history reveals, idea of natural capital has become a pivot of capitalism's 'ecological phase', to return to Artruro Escobar's phrasing. Or, as Apostolopoulou summarizes, nature conservation has undergone a 'profound change in its goals, donors, mottos, communication strategies and tactical alliances, in order to seek a closer alignment with capital'.[32] Conservation is in the process of being thoroughly internalized to the operation of global capital.

If the natural capital approach to ecology evidently provides a somewhat different mechanism for sustainable transition than the high-tech solutions embodied by CM and EVs, the two positions – the economic and the technical – are intimately entwined elements of a hegemonic green capitalism. It is through the development of innovative technologies that involve less intensive use of resources (should this eventuality arrive) that the stock of natural capital can be protected. Conversely, a natural capital approach incentivizes the creation of green technologies that allow business to continue without incurring the costs attendant on pollution or other forms of environmental degradation (should such payments in fact be levied). This marriage of the economic and the technical is, in essence, the answer to the question of global ecological crisis as it is most commonly expressed in mainstream politics. The cynical counterpoint is that each of the mechanisms in its own way (and perhaps most crucially in combination with the other) allows for the continuation and expansion of corporate profit by encouraging the fantasy that unlimited economic growth on a finite planet remains possible. Or to apply Apostolopoulou's provocative framing of market-based forms of conservation, both technological and economic mechanisms embody an 'extreme technomanagerial optimism and its naïve faith [in] capitalism's ability to infinitely reproduce itself'.[33] Natural capital may not be a technology as such, but it is one of the key techniques of sustainable transition understood as a vital hinge of capitalism's durability.

There are numerous specific contexts for and expressions of the idea of natural capital. The UK's aspirations to reach net zero greenhouse gas emissions by 2050 are, for instance, 'underpinned by a natural capital approach'.[34] Carbon markets, through which credits purchased by polluters are directed towards enterprises that remove greenhouse gases from the atmosphere, have been around in some form since the signing of the 1997 Kyoto Protocol. Among the highest profile and most contestable of natural capital's applications is its role in addressing the issue of biodiversity loss. That the world is in the grip of the sixth extinction – an unprecedented anthropogenic extinguishing of varieties of life – is a key theme in environmental and animal ethics and one that reverberates through all aspects of social and political life. Extinction poses massive material and philosophical questions, 'wounding our profound dependence on [a] diverse non-human multitude, not only economically or ecologically but cognitively, culturally and spiritually', as Matthew Chrulew and Rick De Vos put it.[35] Evidently, the case for biodiversity conservation is supported by diverse rationales. The environmental ramifications of the biodiversity crisis are extensive and unpredictable. The knock-on effects of the loss of a particular species from an ecosystem can be profound. Without viable populations of pollinators, moreover, human civilization per se could become untenable. Philosophically and ethically, the implications are vast too. Each extinction is a tragic cessation of a unique perceptual universe, embodied in the particular organization, experience and culture of a species. As more of these are lost, humanity is faced, in E. O. Wilson's phrase, with the arrival of the Eremozoic, an 'Age of Loneliness ... where most of life on Earth that we evolved in [is] gone forever'.[36] If the effects and meanings of biodiversity loss are diverse and wide-ranging, so are the causes. Meat and automobility are both part of the story through their impact on habitats and their role in pollution (both locally through various forms of run-off and waste disposal and globally through their contribution to climate change). Development is a problem in many forms (think of resource extraction and infrastructure projects), and the various symptoms of a changing climate, such as ocean acidification, take their toll on species too.

Given the massive distribution of the causes and effects of extinction across distinct and intertwining discourses and practices, it is a problem that defies a straightforward solution. Historically, economics has had little to say about biodiversity, but the development of natural capital approaches has encouraged a raft of new economic mechanisms and policy measures. Biodiversity loss is, according to Helm and Cameron Hepburn, 'one of the greatest economic problems of this century'.[37] There are, for Helm and Cameron, two reasons for this. The first is that 'it is economic growth and development that has caused biodiversity loss'; the second is that 'future losses of biodiversity and ecosystems may significantly reduce the productivity of our economic systems'.[38] Among the earliest and most notable international attempts to move towards economic solutions for biodiversity loss came with the commissioning of The Economics of Ecosystems and Biodiversity (TEEB) project in 2007 that set out under the tagline 'valuing the invaluable'.[39] TEEB concluded by postulating three levels of action: recognizing value, demonstrating value and capturing value.[40] 'Recognizing value' involves identifying social attitudes that are already enough to 'ensure conservation'; the example in TEEB's statement of its approach is 'the existence of sacred groves in some cultures'. 'Demonstrating value' refers to the calculation of economic values embodied in biodiversity which might previously have been invisible to in decision-making processes. The last of these, 'capturing value', underpins a significant raft of policy shifts that operate through the 'introduction of mechanisms that incorporate the values of biodiversity and ecosystems into decision-making through incentives and price signals'.[41] Central here is the idea of biodiversity offsetting, explained in the UK government's definition as 'conservation activities that are designed to give biodiversity benefits to compensate for losses – ensuring that when a development damages nature (and this damage cannot be avoided …) new nature sites will be created'.[42] Characteristically, in much the same way to the operation of carbon credits, a developer will pay a third party to implement the compensation so that the total amount of habitat is not diminished, even if specific locations are destroyed. In this spirit, the Environment Bank offers developers the option of buying 'biodiversity units' from their 'growing network of Habitat Banks' as the 'most cost effective' means of offsetting biodiversity loss.[43] By protecting habitat in this way and mitigating one of the prime causes of extinction, such innovations promise to slow biodiversity loss.

In the UK, biodiversity offsetting took root in 2012 with a series of pilot schemes. In due course, the idea of no net loss (NNL) expressed in these schemes was extended to the principle of biodiversity net gain (BNG) which became law in the UK under the 2021 Environment Act to ensure that 'habitats for wildlife are left in a measurably better state than they were before the development'.[44] As with other proponents of natural capital approaches, those engineering the practice of biodiversity accounting have been keen to add caveats to their approach that anticipate criticisms about the disappearance of rich and complex understandings of the natural world into the abstract, oversimplified domain of economic calculation. TEEB's developers, for instance, have distanced themselves from what they see as the misconstrual of the economic valuation of biodiversity as a means of '"financializing" nature and its services' and thus exposing the natural world to ever greater depredations from private and corporate interests. Instead, they see TEEB as 'a model for communicating to decision-makers in their own language, dominated by economics, as well as a toolkit for evaluating and integrating good stewardship into their decisions'.[45] Notwithstanding the work that has been done by TEEB and others on anticipating (or as Apostolopoulou prefers 'sidelining') critiques, there is now a sizeable and significant body of work on the limitations of biodiversity offsetting, which, as with the wider discourse of natural capital, fits awkwardly with other perspectives on conservation.[46]

For all the buoyancy of the rhetoric around biodiversity offsetting and net gain, these practices have a lamentable track record. Surveying the results of biodiversity offset schemes in Australia and the Nordic states, Buller notes that 'their record of success has been almost impressively poor' with extensive loss of habitat despite the use of offsets.[47] A large part of the problem is the way in which offsetting unravels established mitigation hierarchies. The expected priorities in proposed development projects are often expressed as avoid, reduce, compensate; attempts should be made to avoid or minimize ecological damage before offsetting comes into play as a method of compensation once the damage is done. In reality, the option to offset renders the expensive and inconvenient earlier steps in the process notably unappealing to developers. Beyond this, criticisms of offsetting take many forms. In a wide-ranging review, Maron et al. list seventeen points of criticism, divided into four categories: philosophical/ethical; social; technical; and governance.[48] In terms of governance, they note 'inadequate monitoring' as a key area of concern, involving a tendency referred to elsewhere as 'set and forget': a commitment to compensate for losses that ultimately produces no action and which points to biodiversity offsetting as mere greenwashing.[49] The technical concerns they raise pivot on concerns about the metrics used in the design of offsets; as Apostolopoulou asks, 'What exactly should be measured ... when calculating ecological gains and losses'?[50] Are the right things being measured? How is it possible to be sure? Does the metric adequately capture the complex interplay between different forms of life? Social concerns focus, among other issues, on the impact on local communities of the replacement of green spaces with, to return to the UK government's phrasing, 'new nature sites' elsewhere. While there is a preference for offsets to be planted as close to the original site as possible, this is not always possible, especially in urban areas, with the result that access to nature is restricted through the offsetting process. Offsetting becomes in this way a factor in changing land use with the effect of, again to quote Apostolopoulou, 'actively remaking the earth in line with the patterns of capitalist growth'.[51]

The technical, governmental and social concerns around offsetting are all elucidated by the first category Maron et al. cite: the philosophical/ethical. Specifically, they note offsetting's failure to 'respect nature's intrinsic values' and the associated danger of 'reframing it as fungible'.[52] Among the earliest and most trenchant refutations of the logic of biodiversity offsetting along these broad lines appeared in Kathryn Yusoff's response to the publication of the 2011 *The Natural Choice* white paper, itself a response to the *UK-NEA* and the document that led to the creation of the UK's biodiversity offsetting pilot schemes. In *The Natural Choice*, biodiversity offsetting was highlighted in familiar language as an example of a 'flexible and innovative' approach to sustainable development that will 'deliver more, better, bigger and joined up networks of habitat' by 'providing a straightforward and cost-effective way to assess the impact of a development and to agree the requirements for compensation'.[53] Yusoff's critique pivots on the way that offsetting's construction of mechanisms of exchange represents a gross oversimplification of the nature of beings and their relationship with the world:

> The *Natural Choice* materializes and sustains ways of thinking about natures as interchangeable autonomous units, divorcing

> things from their places and their intra-actions. It addresses spaces as containers, not as exuberant knots of relations. This action of cutting apart separates both thing and concept at once; it is the lonely spectre of the biotic subject divorced from its lifeworld.[54]

If the environmental humanities is drawn to the aesthetics and politics of entanglement (Yusoff's 'exuberant knots of relations') as key conceptual prop for its ethical commitments to the more-than-human world, biodiversity offsetting is sustained by a process of disentanglement: the divorce of the subject from its life-world that facilitates the doctrine of exchangeability. As Yusoff continues, you cannot simply swap 'a dyke for a ditch, a pond for a puddle, a badger for a baboon'.[55] Here Yusoff's analysis, admittedly, misses the mark to some degree. Biodiversity offsetting and net gain require equivalence; developers probably would not get away with swapping a badger for a baboon, though it might be possible to justify swapping a pond for a puddle. Judging what constitutes equivalence presents its own philosophical problems. Regardless of the criteria of exchange, Yusoff's wider point holds: in translating the meaning or value of any being caught in an offset project into an abstract sphere of calculation, they are 'inscribed into capitalist modes of production as the defining characteristic of their life's work'.[56] Andrea Brock characterizes this effect as one of 'ontological flattening', which is to say the reduction of 'the multi-complexity and diversity of nature(s) to its easily quantifiable properties', which creates 'the invisibilisation of complex social relations and uniqueness for the sake of domination, domestication, categorisation and quantification'.[57] The conceptual roots of Yusoff's and Brock's critiques can be traced back to Maurice Merleau-Ponty's theory of the *Umwelt*, defined, in Louise Westling's summary, as 'the subjective reality created by each organism's dynamic participation in the world around it'.[58] Natural capital accounting represents, perhaps above all, a breach in the understanding of the inextricable relationship between beings and their environments. In this sense, an eco-phenomenology indebted to Merleau-Ponty, focused on the embodied links between beings and worlds, radically undermines the machinations of natural capital. In creating a mechanism for economic valuation, biodiversity offsetting and the more recent policy edict of BNG are involved in deferring the meaning of beings and places as only ever fungible elements of a larger system defined in relation to discourses of capital.

If the overarching aim of *The Natural Choice* white paper is 'long-term sustainable economic growth', it is easy extrapolate out from the logic of offsetting to a larger point about the forms of value at play in green capitalism's attempts to mitigate biodiversity loss.[59] Yusoff is concerned that 'according to the logic of this "natural capital", the nature that does not provide and service us has no place in the world'.[60] After all, as Helm contends, 'conservation ... is about hard choices with economic consequences'.[61] This does not mean that a being that contributed nothing to any form of human economic activity would necessarily be considered expendable under a natural capital approach, but it is tempting to run with the thought experiment. What would be the fate under a neoliberal environmentalism operating through biodiversity offsetting, or even BNG, of a perfectly useless animal? The internet resounds with speculation on what the Nature Blog Network calls the 'fascinating world of seemingly unproductive creatures', though assessments on the uselessness or otherwise of life forms involve an intriguing interplay between forms of value.[62] High in the rankings in Nature Blog Network's list are animals noted for their widely agreed cuteness: pandas are perhaps the poster creature of the useless cute. As the Nature Blog Network summarizes, 'Pandas spend the majority of their time eating, sleeping, and avoiding contact with other pandas. This solitary lifestyle hinders their ability to contribute to the ecosystem.'[63] It is precisely the panda's combination of material pointlessness with cultural centrality (as an icon of the global conservation movement and the template for billions of cuddly toys) that makes it an irresistible case study of processes of valuation. Evidently, even if the panda does not contribute significant ecosystem services, and its body is of no direct use as a food source, it still, to return to Yusoff's language, does not exemplify 'nature that does not provide and service us' and which therefore under the logic of natural capital 'has no place in the world'. Crucially, natural capital valuation can potentially extend to more nebulous forms of value; 'cultural value', for example, is part of the terrain of green capitalism. As the *UK-NEA* explained, it is possible (if challenging) to develop an 'approach to the natural environment that is based on evidence concerning the cultural aspects of human-nature relations', though, crucially, doing so results in the forced conjunction of fundamentally incommensurable forms of value.[64] Even materially useless creatures may be culturally, and experientially, valuable. But how much, exactly, for the skip of the heart at the glimpse of a fawn?

The humanities are – and ought to be – an uncomfortable prospect for proponents of biodiversity offsetting and wider discourses of natural capital. Understanding cultural meanings necessarily extends beyond and casts a critical light back onto reductive economic formulations through analysis of the cultural, social, historical, emotional and ideological contours of economic discourses. The point of the humanities is not calculation but critical thinking. Or, as Sam Ladkin and Robert McKay contend:

> The task of the arts and humanities, both in their creative and educative aspects, is to contest, to challenge, to question, to undermine, to satirise, to offend, to violate, to deconstruct, to degenerate, to critique, to undo, or to suspend dominant and dominating assumptions of value.[65]

Following this trajectory, the humanities provide a necessary complication of the premise of natural capital approaches that operates through an exploration of the interplay between distinct and overlapping discourses of biodiversity loss. It is here that extinction studies comes into view as a field of critical enquiry premised, in Cary Wolfe's words, on the understanding that extinction is '*never* a generic event and … *always* a multi-contextual phenomenon requiring multidisciplinary modes of encounter and understanding' (original emphasis).[66] Or, as Deborah Bird Rose, Thom van Dooren and Matthew Chrulew put it, the aim of extinction studies is to engage with narratives 'that help us to inhabit *multiply*-storied worlds in a spirit of openness and accountability to otherness' (original emphasis).[67] Natural capital approaches to biodiversity are thus only one of the stories that extinction studies exists to navigate. Economic questions exist alongside narratives of loss, the erosion of a sense of place, ideas of the sacred, conceptions of beauty and apprehensions of ethical obligations to other beings. The stakes of extinction transcend human frames of interest, especially those framed narrowly in economic terms.

As a mode of enquiry concerned directly with animals and with the environments they constitute – and are constituted by – extinction studies exists between animal studies and the environmental humanities. Since extinction is evidently an issue with profound impacts on ecosystems, questions of biodiversity have drawn a good deal of attention in the environmental humanities. At the same time, because extinction self-evidently proceeds through animal death, it is also an important theme for the understanding of the cultural representation of animals. These familiar orientations necessitate focus on animals at the level of species and of the individual creature so that endangered species – and most particularly the figure of the endling (more on which in Chapter 9) in which the level of the species and the level of the individual are brought into a final, tragic convergence – are a topic of crucial significance on either side of the environmental humanities/animal studies line.

This does not mean that extinction is the theme through which animal studies and the environmental humanities have been brought into perfect alignment. Ursula Heise, among the most influential environmental humanities scholars on the theme of extinction, suggests that anxieties around extinction have 'typically focused on places and species',[68] rather than on the lives of the particular animals. Tackling the division between animal studies and the environmental humanities head-on, Heise defends an ecological ethic against an animal ethic. It is hard, she contends, to imagine how a framework committed to the moral worth of individual animals could 'possibly determine what the "welfare" of a particular individual means without reference to species'.[69] In critiquing animal studies' approaches to extinction, Heise draws extensively on the culling of invasive species as a key instantiation of the tension between animal and ecological ethics in the context of biodiversity loss. Heise foregrounds the case, for example, of the 'accidental introduction of the notorious brown tree snake, *Boiga irregularis*, to the island of Guam in the 1950s', which 'led to the extinction of most native forest vertebrates, at least a half dozen native bird species, and several native lizard and gecko species'.[70] Situations like these provide a strong conservation rationale for the local eradication of the invasive species. For Heise, Dale Jamieson's claim that 'animal liberation is an environmental ethic' rings 'hollow against the background of such conflicts'.[71] There is no simple solution to many of these issues. As van Dooren notes, 'It is ultimately impossible to reach simple … prescriptions about how ecologies "should be". And so we are required to make a stand for some possible worlds and not others.'[72] Consequently, care for some species is 'intimately and inextricably entangled with various forms of violence' so that it might be more appropriately characterized as 'violent-care'.[73] Negotiating this intractable situation requires nuanced examination of both animal and ecological ethics and the trade-offs between them.

In terms of natural capital approaches to species loss, there might seem, following Heise's line of argument, an easier convergence of biodiversity offsetting with an ecological approach than with a pro-animal approach. It is, after all, the level of the ecosystem and the species that natural capital targets; the key point is that it is the total stock of nature (calculated in part through the diversity of species) that matters rather than any individual creature. This line of enquiry would be misleading, however. Since offset ideology is involved in emptying places out of their specific significance, an environmental humanities critique is most readily located at a landscape scale. Landscapes are particular, non-fungible, culturally meaningful arenas of human and more-than-human interaction that cannot be straightforwardly replaced. Animal studies meanwhile provides a point from which to interrogate the politics of species in the context of biodiversity offsets. Evidently, some species matter more than others. In the UK developers would be legally required to provide compensation for the death and/or displacement of newts but not of rats, mice, pigeons or other common and largely unloved beings (which is similar to the situation in Guam in which conservation posits that a brown snake matters less than a native reptile). The idea of species, then, operates as a means of creating relative value between individual beings: a newt is more valuable than a rat, which is precisely this kind of ideological valorization that animal studies exists to interrogate. Neither the environmental humanities nor animal studies is likely to be readily complicit with the unfolding of natural capital approaches to biodiversity loss, and, as I trace in the following two chapters, the potential alliance between them provides a significant position from which to expose the limitations of market-driven discourses of conservation. In investigating two texts concerned with the representation of endangered species in relation to economic discourses, I argue for an alliance of animal studies and the environmental humanities as a bulwark against neoliberalism's bland simplifications.

Notes

1 E. F. Schumacher, *Small Is Beautiful: A Study of Economics As If People Mattered* (London: Vintage, 1993 [1973]), 3.
2 Schumacher, *Small Is Beautiful*, 5.
3 Schumacher, *Small Is Beautiful*, 4.
4 Schumacher, *Small Is Beautiful*, 9.
5 Schumacher, *Small Is Beautiful*, 9.
6 UK Government, 'Enabling a Natural Capital Approach (Guidance)', 4 February 2025, https://www.gov.uk/government/publications/enabling-a-natural-capital-approach-enca-guidance/enabling-a-natural-capital-approach-guidance, accessed 2 April 2025.
7 Natural England, Press Release, '"Nature Is the National Wealth Service": Natural England Chair Calls for New Approach in Major Report', 9 October 2024, https://www.gov.uk/government/news/nature-is-the-national-wealth-service-natural-england-chair-calls-for-new-approach-in-major-report, accessed 2 April 2025.
8 Schumacher, *Small Is Beautiful*, 33.
9 UN Environment Programme, 'TEEB: Approach and Timeline', https://www.unep.org/topics/teeb/about-teeb/teeb-approach-and-timeline, accessed 2 April 2025.
10 Dieter Helm, *Natural Capital: Valuing the Planet* (New Haven, CT: Yale University Press, 2015), 3, 143.
11 Schumacher, *Small Is Beautiful*, 31.
12 Schumacher, *Small Is Beautiful*, 3.
13 Schumacher, *Small Is Beautiful*, 3.
14 Timothy Morton, *Ecology without Nature: Rethinking Environmental Aesthetics* (Cambridge: Harvard University Press, 2007), 5.
15 Morton, *Ecology without Nature*, 5.
16 Fredric Jameson, *The Seeds of Time* (New York: Columbia University Press, 1994), xii.
17 Mark Fisher, *Capitalist Realism: Is There No Alternative?* (London: John Hunt, 2022), 9.
18 Fisher, *Capitalist Realism*, 34.
19 Adrienne Buller, *The Value of a Whale: On the Illusions of Green Capitalism* (Manchester: Manchester University Press, 2022), 246.
20 Helm, *Natural Capital*, 6.
21 Elia Apostolopoulou, *Nature Swapped and Nature Lost: Biodiversity Offsetting, Urbanization and Social Justice* (Cham: Palgrave Macmillan, 2020), 46.

22 The World Commission on Environment and Development, *Our Common Future* (Oxford: Oxford University Press, 2009), 1.
23 Agenda 21, United Nations Sustainable Development, June 1992, https://sustainabledevelopment.un.org/content/documents/Agenda21.pdf, accessed 4 April 2025.
24 System of Environmental Economic Accounting, 'What Is the SEEA?', https://seea.un.org/content/homepage, accessed 4 April 2025.
25 Lord John Selborne, 'Foreword', in *Synthesis of the Key Findings. UK National Ecosystem Assessment* (Cambridge: UNEP-WCMC, 2011).
26 DEFRA, 'New Plans Promise Flourishing Future for the Natural Environment', 7 June 2011, https://www.gov.uk/government/news/new-plans-promise-flourishing-future-for-the-natural-environment, accessed 1 April 2025.
27 The Environment Bank, 'About Us', https://www.environmentbank.com/more/about-us/, accessed 1 April 2025.
28 https://webarchive.nationalarchives.gov.uk/ukgwa/20130822074033/http://www.defra.gov.uk/naturalcapitalcommittee/files/NCC-Information-Sheet.pdf.
29 Escobar, *Encountering Development*, 205.
30 United Nations Environment Programme, 'Natural Capital Declaration', http://www.naturalcapitaldeclaration.org/the-declaration/, accessed 1 April 2025.
31 United Nations Environment Programme, 'Natural Capital Declaration'.
32 Apostolopoulou, *Nature Swapped and Nature Lost*, 8.
33 Apostolopoulou, *Nature Swapped and Nature Lost*, 8.
34 Natural Capital Committee, 'Advice on Using Nature Based Interventions to Each Net Zero Greenhouse Gas Emissions by 2050', 6 April 2020, https://assets.publishing.service.gov.uk/media/5e986365d3bf7f4123758926/ncc-nature-based-interventions.pdf, accessed 1 April 2025.
35 Matthew Chrulew and Rick de Vos, 'Extinction'. In *The Edinburgh Companion to Animal Studies*. Edited by Lynn Turner, Undine Sellbach and Ron Broglio (Edinburgh: Edinburgh University Press, 2018), 181–97, 183.
36 'Living on Earth: Interview with E. O. Wilson', E. O. Wilson Biodiversity Foundation, https://eowilsonfoundation.org/eowbf-archive/listen-living-on-earth-interview-with-e-o-wilson-on-how-to-save-the-most-species/, accessed 4 April 2025.
37 Dieter Helm and Cameron Hepburn, 'The Economic Analysis of Biodiversity'. In *Nature in the Balance: The Economics of Biodiversity*. Edited by Dieter Helm and Cameron Hepburn, 7–32 (Oxford: Oxford University Press, 2014).

38 Helm and Cameron, 'Economic Analysis of Biodiversity', 7.
39 The Bank of Natural Capital, 'The Economics of Ecosystems and Biodiversity Study (TEEB)', 8 January 2012, n.p., http://bankofnaturalcapital.com/, accessed 14 June 2014.
40 Pavan Sukhdev, Heidi Wittmer and Dustin Miller, 'The Economics of Ecosystems and Biodiversity (TEEB): Challenges and Responses'. In *Nature in the Balance: The Economics of Biodiversity*. Edited by Dieter Helm and Cameron Hepburn, 135–50, 138 (Oxford: Oxford University Press, 2014).
41 UN Environment Programme, 'TEEB: Approach and Timeline', https://www.unep.org/topics/teeb/about-teeb/teeb-approach-and-timeline, accessed 10 May 2025.
42 UK Government, 'Biodiversity Offsetting', 9 April 2013, https://www.gov.uk/government/collections/biodiversity-offsetting, accessed 2 April 2025.
43 'Biodiversity Units', The Environment Bank, https://www.environmentbank.com/what-we-do/biodiversity-units/, accessed 4 April 2025.
44 UK Government, 'Biodiversity Net Gain', 21 February 2023, https://www.gov.uk/guidance/understanding-biodiversity-net-gain, accessed 4 April 2025.
45 UN Environment Programme, 'Approach', TEEB, https://teebweb.org/about/approach/, accessed 2 April 2025.
46 Apostolopoulou, *Nature Swapped and Nature Lost*, 8.
47 Buller, *The Value of a Whale*, 253.
48 Martine Maron, Amrei von Hase, Fabien Quétier, Laura J. Sonter, Sebastian Theis and Sophus OSE zu Ermgassen, 'Biodiversity Offsets, Their Effectiveness and Their Role in a Nature Positive Future', *Nature Reviews* 1 (March 2025), 183–96, 190.
49 Australian Conservation Foundation, 'Set and Forget Offsets Are Killing Biodiversity', https://www.acf.org.au/set-and-forget-offsets-are-killing-biodiversity, accessed 2 April 2025.
50 Apostolopoulou, *Nature Swapped and Nature Lost*, 77.
51 Apostolopoulou, *Nature Swapped and Nature Lost*, 77.
52 Maron et al., 'Biodiversity Offsets', 190.
53 HM Government, *The Natural Choice: Securing the Value of Nature*, 2011, https://assets.publishing.service.gov.uk/media/5a7cb8fce5274a38e57565a4/8082.pdf, accessed 2 April 2025, 22.
54 Kathryn Yusoff, 'The Valuation of Nature: The Natural Choice White Paper', *Radical Philosophy* 170 (November/December, 2011), 1–6, 4.
55 Yusoff, 'The Valuation of Nature', 5.
56 Yusoff, 'The Valuation of Nature', 2.
57 Andrea Brock, 'Securing Accumulation by Restoration – Exploring Spectacular Corporate Conservation, Coal Mining and Biodiversity

Compensation in the German Rhineland', *Environment and Planning E: Nature and Space* 6.4 (2020), 2137.

58 Louise Westling, *The Logos of the Living World: Merleau-Ponty, Animals, and Language* (New York: Fordham University Press, 2013), 16–17.

59 HM Government, *The Natural Choice*, 22.

60 Yusoff, 'The Valuation of Nature', 4.

61 Helm, *Natural Capital*, 3.

62 Nature Blog Network, 'The Top 10 Most Useless Animals on the Planet', https://www.hummingbirdsplus.org/nature-blog-network/the-top-10-most-useless-animals-on-the-planet/, accessed 2 April 2025.

63 Nature Blog Network, 'The Top 10 Most Useless'.

64 *UK National Ecosystem Assessment: Technical Report*, http://uknea.unep-wcmc.org/LinkClick.aspx?fileticket=QLgsfedO70I%3d&tabid=82, accessed 2 April 2025, 680.

65 Sam Ladkin and Robert McKay, 'Against Value', https://occursus.wordpress.com/2012/02/14/against-value-23-2-2012/, accessed 1 May 2025.

66 Rose, van Dooren and Chrulew, *Extinction Studies*, viii.

67 Rose, van Dooren and Chrulew, *Extinction Studies*, 3.

68 Heise, *Imagining Extinction*, 19.

69 Heise, *Imagining Extinction*, 138.

70 Heise, *Imagining Extinction*, 138.

71 Heise, *Imagining Extinction*, 140.

72 Thom van Dooren, *Flight Ways: Life and Loss at the Edge of Extinction* (New York: Columbia University Press, 2014), 60.

73 van Dooren, *Flight Ways*, 111.

CHAPTER 8

Comedy, capital and the poetics of encounter in Douglas Adams and Mark Carwardine's *Last Chance to See*

Since the late 1970s there has been a significant wave of non-fiction narratives about endangered species that cohere into what Graham Huggan has described as the 'new subgenre' of ecotravel writing.[1] Acclaimed texts like Peter Matthiessen's *The Snow Leopard* (1978) and Dian Fossey's *Gorillas in the Mist* (1983), for example, attested to, and in turn stimulated, public interest in the imperilled lives of charismatic megafauna which developed alongside increasing understanding of the science of biodiversity and conservation, facilitated by key studies such as E. O. Wilson's 1988 edited collection *Biodiversity*. Wilson's volume emerged from the National Forum on Biodiversity, held in Washington, DC in 1986 with an 'immediately perceived impact on the public'.[2] For Wilson, by 1980 enough data had been accumulated 'on deforestation, species extinction, and tropical biology to bring global problems into sharper focus and warrant broader public exposure'.[3] In the same period David Attenborough's life trilogy – *Life on Earth* (1979), *The Living Planet* (1984) and *The Trials of Life* (1990) widely lauded as 'landmark wildlife series' – consolidated the role of biodiversity, and wider ecological themes, in mainstream media culture, providing a visual complement to the textual form of the ecotravel narrative.[4]

The increased public interest in endangered species and the challenges of conservation in this period pivot on a well-remarked compensatory relationship between biodiversity loss and its representation. As Akira Mizuta Lippit observes in a much-quoted passage, 'Animals recede into the shadows of human consumption and environmental destruction ... ecospheres are vanishing, species are moving toward extinction.'[5] Rather than simply fading into obscurity, in Lippit's analysis, 'animals never *entirely* vanish, but exist in a state of *perpetual vanishing*' (original emphasis).[6] For Lippit, 'modernity finds animals lingering in the world *undead*' (original emphasis); the animal becomes 'a lost object' to 'be mourned'.[7] In exploring how animal being has come to be 'constituted by that state of disappearing',[8] Lippit draws on John Berger's influential analysis of the ways in which the increasing absence of animals from daily life in the nineteenth century activated a visual demand that was, in part, responsible for the development of zoos (institutions with historical links with the wildlife documentary and ecotravel writing). Because animals are gone, we are compelled to look for them so that a 'new breed of animals now surrounds the human populace – a genus of vanishing animals'.[9] The extinction crisis thus creates an imperative to catch creatures in textual and visual representation as affecting engagements with animal life that are necessarily structured by the realization of mass animal death.

The title of Douglas Adams and Mark Carwardine's comedy ecotravel narrative *Last Chance to See* condenses this cultural context into a neat proposition. We are at a point in history which provides the final opportunity to witness many creatures poised on the brink of extinction. The problem is not just that these creatures are disappearing (with all the ecological and ethical implications that carries) but also that we will no longer be able to witness them. It is not enough for animals to survive, they must be looked at. In this way, *Last Chance to See* provides a significant case study in the politics of representation of endangered species, though it also strikes a notably different tone from what Ursula Heise describes as the 'genre templates of elegy and tragedy' that are, understandably, most commonly deployed in extinction narratives.[10] *Last Chance to See* is, by contrast, conservation in a 'comic rather than an elegiac mode'.[11] Heise offers a brief but significant account of the text (more on which in due course) that pivots on its importance as a counterpoint to overly familiar, even hackneyed environmentalist tropes, in tune with Lippit's emphasis on the state of vanishing. For Heise, extinction narrative suffers from a 'declensionist' perspective in which 'the awareness of nature's beauty and value is intimately linked to a foreboding sense of its looming destruction'.[12] In 'breaking away from doom and gloom scenarios' (though as we shall see not entirely),[13] *Last Chance to See* is a text that meets Heise's desire for accounts that provide a 'more affirmative vision of our biological future'.[14] Questions of mood and genre are explicitly situated in Heise's discussion at the cusp of animal studies and ecological approaches to extinction and reveal a stridently partisan ecological critique of animal ethics. Reading the text in dialogue with the emergence of discourses of natural capital allows, however, for a differently inflected argument that, against Heise's reading, identifies animal ethics as a central part of the political force of *Last Chance to See.*

Last Chance to See was first conceived by Adams, the much-loved British science-fiction novelist, and the zoologist Carwardine for a radio series in 1989 before becoming a 1990 book by Adams and Carwardine. In 2009, several years after Adams's untimely death, *Last Chance to See* was revived with the actor and comedian Stephen Fry replacing Adams and working alongside Carwardine to produce a TV series and then a follow-up book that returned to the scene of many of Adams's and Carwardine's earlier adventures. The 1990 book version I focus on here is structured around five main sets of animal encounters (and a shorter reflection on an earlier trip to Madagascar to look for aye-aye lemurs). In Indonesia, Adams and Carwardine meet Komodo dragons; in Zaire (now the Democratic Republic of Congo), they visit mountain gorillas and Northern white rhinos; in New Zealand, they locate kakapos (a large, flightless parrot); in China, they fail to locate any Yangtze river dolphins (now extinct); and in Mauritius, they are introduced to the world's rarest type of fruit bat. The book consists mainly of Adams's first-person narrative with Carwardine contributing an afterword from his more formally scientific perspective.

Adams is most celebrated for his science-fiction comedy series *The Hitch Hiker's Guide to the Galaxy* (1979); despite evident generic differences from *Last Chance to See*, there is a strong thematic continuity between the texts in their shared interest in both species and environmental politics. *Hitch Hiker's* pivots on the limitations of anthropocentric hubris, expressed in the famous twist that the world is actually 'commissioned, paid for, and run by mice', who are not insignificant 'little white furry things', as is generally supposed, but rather 'protrusions into our dimension of hyper-intelligent, pan-dimensional beings'.[15] This ego-puncturing assault on human exceptionalism contains an ecological angle which informs the comic set piece that opens the *Hitch Hiker's* novels. Arthur Dent, protesting against the demolition of his house in the West Country to build a bypass through the countryside, discovers a far larger problem: the Earth itself is to be demolished by the Vogons (a race of aliens with responsibility for galactic planning) as part of the construction of a 'hyperspatial express route'.[16] If that seems unfair, as the Vogons point out, 'all the planning charts and demolition orders have been on display in your local planning department in Alpha Centauri for fifty of your Earth years, so you've had plenty of time to lodge any formal complaint'.[17] As nimbyism is expanded from a local to a cosmic scale, Adams connects the novels' playful interrogation of anthropocentrism with a satire on the bureaucratic infrastructures of institutional power. It is not just ontology that reduces the status of the human in the world of Adams's novels – the fact that mice are more intelligent and powerful than *Homo sapiens* – but also their subjection to administrative processes. Dent is powerless in the face of Vogon bureaucracy. While anyone is welcome to complain, it is impossible to do, and in any case, there is no point.

Of course, had the Vogons arrived after the UK's 2021 Environment Act had come into force, they would at least have been required to offset the loss of biodiversity involved in the destruction of the entire planet. It might seem an egregious act of overreading to see *The Hitch Hiker's Guide to the Galaxy* as a prescient critique of discourses of natural capital, but there is a precedent for this approach. In a 1993 essay on Vogon economics, John Adams ponders the bureaucratic processes by which the demolition of the Earth might have been approved. Adams speculates that although *The Hitch Hiker's Guide* 'fails to say whether Alpha Centauri's planners used cost benefit analysis, they must have done'.[18] Cost-benefit analysis – the process of weighing a project's advantages against its disadvantages – is closely related to natural capital; specifically, natural capital accounting aims to provide a mechanism for understanding the balance of advantage and disadvantage in ecological terms, by drawing attention to costs (such as those generated by pollution) that might previously have appeared invisible to decision makers. John Adams uses the case of the Vogons to reflect on the application of cost-benefit analysis to climate change and the emerging hypothesis in the 1990s that a 'monetary assessment is crucial to design the optimal policy response'. Adams's argument is by now a familiar one. Understanding ecological issues in the context of 'the promotion of world economic growth' can produce situations in which conservation is ruled out as uneconomic. The problem with this position – it hardly needs saying – is that you can't have an economy without a functioning ecology. John Adams's punchline is that 'Vogon economists have another planet to which they can retreat' if their policies fail.[19] For the Vogons, there *is* a Planet B.

John Adams's speculation on the limitations of natural capital approaches might be taken further. As it turns out, the Earth can be replaced. Rather than a self-existing planet, the Earth is in fact a supercomputer designed to interpret the answer to the question of life, the universe and everything given by the earlier supercomputer Deep Thought. (Deep Thought's answer to the question of life, the universe and everything is the famously mysterious forty two.) Since the Vogons destroyed Earth just before it was due to make its revelation, the people who made the original planet/supercomputer have to make another one. Adams's comedy is not straightforwardly appropriable as a direct satire on twenty-first-century practices of biodiversity offsetting, but the key themes of singularity and replaceability (in concert with bureaucratic bombast and ecological violence) lead into that broad territory, particularly via the deep emotional attachment Dent feels towards the particularities of his home and his culture: 'Nelson's column had gone and there would be no outcry because there was no one left to make an outcry'; 'every Bogart movie has been wiped'.[20] The Vogons have destroyed a specific and irreplaceable singularity that can nonetheless be replaced. If it is not strictly an offset, *Hitch Hikers'* will nonetheless be read in dialogue with the economic–environmental discourses taking shape in Thatcher's Britain. There is no alternative, to return to a favourite phrase of Thatcher's, to the construction of the hyperspatial express route, but miraculously the damage is undone.

Adams brings a similarly quirky and subversive imagination to the machinations of global capital in *Last Chance to See*. Just as *Hitch Hikers'* is a product of the early Thatcher years, Adams's and Carwardine's travels take place at an historical juncture in the development of international policy about biodiversity during which discourses of global capital begin to subsume political debates about extinction on the world stage. The launch of the Convention on Biological Diversity (CBD) in 1992 was a pivotal moment for the formation of postcolonial critique of mainstream, international approaches to biodiversity loss. For Vandana Shiva, rather than a 'dramatic step forward' in postcolonial environmental politics, the CBD comprised only a reaffirmation of the old world order supporting the familiar vested interests of the Global North in the guise of multinational corporations. Her evaluation opens with the assertion that the convention 'started out primarily as an initiative of the North to "globalise" the central management and ownership of biological diversity ... so as to ensure free access to the biological resources which are needed as "raw material" for the biotechnology industry'.[21] The CBD's vision of a global policy of biodiversity management in this analysis stands to renew rather than to overcome the legacies of colonialism. This is a question of representation as much as of politics. How does the primacy of capital in discourses of biodiversity become a matter not just of how conservation is legislated for but also of how forms of life are imagined? The development of sustainability as a hegemonic discourse of global capital for Shiva involves profound cultural effects. The title of the book in which she contends with the CBD's postcolonial politics makes this association strongly: *Monocultures of the Mind* argues that the 'dominant political system' of 'commercial capitalism' negates local knowledge to encourage a homogeneous, globalized system of knowledge.[22] It is here that the question of textual form – and its histories – comes back into view.

Emerging via the institutional might of the BBC and with a focus on the tropical and (for the most part) postcolonial world, *Last Chance to See* is unavoidably connected to empire. As Huggan notes, environmental travel writing is a genre 'haunted by its own imperial/colonial spectres'.[23] The overarching structure of the journey into the postcolonial wilds shows Adams re-enacting the nineteenth-century literary modes of exploration and adventure through which the natural historian often functioned as the vanguard of imperial expansion. In repackaging this trope for a late-twentieth-century audience, Adams expresses the text's formal debt to a colonial past via an engagement with ecotourism as the neo-colonial practice through which the Western readership might realize the 'last chance to see' these vanishing creatures.

Ecotourism might immediately appear to function as a celebration of the diversity and aesthetic appeal of more-than-human life, but it is also, in its quest for the world's vanishing animals, built on the apprehension of death. The powerful demand for the cultural consumption of the diminishing variety of the Earth's biota follows a capitalist logic of scarcity. Endangered species offer a powerful boon to ecotourism precisely because of their endangerment; as Heise contends, the more endangered a 'species is, the more valued it becomes, in a logic that resonates both with the capitalist valuation of scarce resources and with the cultural fascination, inherited from the Romantic age, with impending death – the aura of "the last"'.[24] As a cultural practice situated on the cusp of destruction and survival, ecotourism can be taken as a form of dark tourism: travel to sites of earthquakes or war zones, for instance, to witness the spectacular unfolding of trauma. Since ecotourism revolves around the particular significance attached to rare or endangered forms of life, it effectively operates through a double commodification of animal life. Animals and the environment are harmed through habitat loss in the process of the extraction of material value which in turn adds cultural value to what remains.

The wildlife documentary exists in this space (and it is worth recalling *Last Chance to See*'s later TV adaptation here) as a cultural form linked with discourses of capital. As Richards notes, notwithstanding the public service ethos of the BBC, the BBC Earth brand launched in 2009, in the wake of Attenborough's growing status, 'was designed to exploit the vast revenues generated from the sale of products related to landmark and other wildlife series'.[25] Behind this is the wildlife documentary's function as a commodity which, in Huggan's terms (reminiscent of Lippit's argument), works through its generation of the effect that '"disappearing" wildlife magically reappears'.[26] The trope of the vanishing animal can be thought of, in Nicole Shukin's terms, as 'profoundly idealizing', a representational convention which 'allows capital to largely go missing as motive force'.[27] Global capital thereby becomes a crucial if somewhat obscured element of the representation and experience of endangered species across the interlinked colonial forms of ecotourism, the wildlife documentary and ecotravel writing.

Against these situational entanglements of ecotravel writing and (neo)colonial ideology, *Last Chance to See*, rather than silencing the operations of global capital, derives a good deal of its comedy from critiquing its flattening effects. *Last Chance to See* is explicit in its engagement with the long historical processes of colonization, decolonization and globalization in both ecological and cultural terms. The decline of the kakapo in New Zealand, for example (the basis of the fourth journey), was one of empire's many unforeseen ecological consequences; as Adams explains, when 'European settlers arrived and brought cats and dogs and possums with them, a lot of New Zealand's flightless birds were waddling for their lives'.[28] Much of the book's sardonic humour comes from its account of the ironies of global tourism. Adams's descriptions of the elaborate intrigues of postcolonial bureaucracy in the issuing of visas and other permits recall the galactic planners of *Hitch Hikers* and provide a sardonic take on the legacies of empire in the tourist industry. The visit to Indonesia is particularly elucidating for its depiction of capital, postcolonial tourism and endangered species.

En route to Komodo to find the fabled dragons, Adams and Carwardine alight in Bali, that most extensively marketed of tourist destinations. Particularly, they find themselves in the 'part of Bali which has been made almost exactly the same as everywhere else in the world for the sake of people who have come all this way to see Bali' (15). The monoculture ushered in by mass global tourism produces a world of 'gift shops and hamburger bars', seemingly interchangeable to Adams's mind with Spain or Greece and populated by the same gangs of inebriated visitors (15–16). When Adams and Carwardine arrive in Komodo, encounters with the dragons are equally mediated by global capital. The spectacle of a live goat (more on which later) being fed to a dragon in front of a group of mainly American tourists who have been choppered in to this remote Indonesian island is a rich and knowing moment. As the head of the dragon becomes wet with the thick green liquid from the goat's stomach, one of the watching tourists shouts a surprising response to his friend: 'Al? Al, take a look at these binoculars and see how heavy they are!' (42). What draws the man's attention is not the grisly spectacle he has paid to witness but the technological apparatus that is there to facilitate the intimacy of his experience. Adams is clearly dismayed and amused by a scene that is characterized both by an intense scopophilic desire and an overwhelming indifference: a hollow visual appetite that desires the world but views it with detachment.

For all the tourist's enjoyment of his binoculars, the experience of the Komodo dragon is ultimately disappointing. As another tourist complains: 'I like the landscape ... The dragons are just thrown in. If you were walking by yourself and you came across one that might be different, but it's kind of like a puppet show' (42–3). If Adams and Carwardine's title evinces the spectacular lure of endangered species, the episode in Komodo suggests that there also needs to be more to the encounter than the curated meeting with an animal. It is not enough to witness the creatures in the heavily mediated environment of the tourist; the meeting needs an extra element, of surprise or of a larger, more earnest quest. The image of the 'puppet show' is a forceful one. Set up for tourists like this, the Komodo dragon is emptied of its 'meaning'; part of the enticement of endangered animals is transferred to their habitat and therefore to a larger sense of the postcolonial environment as a wilderness worthy of a true adventure. Certainly, this kind of ecological imaginary has proved to be a remarkably durable aspect of tourist culture (there is no shortage of companies offering adventure holidays characterized by their distance from metropolitan centres). Part of the role of the postcolonial explorer is to access these wildernesses on the audience's behalf, to attain a more authentic encounter with the dwindling animal world. The role of ecotravel writing is to struggle towards a more resonant experience than a mere 'puppet show', though reaching beyond the puppet show is itself a profoundly colonial gesture. *Last Chance to See*'s satire on ecotourism is complemented by Adams's bathetic narration of the protagonist's failure to match up to the image of the explorer; their arrival in Komodo features a number of 'blow[s] to our sense of intrepidness' (30). In this way, *Last Chance to See* offers a multifaceted satire of the disappearance of endangered species – and the quests to witness them – into the operations of capital.

Importantly, bathos infuses Adams's depiction of the moments of human–animal encounter that the textual form of the ecotravel narrative demands. Encounters with endangered species in extinction narratives are evidently highly charged narrative events that carry the sense of a climax or epiphany in a way evocative of the form's colonial antecedents. Although the gun is now replaced by the camera or the pen, meetings with rare animals echo the heightened energy characteristic of the hunt. Against this pattern, the poetics of encounter such writing ordinarily moves toward is rendered unconventionally in *Last Chance to See*. Adams is no macho hunter. Rather, in the emotionally intensified moments of encounter with rare animals the text is structured around, Adams makes use of a technological frame of reference that adds complexity to a reading concerned with tracing the relationship between ecological, animal and economic discourses in the context of extinction.

Adams is remarkably consistent in the framing of meetings with endangered animals in mechanomorphic terms (which is to say in Garrard's definition, the 'representation of animals as machine-like').[29] Watching a rhinoceros grazing in Zaire is like 'watching a JCB excavator quietly getting on with a little weeding' (94); its 'huge muscles move easily under its heavy skin like Volkswagons parking' (95); it hurtles off 'like a nimble young tank' (96). Meeting a mountain gorilla evokes the feeling of 'being watched by a truck' (69). Similarly, a Philippine monkey-eating eagle is 'a wildly improbable-looking piece of flying hardware that you would more readily expect to see coming in to land on an aircraft carrier than nesting in a tree' (173). In a more extended metaphor, the kakapo is compared by Adams to the ill-fated British motorcycle industry: 'It had things its own way for so long that it simply became eccentric. The motorbike industry didn't respond to market forces because it wasn't particularly aware of them.' Problems arise when highly competitive foreign machines appear: Japanese motorbikes for the British motorcycle industry, or, in the case of the kakapo, cats, stoats and other non-native species (113).

Casting these creatures in machinic terms has subtle ideological implications. Just as the satire on the tourist gaze in Komodo produced comedy as anti-capitalist critique, so the poetics of encounter elsewhere in the text operates through resistance to a certain commodification at work in the epiphanic mode of extinction writing. As Carwardine takes pleasure in explaining, *Last Chance to See*'s difference from a 'normal' nature documentary helps to 'make conservation accessible to people who wouldn't normally care about endangered species' via a 'hilarious but thought-provoking insight into the disappearing world around us'.[30] Given his celebrity as a science-fiction comedy writer and a self-professed 'gadget freak' (36), Adams's preferred metaphorical register is unsurprising. Importantly, the key element of the motif is not the technological register per se but the sense of machines that are awkwardly attuned to their surroundings and evocative of failures of efficiency or design (as in the case of the out-of-touch British motorcycle industry). Heise sees in this pattern a particular ethics of conservation: 'It is precisely this inefficient, irrational unadaptedness of the natural world that makes it attractive and worth preserving for the narrator – the sheer unlikelihood of it ever having made it to the present day.'[31] Consequently, she argues, 'the idiosyncracies of the sociocultural realm mirror and extend the contingencies of ecology and evolution'[32] so that we are left with 'an essentially comic awareness of the contingent events, habits and bodies it took to produce both humans and nonhumans in their present form'.[33] Heise's analysis emphasizes how *Last Chance to See* operates at arm's length from an emerging economic rationale for biodiversity conservation; Adams's quirky view is in a sense diametrically opposed to a commercial emphasis on usefulness by relishing whatever is purportedly useless. As such, the text produces an important corrective to the reductive economic vision of the CBD and the Brundtland Report in two ways: it resists extracting cultural capital via a conventional poetics of encounters, and its figuration reveals an attraction to awkwardness and inefficiency that refuses a discourse of utility.

Heise concludes her discussion of Adams's and Carwardine's text in upbeat terms: rather than a 'well-functioning natural realm disrupted by the advent of modern society, *Last Chance to See* implies a view of nature and culture as parallel and intersecting histories of experiments that continually succeed and fail'. Accordingly, it points 'to an understanding of extinction not only as narrative endpoint, but as the possibility of new beginnings – not the end of nature so much as its continually changing futures'.[34] The conclusion of Heise's argument works coherently within the terms of the environmental humanities by tying ethics to wider ecosystemic, evolutionary logics. Thinking through a specifically animal-centred ethics, however, makes Heise's line of reasoning less compelling. To think of extinction as part of an ongoing play of planetary life as Heise asserts fails to attend sufficiently to the particular animal deaths through which extinction proceeds or to the geopolitical contexts in which this happens.

At one level Heise's argument is a matter of ecological fact: species go extinct; new species emerge; beings and habitats are replaced by other beings and habitats. Heise acknowledges that the current extinction crisis is different in scale and cause from the ongoing pattern of background extinctions, but there is something like an ethics – or even economics – of fungibility at work in her recourse to the prospect of 'our continually changing futures' which risks mirroring or even endorsing emerging neoliberal practices, such as biodiversity offsetting, by which creatures are understood to be exchangeable in the service of human interests. In casting the creatures it describes as generic and in the case of the Volkswagen mass-produced figures, Adams's techno-cultural imagination might appear to risk sidelining the creaturely dimension of the biodiversity crisis, which is to say extinction's arrival through the pain and death of individual sentient beings with an urgent interest in their own survival.

Importantly, however, the machinic register is complemented by an insistence of beings as non-exchangeable ethical subjects rather than ecological units that Adams develops through comic speculations on animal experience which knowingly play with anthropomorphism. Adams is particularly keen to assert an awareness of an unknowable animal consciousness which (like the realization of the power of mice in *Hitch Hiker's*) unsettles human exceptionalism. Face to face with a gorilla – that most overdetermined of beasts – Adams reflects that we 'look them in the face and we think, "We know what they're like", but we don't. Or rather we actually block off any possible glimmering or understanding of what they may be like by making easy and tempting assumptions' (75). Similarly, looking a Komodo dragon in its 'unwavering and disinterested eye', Adams recounts a set of anthropomorphic stereotypes about lizards (emotional coldness and malignity) only to insist that the dragon 'didn't know anything about the horror, the guilt, the shame, the ugliness that we ... were trying to foist on it'. Instead, it carries on 'going about its lizardly business in a simple, straightforward lizardly way' (33), while Adams reflects on the 'profoundly disturbing experience' of 'watching an eye that is watching you' (32). Adams leaves space open for the realization of animal interiority beyond the human gaze, even if – in fact, precisely because – that experience is closed to human apprehension. Turning back to Adams's techno-cultural figuration from this perspective reveals the trope of the machine as a knowing exemplification of the limitations of making sense of animals in anthropomorphic terms. To return to Mark Fisher's terminology, animals are in a sense precorporated into economic modes of signification by the image of the rhino moving like a Volkswagen (et cetera); animals may appear, in this sense, as a *product* of nature. But in Adams's comedic encounters this imagery is signalled as an anthropomorphic construction of beings that exceed these figurations. Looking animals in the eye in this way embodies the stakes of extinction and shows that before we affirm the 'possibility of new beginnings', there is a vulnerable present to attend to, which, crucially, extends beyond the charismatic creatures at the centre of the narrative. In Komodo Adams is attentive not just to the dragons but also to other creatures they share their journey with: 'Four chickens [that] sat in the prow of the boat and watched us' (27) are not just food but also the occasion for a meditation on the ethics of meat and the sentience of the birds. Similarly, the ill-fated goat that lures the dragons to the tourists is the focus of an extended meditation as it evinces an 'appalling dread' on the path to its death, struggling 'desperately against the tugging of the rope, bleating and crying' (39). It is not just the endangerment of species that constitutes the ethical force of *Last Chance to See* but also this wider attention to the experience of vulnerability that appears at the edges of the main narrative drama.

For all the merriment of Adams's writing, *Last Chance to See* leaves the force of its ethical commitment in no doubt. The overarching message of the text is drawn out across three successive endpoints: the final passage of Adams's narration of the travels; at the end of a parable Adams closes with; and then in the final chapter written by Carwardine titled 'Mark's Last Word'. If what makes *Last Chance to See* distinctive is its comic register, these endings all strike a more conventional elegiac note that returns to the declensionist position Heise observes as the wider trend of extinction narratives. Adams's parting evocation of Mauritius encapsulates a mournful atmosphere that counterpoints the humour elsewhere:

> At dusk that day we stood by the side of another road, where we had been told we would have a good view, and watched as the world's rarest fruitbats left their roost in the forest and flapped

> across the darkening sky to make their nightly forage among the fruit trees ... I have a terrible feeling that we are in trouble. (195)

As the last episode in Adams's and Carwardine's travels, the crepuscular setting for the fruit bats roosting is evidently gauged to be resonant: the sun setting, as it were, on another species. The bats flapping across 'the darkening sky' operates metonymically as a sign of the larger catastrophe. This, as Heise argues, is a common ingredient of extinction discourse: in both science and art 'species serve as proxies for ecosystems and biodiversity'.[35] The global frame implied by Adams's fruit bat emerges again in the concluding chapter of Adams's narration when he relates the story of the Sibylline books as an analogy for the ethical stakes of extinction. The story runs that an old beggar woman successively burns the twelve books containing 'all the knowledge and all of the wisdom of the world' (196) because the residents of the city she visits are too deeply under the sway of gold to think of the need of wisdom and to buy the books from her. The story ends with one book remaining and the people of the city left to survive with the 'remaining twelfth of all the knowledge and wisdom that had been in the world' (199). As an ecological parable about extinction, the story makes a political point: it is the profit motive that keeps us from apprehending more profoundly meaningful forms of value.

Carwardine's *crie de coeur* in the final chapter provides his gloss on the significance of extinction. Having cited a familiar litany of anthropocentric reasons for conservation as necessary for 'our own survival' (205), Carwardine concludes with the reflection that

> there is one last reason for caring, and I believe that no other is necessary. It is certainly the reason why so many people have devoted their lives to protecting the likes of rhinos, parakeets, kakapos and dolphins. And it is simply this: the world would be a poorer, darker, lonelier place without them. (206)

Carwardine's conclusion retains elements of anthropocentrism but in a soft guise: one that privileges affect and aesthetics over use value. 'Poorer' functions metaphorically; the richness it counters is that of a fading biological abundance. 'Darker' adds an aesthetic dimension, and 'lonelier' implies a sense of community with other creatures, based on a presumption that human fulfilment relies on an intimacy with other forms of life (think back to Wilson's coinage of the Eremozoic). The book ends with environmentalism as affect, with a feeling for the world and the creatures in it (or at least those creatures in it that we feel moved to identify with) as an antidote to the flattening effects of global capital. Carwardine's final chapter is the last word in the double sense of being literally the book's end pages and also *Last Chance to See*'s resonant philosophical conclusion.

What is significant about each of these three endpoints is their utilization – in familiar ecological terms – of the category of world as the key ethical criterion. The metonymic logic of the fruit bat scene points to a larger frame of reference just as the two succeeding endings explicitly conceive of biodiversity loss in a planetary frame (the *world* without wisdom in the parable of the Sibylline books and the dark lonely *world* of 'Mark's Last Word'). Thus, the tragedy of extinction is ultimately posed macrologically at these decisive moments in the text. As satire makes way for sincerity, the key message is an ecological one. At issue here is the *world* without the *likes* of these animals. Such an orientation towards the global scale expresses the all-encompassing ethical urgency of the extinction crisis. It is here that the interplay between registers in the book appears as central to its force across the animal studies/environmental humanities cusp. The ecological tragedy of extinction emerges from the comedy of animal being. It is the combination of these perspectives that solidifies the text's resistance to neoliberal and neocolonial modes of representing nature and foregrounds the necessity of the animal ethics for a radical ecological approach to the question of extinction.

Notes

1 Graham Huggan, *Extreme Pursuits: Travel/Writing in an Age of Globalization* (Ann Arbor: University of Michigan Press, 2009), 52.
2 E. O. Wilson, 'Editor's Foreword'. In *Biodiversity*. Edited by E. O. Wilson and Smithsonian Institution Staff, v–vii, v (Washington, DC: National Academy Press, 1988).
3 Wilson, 'Editor's Foreword', v.
4 Morgan Richards, 'Global Nature, Global Brand: BBC Earth and David Attenborough's Landmark Wildlife Series', *Media International Australia* 146.1 (February 2013), 143–54, 144.

5 Akira Mizuta Lippit, *Electric Animal: Towards a Rhetoric of Wildlife* (Minneapolis: University of Minnesota Press, 2000), 1.
6 Lippit, *Electric Animal*, 1.
7 Lippit, *Electric Animal*, 1, 3.
8 Lippit, *Electric Animal*, 3.
9 Lippit, *Electric Animal*, 3.
10 Heise, *Imagining Extinction*, 14.
11 Heise, *Imagining Extinction*, 51.
12 Heise, *Imagining Extinction*, 7.
13 Heise, *Imagining Extinction*, 53.
14 Heise, *Imagining Extinction*, 13.
15 Douglas Adams, *The Hitch Hiker's Guide to the Galaxy* (London: Pan, 1979), 125.
16 Adams, *Hitch Hiker's*, 30.
17 Adams, *Hitch Hiker's*, 31.
18 John Adams, 'Vogon Economics and the Hyperspace Bypass', *New Scientist*, 18 September 1993, https://institutions.newscientist.com/article/mg13918915-200-forum-vogon-economics-and-the-hyperspace-bypass-john-adams-on-a-debate-in-which-scientific-uncertainty-is-being-transformed-into-economic-farce/, accessed 2 April 2025.
19 Adams, 'Vogon Economics'.
20 Adams, *Hitch Hiker's*, 51.
21 Shiva, *Monocultures of the Mind*, 151.
22 Shiva, *Monocultures*, 9.
23 Huggan, *Extreme Pursuits*, 8.
24 Heise, *Imagining Extinction*, 72.
25 Richards, 'Global Nature, Global Brand', 150.
26 Huggan, *Extreme Pursuits*, 83.
27 Shukin, *Animal Capital*, 13.
28 Douglas Adams and Mark Carwardine, *Last Chance to See* (London: Arrow, 2009 [1990]), 105. Subsequent references in parenthesis.
29 Greg Garrard, *Ecocriticism* (Abingdon: Routledge, 2012), 208.
30 Mark Carwardine, '*Last Chance to See*', https://www.markcarwardine.com/last-chance-to-see.html, accessed 11 October 2019.
31 Heise, *Imagining Extinction*, 52.
32 Heise, *Imagining Extinction*, 53.
33 Heise, *Imagining Extinction*, 53.
34 Heise, *Imagining Extinction*, 54.
35 Heise, *Imagining Extinction*, 53.

CHAPTER 9

Disentangled creatures in Ned Beauman's *Venomous Lumpsucker*

Ned Beauman's *Venomous Lumpsucker* (2022) could well be the first novel explicitly about natural capital accounting. Although its form contrasts markedly with the non-fiction travel narrative *Last Chance to See*, there are notable consanguinities between the texts through a shared interest in the bureaucracy and economics of endangered species and in their satirical, self-reflective engagement with the politics of representation in the context of extinction. Given its intimate engagement with the neoliberal environmentalisms of the early twenty-first century, *Venomous Lumpsucker* develops out of from a key moment in the discourse of sustainable transition, following on from *Last Chance to See*'s emergence from the first heyday of sustainability in the 1990s. In this sense, they represent sequential stages in the development of green capitalism.

Set fifteen to twenty years in the future (though no exact date is given in the text), at a time when the '2°C warming era' has taken hold and 'fires and floods and pandemics and riots and wars' are devastating the planet,[1] the story follows the adventures of Mark Halyard, an Australian 'Environmental Impact Coordinator (Northern Europe) at the Brahmasamudram Mining Company' (14), and Karin Resaint, a 'species intelligence evaluator' from

Switzerland (41). As Beauman explains, *Venomous Lumpsucker* circulates around a 'debate between these two characters about … the moral weight of species extinction', framed by the invention of an elaborate system of extinction credits that allows countries and corporations to submit vouchers to legally eradicate a species, thus paying lip service to species conservation while continuing business as usual.[2] Inspired, Beauman explains, by the carbon credit system, though with marked resonance for biodiversity offsetting in its depiction of the use of free market mechanisms to regulate species extinction, it is 'a book about the failure of global climate finance instruments'.[3] Although the novel's comedy is based to a large extent on the absurdity of its imagined financial machinations, 'most of the details', Beauman insists, 'are true to life'.[4] *Venomous Lumpsucker* is a deftly constructed and conceptually sophisticated literary novel, but the satire takes care of itself, based on the irony inherent to the premise of offset ideology that conserving corporations might be a way of conserving endangered species.

At the heart of the novel's dystopic extrapolation of neoliberal approaches to conservation is the eponymous, fictional fish – *Cyclopterus venenatus* – the venomous lumpsucker, 'one of the most intelligent creatures on the planet' (43). Lumpsuckers are remarkable for their awareness of 'their own population size' and their ability to 'make group decisions based on it'. What is more, 'they're vindictive' (111). If their population is harmed, they 'take revenge, not necessarily against the perpetrator, but against some passing member of the perpetrator's species' (111). Pushed to the brink of extinction by warming seas, the lumpsucker is clinging on in 'one little stretch of the Swedish coast' among the 'bouldery reefs' that constitutes its habitat (20). The Brahmasamudram Mining Company, however, has plans for precisely this area of the Baltic seabed. Specifically, it aims to extract 'ferromanganese nodules' (20), mineral deposits rich in the rare metals used in EV batteries and other smart technologies (though the novel never takes us into the specific question of their use). Since this activity is likely to endanger the remaining population of lumpsuckers, Resaint is brought in to evaluate whether the fish exceeded a 'certain level of "intelligence"' (4). The necessity of this task is determined by the specific bureaucratic processes of the governing body that oversees the system of extinction credits, the World Commission on Species Extinction (WCSE). Ordinarily, the eradication of a species requires the payment of one extinction credit which, trading at the start of the novel at €38,432, is small beer for a global mining company. But if the species is proven to be intelligent, the cost increases to thirteen extinction credits. Resaint is preparing to certify the fish as intelligent (and thus thirteen times more expensive to exterminate), when as a result of a software error, the company's autonomous mining vehicles (AMVs) accidentally destroy the lumpsucker's habitat. The AMVs, it seems, 'have just eradicated the species in one fell swoop' (20).

The novel's intrigue revolves to a significant extent around the possibility of finding a surviving population of venomous lumpsuckers that has evaded the blunders of the Brahmasamudram Mining Company and the wider collapse of global ecosystems. In its focus on green capitalism as the background to this quest, *Venomous Lumpsucker* coheres, in the words of Kevin Power, with Beauman's status as an author of 'systems novels', which is to say texts concerned with the systematization of the world through ideological-material networks or, as Power puts it, with 'the ways in which human beings tend obsessively to instrumentalise the world'.[5] This focus on wider systemic issues underpins the novel's interest in the meanings of animals, the interplay between economic and inherent forms of value and the balance of anthropocentric and counter-anthropocentric rationales. In this task Beauman draws extensively on the territory and terminology of extinction studies, acknowledging a particular debt to Thom van Dooren's *Flight Ways: Life and Loss at the Edge of Extinction* (2014).[6] Central to *Venomous Lumpsucker*, and to *Flight Ways*, is the environmental humanities trope of entanglement (and by extension disentanglement), but there are also moments in the novel that can be read (a little more speculatively) in dialogue with Derrida's pivotal work on the abyssal structure of human–animal difference that has proved so influential in animal studies. Although the satire is bleak – and all the bleaker for its close reference to the historical unfolding of green capitalism – the novel's misanthropic, anti-capitalist edge involves a close attunement to animal and ecological ethics in which patterns of consumption (eating and being eaten) come to the fore.

Both Halyard and Resaint have strong, and strongly opposing, reasons for wanting to keep the lumpsuckers alive that represent the heart of the novel's narrative and philosophical exploration of the meaning of species extinction in the age of green capitalism. For Halyard, the lumpsuckers' survival, or otherwise, is all to do with money and particularly to do with his own perilous situation as the perpetrator of a 'medium-sized financial crime' (31). At the root of Halyard's predicament are the financial structures of the extinction industry which need some further explanation to make sense of the novel's intricate plotting.

After the death of Chiu Chiu, the world's last giant panda, China takes a lead in the formation of the WCSE, signed by '196 other states' with the aim of ensuring that the 'giant panda will be the last species ever driven to extinction by human activity' (14). Despite China's determination to make Chiu Chiu the 'endling of endlings' (14), it quickly became clear that for 'the sake of growth and prosperity ... it was necessary for some minimum number of species to be lost each year' (21). Consequently, the Chinese government is 'helped to understand that a free market solution, responsive to stakeholders of all kinds would be the fairest and the most efficient way forward' (21). This is where extinction credits come in:

> Every year, a certain number of extinction credits were allocated at no charge by the WCSE, while others were auctioned off, and afterwards they could be bought and sold on the open market. The idea was that the supply of credits would be gradually ratcheted down, so the price would creep up until they were pretty much unaffordable, and people would simply have to use their ingenuity to avoid driving species to extinction. (22)

Fortunately for the world's financial elites, under the WCSE's 'nimble free market solution' (22) corporations can remain focused on profit. Unfortunately for the world's creatures, the extinction credit system only makes it easier for nations and corporations to kill them. There were 'so many allowances, indulgences, exceptions and delays that the intended scarcity of extinction credits had never actually come to pass' (22–3). Consequently, there were 'fewer barriers now to eradicating an endangered species than there had been at any time since laws of this kind were first enacted in the mid-twentieth century' (22). As one of the novel's activists summarizes as he interrogates Halyard, the 'suits always win and the animals always lose' (90).

The disappearance of conservation into the broken system of extinction credits creates the context for Halyard's crime; his opportunity comes with a 'radical change in the WCSE criteria for the extinction of species' (28). In essence, the WCSE's policy innovation is that 'even if a species didn't have a single living individual left on earth, it should still not be considered extinct, as long as it had been the subject of what was called "multimodal preservation"' (28). Multimodal preservation, Halyard explains, is essentially 'scanning an animal's brain and putting it into a computer' (16); DNA sequences, MRI scans and information about habitat and behaviour are 'uploaded to servers' and tissue samples deposited with biobanks. Thus a 'physical body breathing its last was not the same thing as the End' (28); 'in a legal or regulatory context ... the species was in some sense *not yet lost* (17, original emphasis). The WCSE's new plan exemplifies the victory of corporate ideology over reality in an absurd culmination of neoliberal processes of abstraction that recalls the force of bureaucracy in Douglas Adams's *Hitch Hikers'* series. Evidently, the WCSE's reform is going to be a boon to 'companies like Brahmasamudram Mining, who would merely need to arrange for the multimodal taxidermy of a species like the venomous lumpsucker, instead of either tiptoeing around its habitat or expending the extinction credits necessary for its legal disposal' (30). In this way, the twin pillars of neoliberal environmentalisms – finance and technology – work together to create a system in which the devastation of the planet can be repurposed for corporate profit.

Crucially for Halyard, the forthcoming change in the WCSE's criteria is widely expected to cause a significant drop in the price of extinction credits. At the time of the first rumours of the WCSE's impending reform, extinction credits were trading at €67,000. Since the lumpsucker is thought to be intelligent – subject to confirmation by Resaint's assessment – the Brahmasamudram Mining Company had budgeted for thirteen extinction credits as 'the maximum number that might be required if the venomous lumpsucker did in fact get eradicated' (52). So if Halyard could 'discreetly borrow the credits from his own department, sell off all thirteen at €67,000 each' and direct the resulting €871,000 to a 'crypto account', he would just need to 'wait a few months until the price tumbled', buy back the extinction credits after their price has crashed following the change in criteria for extinction, return them to his employers and pocket the difference. With extinction credits already down to €38,432, everything looks rosy for Halyard.

The novel's pivotal moment comes with a series of cyber-attacks on the world's six major biobanks. A computer worm takes control of the biobank's IT systems, switches off the freezers and cranks 'the facility's heating system until those freezers turned into ovens' (53). The result is that 'millions upon millions of frozen tissue samples' are 'cooked into useless snot' (54). To make things worse, the worm also deletes 'every file ever uploaded by the biobanks' (54). Halyard realizes that without the biobanks the WCSE reforms are 'dead' (56). Accordingly, the price of extinction credits rises instead of falls, quickly leaping from €38,432 to €287,057. If the venomous lumpsucker is extinct, Halyard owes his employers the cost of thirteen of these credits. His only hope to avoid detection is if the lumpsucker is not in fact extinct and Brahmasamudram Mining does not need to use the credits. Then Halyard at least has some time to concoct a plan for balancing the books before his employers notice the missing credits. So Halyard needs to find some lumpsuckers pronto to avoid financial ruin and stay out of jail.

Beauman's satirical extrapolation of the logic of biodiversity offsetting into an elaborate financial crime caper pivots on the subordination of materiality to data integral to neoliberal conceptions of natural capital. In the green information age represented by multimodal preservation, physical existence barely matters. Against this, facing the prospect of imprisonment, Halyard reflects on 'one of the terrors of the era': the 'suddenness with which life could become *physical*' (52, original emphasis). High-functioning professionals like Halyard are 'safe and serene and almost untethered to the earth. Your body is nothing, really: it's just the part of you that gets tired at the gym' (53). Suddenly, with jail beckoning, Halyard is exposed to the possibility of 'physical degradation, physical constraint, physical danger' (53). In this way, Halyard's situation represents an inversion of the plight of endangered species under the WCSE's plans: while the problem for animals is that their physical being is replaced by its simulation in multimodal preservation, the problem for Halyard is that his safe, 'untethered' life will become retethered to the material circumstances of his existence. If his crime is facilitated by a dematerialization of animals, the penalty for Halyard will be his rematerialization into the realm of the physical.

As the image of a life 'untethered to the earth' suggests, *Venomous Lumpsucker*'s play between embodiment and abstraction has an explicit connection to the environmental humanities' motif of entanglement. The novel's explanation of the WCSE's planned reforms is expressed in precisely these terms in an extended thought experiment about the precise point at which extinction might be said to have occurred that resonates strikingly with van Dooren's account of the death of Martha, the last passenger pigeon, in the Cincinnati Zoo in 1914. While van Dooren sees the death of an endling like Martha as an 'important and profound' event, such an occurrence still does not capture 'the immensity and significance of extinction'.[7] To deem a creature 'extinct or not solely on the basis of the presence in the world of at least one individual of that kind/lineage' is to fail to 'acknowledge their entangled complexity'. For van Dooren, a species is not 'somehow "ongoing" because one individual continues to draw breath in a zoo' because the bird's 'entangled relations ... *are* this particular life form and its form of life' (original emphasis).[8] In *Venomous Lumpsucker*, the WCSE's development of the idea of 'multimodal preservation' serves as the ironic solution to the philosophical tension van Dooren identifies between the survival of a single creature and the meaning of extinction. If the problem for van Dooren is the need to acknowledge the entanglement of creatures in their life-worlds, the solution for the WCSE is to reproduce entanglement in a virtual format.

For the WCSE, a 'physical body breathing its last was not the same as the End'. The 'End', in fact, 'could come before and it could come after' (28). It 'could come before', as van Dooren might have written, 'because a species was not just a set of bodies. It was a set of habits, relationships, territories, entanglements' (28). Once the environment that constitutes these evolutionary interactions is gone, the species might as well be considered extinct; the 'death of the last holdout was in some sense a mere formality' (29). Conversely, in the world of the WCSE, 'an animal which at present happened to have a living population of zero' might not be considered extinct if its preservation as a 'virtual specimen in a virtual environment ... preserved the memory of those habits, relationships, territories and entanglements from before they unravelled' (29–30). Which, the narrative asks, is more extinct? While these philosophical speculations wind up with the conclusion that the 'population-zero animal ... was more extinct' (30), the crucial point is that even asking the question indicates a 'worldwide shift in attitudes' that provides the WCSE with 'enough of a pretext' to 'loosen its criteria' so that, in an ironic extrapolation of van Dooren's argument, the simulation of a creature's entanglements can be considered the survival of the species. The problem, of course, is that the informational and biotechnological processes that enable the simulation of entanglement are ideologically loaded mechanisms of disentanglement that work by reducing a being to disembodied data.

The ethos of disentanglement central to natural capital approaches to conservation has significant ramifications for other forms of human connection to the world in *Venomous Lumpsucker* that have traditionally been seen, though by no means universally, as expressions of ecological entanglement. Food, for example, is a recurrent theme of the novel. Halyard's crime is motivated by his intention to 'spend the profits on some combination of debt service and dazzling gluttony' (52). Moreover, the need to service his debts is in itself created by his appetite for culinary excess as someone 'voracious, forensic, worshipful towards good meals and caustic towards bad ones, decadent in the sense of pursuing sensual pleasure with great seriousness and conviction' (45). As the world's ecological disaster deepens, it becomes harder, and more expensive, for Halyard to satisfy his Epicureanism: 'In Ontario, the heat dried up the sap in the maple trees; in Kenya, it wilted the coffee plants and invigorated their pests; in Champagne, it broke down the acid in the grapes' (46). Under such gastronomically desperate circumstances, Halyard is reduced to taking a medication called Inzidernil – 'the painkiller of the palette' (285) – which has the effect of making depressing food feel less depressing. The prospects for his dietary future look bleak until he samples a piece of cultured bluefin tuna made by a biotech specialist called Warkentin (who, in another example of Beauman's engagement with academic debates related to the novel's themes, shares his surname with Traci Warkentin, a Canadian environmental philosopher who published some of the earliest scholarly accounts of cultured meat). Sceptical at first that Warkentin's tuna will be anything like the original, Halyard is moved to tears by its perfection (196). The disentanglement of conservation from the lived experience of the world thus finds a counterpart in the depiction of CM as a product that familiarly signifies ecological collapse and the human alienation from the natural world. There is no sense for Halyard that eating meat represents – in an ecocarnist mode – a holistic connection with the environment. All that matters to him is pleasure.

The severing of the ecological connection between human and world through food culminates at the novel's denouement with a speculative depiction of the future of hunting in the information age. Halyard and Resaint's quest for the lumpsucker takes them to a new nature reserve in Cornwall that is being filled with 'endangered and extinct species' by the billionaire Ferenc Barka (240). Barka is, as Paul March Russell glosses, 'a crypto-fascist, Elon Musk-like villain' whose aim in assembling the world's beleaguered creatures is not to save them but to hunt them.[9] Although hunting is a perennially controversial topic among environmentalists, it retains a status in some circles as the exemplary expression of ecological holism: the intimacy of predator and prey as the ancient connection of human and animal and through that of human and world. As the website *Why Hunt?* puts it, for many hunters, hunting 'is an extension of their ethical relationship with the land or a demonstration of their commitment to conservation'.[10] The consummation of this ethos is usually taken to exist in the consumption of the hunted beast as the demonstration of a land ethic, indebted to Aldo Leopold among others. Barka's motivations are less conventional, however.

On realizing Barka's violent intentions towards the remarkable menagerie he has created, Resaint asks him with exasperation, 'You brought all these animals here just to kill them?' (27) Barka's answer, based on the work of the 'computational physicist' Alvin Ip, represents the novel's most absurd and surprising expression of the disentanglements of late capitalism. According to Barka, Ip

> has proven that the amount of information in the universe is constant, just like matter and energy. Which means that when you destroy information in one place, you're forcing new information to come into existence somewhere else. That's what this is. Imagine a species as a bundle of information. When you eliminate the last of that species – as long as you make sure that there's no trace of it left anywhere else – you're destroying an enormous quantity of information. Which really means you're *creating* an enormous quantity of information. When I killed that last turquoise-throated puffleg this morning, I could almost feel the information shattering, dissipating, condensing,

recrystallising. Like a supernova. It's one of the most profound experiences a human being can have. (270, original emphasis)

It is at this revelatory moment that Resaint and Halyard realize that Barka was behind the biobank attacks, his motivation being that multimodal preservation eroded the purity of his intervention in what he calls 'the informational topology of the universe' (270). The point for Barka is that the 'kill needs to take the species to absolute zero' (271). Barka's postmodern version of the hunt represents the ultimate expression of market-driven processes of abstraction in the novel. If a creature comes to represent only a certain number of credits, it is essentially only a numerical value in an informational ecosystem. Accordingly, the ostensible, ecocarnist intimacy of hunting is reformulated as an equation that is still ironically celebrated for the profundity of the experience: ecological holism reformatted for the information age.

If Halyard and Barka represent disentangled subjects, Resaint by contrast embodies – or aims to embody – a complex apprehension of the entanglements between the human and the animal in the context of extinction which underpins her idiosyncratic motivations for saving the venomous lumpsucker, though getting to this key point requires a patient exposition of her back story. Early in her career as a 'species intelligence evaluator', Resaint had 'found it easy not to care about extinction' (96). Arguments about the human sense of loss attendant on species extinction fall flat; most endangered species passed into oblivion without anyone noticing so that 'nobody could pretend to miss them' (97), and even if they did, the 'churn' of extinction had been going on forever so to 'wring your hands over it would be absurd' (97). 'Technical arguments' about the impact of species extinction on ecosystems were equally unconvincing to Resaint; 'most biodiversity was redundant', doing nothing that could not be done by another species and in any case in an era of runaway climate change, 'ecosystems had bigger things to worry about' (97). Instrumentalist arguments about the potential value of species for big pharma were no more persuasive. While 'biodiversity enthusiasts' try to talk to 'capitalists in the language of capitalism', it 'wasn't a strong pitch': only 'a tiny minority of species had anything unique and packageable to offer', and even then the 'most exciting discoveries were now being made by algorithms working millions of times faster than evolution could' (98).

Resaint's cynical views on the meanings of extinction are transformed, however, by her research into *Adelognathus marginatum*, a parasitic wasp from Western Ukraine threatened by an agricultural company's plans to introduce a pest-resistant variety of sunflowers. *Marginatum* is notable for its 'particularly devious method of self-perpetuation' (99), laying its eggs inside a spider so that its larva, once hatched, can feed on the spider's blood. The spider, meanwhile, subject to mind control by hormones released into its body by the larva, builds a convenient cradle in which the larva can pupate. Although parasitic wasps might usually be considered 'repugnant to the soul' (103), Resaint is led by *marginatum*'s ingenious adaptation to its environment to a profound realization of its 'inherent value' based on a sense of wonder at the evolutionary processes the wasp embodies: 'How could this brilliant, intricate, hilarious thing – the fluke result of an unrepeatable process, the legacy of some dizzying number of past individuals, all of them, in hindsight, striving unconsciously towards a single invention – not be valuable in itself?' Thinking beyond narrow anthropomorphic arguments against extinction, Resaint sees the impending loss of *marginatum* as a 'terrible loss to the universe' (104) and part of what she refers to as the 'Black Hole':

> If evolution gave her a sense of the sublime – so many billions of animals over so many millions of years, just to devise one species – then the extinction crisis did too. She called it the Black Hole not just because it was like a vast leak into which so much was irretrievably disappearing, but even more so because in moral terms it was a cosmic singularity, a region of infinite horror ... The Black Hole was shrouded in its own enormity: you couldn't properly examine it because it just swallowed up your regard in its blackness. It was a breach like no other breach that had ever preceded it, a breach that could not be measured on any existing scale. The diversity of life on earth was (as far as anyone knew) the most majestic thing in the universe, and human beings were (as far as anyone knew) the only living things with the capacity to appreciate that majesty, and yet human beings were also the ones who were stamping that majesty out. (107)

Resaint's attention to evolutionary aesthetics – the appreciation of the majestic diversity of life on Earth, embodied in the wasp's intricate attunement to its world – evidently contrasts sharply with the crude, self-interested calculations behind Halyard's interest in conservation. If Resaint's argument pivots on the realization of the 'cosmic singularity' of each species, Halyard's position is based on its exchangeability. Or, to put it another way, Resaint's evolutionary ethics is based on wonder in marked contrast to Halyard's economic focus on calculation.

Wonder is an integral element of the evolutionary imagination. Philip Armstrong's analysis of its meaning in the philosophical, artistic and textual representation of animals makes a useful companion piece to *Venomous Lumpsucker* particularly through the tension he identifies between René Descartes and Charles Darwin. While Descartes in *The Passions of the Soul* (1649) makes a connection between wonder and scientific method, Armstrong sees the link as experientially limited: 'Descartes seems most often entirely determined to impose his mathematical-mechanical model for understanding the world, so that for him wonder becomes replaced by a fixed system of meaning.'[11] Halyard's recourse to offset ideology works in similar terms by inserting the world into a financial model that fixes the meaning of beings in economic terms. In juxtaposition, Armstrong notes that Charles Darwin's formulation of natural selection is 'pervaded by a "poetics" of wonder' which connects to the Darwinian emphasis on entanglement.[12] Darwin's parting invitation at the conclusion of *On the Origin of Species* to 'contemplate a tangled bank' leads him to the book's resonant final words: 'Whilst this planet has gone cycling on according to the fixed law of gravity, from so simple a beginning endless forms most beautiful and most *wonderful* have been, and are being evolved' (emphasis added).[13] While Halyard's Cartesian ethos can have no space for beauty, an aesthetic sense is evidently central to Resaint's realization of the meaning of extinction which in turn leads her to a deep ethical orientation towards the more-than-human world. Armstrong's conclusion that 'wonder offers the kind of disposition that has great potential to contribute to the urgent task of recalibrating our species' relation to others' fits neatly with Resaint's epiphany in her researches into the parasitic wasp.[14]

The Black Hole of Resaint's imagination is the inevitable corollary of the ethics of wonder as the monolithic emptiness that contrasts with the 'brilliant, intricate' diversity of life. As 'a breach that could not be *measured* on any existing scale' (emphasis added), the Black

Hole evidently constitutes a domain beyond natural capital: a form of loss irreducible to any calculation. When Resaint reflects of the Black Hole that 'you couldn't properly examine it because it just swallowed up your regard in its blackness', her evolutionary ethics recalls Derrida's formulation at being seen naked by his cat of confronting a 'gaze behind which there remains a bottomlessness ... uninterpretable, unreadable, undecidable, *abyssal* and secret' (emphasis added).[15] Though the twin images of the Black Hole and the abyss are conceptually similar, the occasion for the two reflections are somewhat distinct: the direct encounter between philosopher and cat in Derrida's apprehension of the animal's abyssal gaze versus Resaint's image of the planetary process of biodiversity loss. Going deeper into Derrida's abyss, however, draws out some of the crucial implications of Resaint's evolutionary aesthetics.

Derrida picks up on the theme of biodiversity loss in *The Animal That Therefore I Am* (and elsewhere in his later work) as an aspect of the 'unprecedented Transformation' of the Earth that 'we who call ourselves men or humans' have produced: part of an 'alteration ... in the being-with shared by the human and by what the human calls the animal' that 'has been accelerating, intensifying ... for about two centuries, at an incalculable rate and level'.[16] The 'number of species endangered because of man', Derrida notes, 'takes one's breath away'.[17] Extinction forms part of the context for Derrida's reflection on what he calls 'the question ... of the living animal', a theme which, for him, 'will always have been the most important and decisive question'.[18] Derrida is concerned with how 'the gaze called "animal" offers to my sight the abyssal limit of the human: the inhuman or the ahuman, the ends of man, that is to say the bordercrossing from which vantage man dares announce himself to himself".[19] 'The animal' in this way is a point at which the human both meets its limit and constructs its own being; the abyss is the emptiness out of which the appearance of the fullness of 'man' emerges.

In part, Derrida's trope of the abyss constitutes his response to Martin Heidegger who in his 'Letter on Humanism' identifies 'living creatures' as 'in a certain way most closely akin to us' but 'at the same time separated from our ek-sistent essence by an abyss'.[20] Heidegger's unfamiliar usage 'ek-sistent' encapsulates the radical untraversable depth of this separation. Thought, Heidegger explains, in terms of ecstasis (a literal 'standing outside'), 'ek-sistence means standing out into the truth of Being'.[21] The abyss, for Heidegger, is an image of profound separation which Calarco summarizes as 'metaphysical anthropocentrism', characterized by an 'uncritical reliance on a logic of opposition in differentiating human beings from animals'.[22] The precise nature of Derrida's response to Heidegger has been subject to extensive debate, but the key distinction between their uses of abyss is that between separationism in Heidegger (the untraversable gulf of the human and the animal) and a more ambivalent function in Derrida's work which neither entirely asserts nor abandons the distinction between the human and the animal. The abyssal limit, for Derrida, is not a gulf or a 'single indivisible line' but a 'plural and repeatedly folded frontier' understood as having a 'foliated consistency'.[23] As David Wood summarizes, the abyss for Derrida 'is not one thing, but many and varied'.[24] The significance of this complex framing is amplified in 'But As for Me, Who Am I (Following)' when in a discussion of Paul Valéry, Derrida writes that the 'animal abyss' (a phrase from Valéry's 'Silhouette of a Serpent') is 'not a hole, a gulf, but too much being'; it 'brings to light not nonbeing but being, a spark in the place of nothingness'.[25] The abyss then is not a vacuum that marks out a metaphysical compartmentalization in which beings are discovered in their isolation from one another but rather a potentiality from which beings in their incontrovertible differences emerge. That the limit of the human should be abyssal, then, identifies the human as one among a multiplicity of lines or folds between beings all of which are enclosed within and modulated by a kind of ontological groundlessness.

The abyss in this way can be taken as an evolutionary figure which facilitates readings of the interplay between deconstruction and evolution explored by Timothy Morton. For Morton, just as deconstruction shows how texts cannot be 'said to have a single, independent and lasting identity', so the 'further scholarship investigates life forms … the less those life forms can be said to have a single, independent and lasting identity'.[26] Conceiving of the human in these terms – as part of foliated, multiplicity of lines and limits – means to realize, as Wolfe concludes (to an argument that proceeds along different lines than this), that '"we" are not "we"; we are not the "auto–" of the "auto-biography" that humanism gives to itself. Rather "we" are always radically other, already in– or ahuman in our very being.'[27] The designation of the 'abyssal limit of the human' both destabilizes the idea of the human and provides grounds for a renewed sense of responsibility towards the other abyssal subjects with which we share the planet. David Wood's summation of Derrida's ethics of the future provides a resonant hint back to the domain of the biodiversity offset. For Wood, in Derrida's thought 'ethics ... begins at the point at which calculation breaks down'.[28] It thus becomes difficult to think of 'the other' as an object or element of exchange; it means that we must 'reproblematize', as Derrida puts it, how we think of 'man', 'animal' and 'world'.[29] Thinking abyssally reinvigorates awareness of a shared finitude in a time of unprecedented peril. Living with attention to the shared emptiness of heterogeneous beings invites a greater determination to live harmlessly, in what Derrida calls the 'dream of an absolute hospitality' that stands in marked contrast to the violence of market-driven approaches to biodiversity.[30]

Resaint's Black Hole coheres with such abyssal thinking in three ways. First, the Black Hole complicates the conception of the human by figuring a sublime emptiness that swallows the human gaze. Second, in its emptying of the human it creates a set of ethical relations that are irreducible to anthropocentric rationales or to the ideological drive of calculation. Third, it provides a template for responsibility. As Derrida explains, the 'limit to calculability [is] the condition of praxis, decision, action and responsibility'.[31] It is the realization and the enactment of responsibility that provides the key to Resaint's strikingly dark reasons for wanting to ensure that the venomous lumpsucker remains extant as wonder leads her towards a compulsion to produce some kind of ecological justice. The result of Resaint's research into animal intelligence and extinction is the realization that 'humans deserved a terrible punishment for their crime' and that 'this punishment ought to be enacted by that crime's victims'. Crucially, 'that enaction could be meaningful only if those victims recognised it for what it was' (108). It is here that the lumpsucker's unique characteristics come into play. Its awareness of its own population size, plus its determination to wreak revenge, plus its venom allows Resaint to formulate a plan to sacrifice herself by being killed by lumpsuckers. As Halyard summarizes with incredulity, Resaint's plan is to be 'executed by a fish' (111) as a kind of karmic resolution of the violence of the Anthropocene. Or, as Resaint puts it, allowing the animals to 'score a point, just once' (112).

Beauman's explanation of his thinking behind Resaint's multispecies suicide contains a significant echo of the premise of *Last Chance to See*. Referring to his own encounters with animals while travelling, Beauman identifies an awkwardness in the sense that a 'wild animal is gifting me with this joyful experience'. Instead of taking for granted the casual satisfactions of the touristic gaze, Beauman offers a compelling counter-argument that he addresses to the animal:

> I shouldn't be able to turn up and just blithely have a fun time watching you and you don't get anything out of it and then I get to go home and tell people about it ... I turn up and you rip me to shreds and that's the end of my life and you get to feast on me.[32]

Beauman's response, here and in the novel, adds an idiosyncratic twist to the cultural dynamics of the representation of encounters with animals in the Sixth Extinction. Rather than adding cultural capital to such moments (via the logic that scarcity increases value), extinction for Beauman makes such meetings ethically horrifying. The counter-intuitive reading of ecotourism as dark tourism comes starkly into the foreground here as Beauman presents an absolute refusal of the commodification of animals and a repudiation of the human.

Accordingly, when Resaint visits an uninhabited Baltic island with her lover Selim, she comes across a turnstone nest – 'four olive-coloured eggs in a wreath of straw' – and wonders what it would be like to 'smithereen' them 'while the mother was right there watching you' (245). The point of such a senseless act of cruelty would be to make the bird 'understand just for a moment what she [Resaint] was' (246). The need to do this is created by the routine obfuscation of human responsibility through the understanding that any individual's 'contributions were so fragmentary and indirect' (246). Destroying the turnstone's nest provides an escape from ambiguity and deniability into a frank acknowledgement that the 'murder of animals was an enormous collaborative project, perhaps the fundamental human project' (246). Moreover, the turnstone's 'understanding itself was not enough' (246). What she really wants is 'for the turnstone to stamp on her' (247). Resaint's planned sacrifice is both an intensely personal position and an act that works at the level of species. While the novel's satire is directed committedly towards green capitalism, there is also a consistent critique of humanity per se as Resaint foregrounds misanthropy as an emotional and intellectual response to extinction.

As it turns out, Resaint does not get quite what she is looking for. She is never able to find any lumpsuckers to kill her and to revel in their vengeance, nor does the turnstone stamp her to death. But her fate still evokes a suitably counter-anthropocentric frisson. Escaping from Barka with Halyard and Warkentin, she slips and falls onto a ledge. With time pressing and Barka in pursuit, there is no time to rescue Resaint who remains 'warm, but defenceless, and perfumed with shed blood' (279). Halyard watches as various creatures from Barka's collection investigate her, though 'which species he couldn't possibly guess' (279). Unable to help, he 'left her to them. The endangered and the extinct, the remnants and the endlings. The only living things that mattered to her. She would lie there uncomplaining as they ate her flesh' (280). The story ends with a moment of entanglement that reverses the usual ecocarnist logic. Rather than entanglement providing a justification for human violence against animals – we should eat meat because we are part of nature – the scene works by exposing the edibility of the human in a close echo of Val Plumwood's famous account of narrowly evading being eaten by a crocodile.

Nearly being eaten provides Plumwood with a unique perspective on what it means to be human. To be human, in short, is to be meat:

> I was suddenly transformed in the parallel universe into the form of a small, edible animal whose death was of no more significance than that of a mouse, and as I saw myself as meat I also saw with an incredible shock that I inhabited a grim, relentless and deplorable world that would make no exceptions for me, no matter how smart I was, because like all living things, I was made of meat, was nutritious food for another being.[33]

(Nearly) being eaten is perhaps the idea above all that brings pro-animal and ecological perspectives into alignment as an exemplary manifestation of the human entanglement in the world that also reveals the mythic structure of human exceptionalism. Beauman's adjustment of the scene by adding the twist that the human is being eaten by endlings, not just by any animal, fulfils Resaint's desire for some equivalent punishment for the violence done to the world's endangered species but also perhaps makes a subtle political point. Vengeance is wreaked not on capital but on the human in the form of Resaint as a sample of the 'fundamental human project' of species extinction. On the one hand, a juster vengeance – a clearer moral for the novel – would be the collapse of the global markets as the ethical resolution of the violence of the Capitalocene. On the other hand, that the human has to stand in for the economic system as the sacrificial victim foregrounds the materiality that underpins the abstractions of green capitalism. For all Barka's fantasy of the informational topology, and the WCSE's financial jiggery-pokery, the main narrative (before its two appendices) culminates with the word 'flesh', a word which bestrides the human and the animal as a descriptor of a shared vulnerability. The human, as much as the animal, is sacrificed to the operations of green capitalism. *Venomous Lumpsucker* in this way demonstrates how the operations of systems are embodied at the level of the creature so that the novel ends with a conjunction of animal and ecological ethics under but against the abstractions of green capitalism.

Notes

1 Ned Beauman, *Venomous Lumpsucker* (London: Sceptre, 2022), 14, 47. Subsequent references in parenthesis. For the author's explanation of the dating of the novel's events, see V. Morris and J. Skene (hosts), 'Episode 51 – Novelist Ned Beauman on Venomous Lumpsuckers and the Price of Extinction', *When We Talk about Animals*, https://www.whenwetalkaboutanimals.org/2023/04/11/ep-51-ned-beauman/#more-2030, accessed 1 May 2025.
2 Morris and Skene, *When We Talk about Animals*.
3 Morris and Skene, *When We Talk about Animals*.
4 Morris and Skene, *When We Talk about Animals*.
5 Kevin Power, '*Venomous Lumpsucker* by Ned Beauman Review – a Cerebral Eco-Thriller', *The Guardian*, 14 July 2022, https://www.theguardian.com/books/2022/jul/14/venomous-lumpsucker-by-ned-beauman-review-a-cerebral-eco-thriller, accessed 1 May 2025.
6 For a discussion of Beauman's sources, and his engagement with van Dooren's work, see Morris and Skene, *When We Talk about Animals*.
7 Thom van Dooren, *Flight Ways: Life and Loss at the Edge of Extinction* (New York: Columbia University Press, 2014), 11.

8 Van Dooren, *Flight Ways*, 11.
9 Paul March-Russell, 'Après le Déluge', *Foundation* 53.147 (2024), 76–82, 77.
10 'Why Hunt?', https://why-hunt.org/, accessed 1 May 2025.
11 Philip Armstrong, '"The Wonderment of This Taxonomy". Animals and Wonder from the Pre-Modern to the Modern'. In *Exploring the Animal Turn: Human–Animal Relations in Science, Society and Culture*. Edited by Erika Andersson Cederholm, Amelie Björck, Kristina Jennbert and Ann-Sofie Lönngren, 155–70, 161 (Pufendorfinstitutet: Lund, 2014).
12 Armstrong, '"The Wonderment of This Taxonomy"', 161.
13 Charles Darwin, *On the Origin of Species* (New York: Collier and Son, 1909 [1859]), 528–9.
14 Armstrong, '"The Wonderment of This Taxonomy"', 170.
15 Jacques Derrida, *The Animal That Therefore I Am*, trans. David Wills (New York: Fordham University Press, 2008), 12.
16 Derrida, *The Animal That Therefore I Am*, 24–5.
17 Derrida, *The Animal That Therefore I Am*, 26.
18 Derrida, *The Animal That Therefore I Am*, 34.
19 Derrida, *The Animal That Therefore I Am*, 12.
20 Martin Heidegger, *Basic Writings* (San Francisco, CA: Harper, 1993), 230.
21 Heidegger, *Basic Writings*, 230.
22 Matthew Calarco, *Zoographies: The Question of the Animal from Heidegger to Derrida* (New York: Columbia University Press, 2008), 48.
23 Derrida, *The Animal That Therefore I Am*, 30.
24 David Wood, 'The Eleventh Plague: Thinking Ecologically after Derrida'. In *Eco-Deconstruction: Derrida and Environmental Philosophy*. Edited by Matthias Fritsch, Philippe Lynes and David Wood, 29–49, 41 (New York: Fordham University Press, 2018).
25 Derrida, *The Animal That Therefore I Am*, 66.
26 Timothy Morton, 'Ecology as Text, Text as Ecology', *Oxford Literary Review* 32.1 (2010), 1–17, 1.
27 Cary Wolfe, 'Human, All Too Human: "Animal Studies" and the Humanities', *PMLA* 124.2 (2009), 564–75, 571.
28 David Wood, 'On Being Haunted by the Future', *Research in Phenomenology* 36 (2006), 274–98, 280.
29 Derrida, *The Animal That Therefore I Am*, 54.
30 Derrida, *The Animal That Therefore I Am*, 37.
31 Cited in Wood, 'On Being Haunted by the Future', 277.
32 Morris and Skene, *When We Talk about Animals*.
33 Val Plumwood, *The Eye of the Crocodile* (Canberra: ANU Press, 2012) 13–14.

Conclusion: The aporias of green capitalism

Thinking through the interconnections between ecological and pro-animal critical approaches might – idealistically – support a politics beyond the narrow economic frame Beauman satirizes in *Venomous Lumpsucker*. The role of literature, and literary criticism, in this context is to encourage and enact forms of attention that emerge beyond mechanisms of calculation that can only stand in for ethics as a neoliberal substitute for a serious-minded commitment to living wisely and hospitably in the world and with its creatures. Market-based conservation erodes the interlinked significance of both relationships and singularities: neither a being's place in its life-world nor its individual, embodied experience of itself and its entanglements can be meaningfully accounted for within the discourse of natural capital. Nor is blind faith in unrealized techno-fixes anything other than an abnegation of responsibility and a deferral of individual and communal agency to the bleak ideological drives of global capital. The risk of this deferral to business as usual is that, as Theodor Adorno writes, 'exchange value ... dominates human needs and replaces them; illusion dominates reality'. In late capitalism 'this illusion is what is most real': it is the 'formula used to bewitch the world'.[1] Sustainable transition is a phantasmal projection of techno-capitalist imaginaries onto the world and its creatures; as such, it represents a form of inattention that highlights the force of the arts and humanities (at the very moment that they are being eroded) as ways of attending, with care, to animals and the world.

Perhaps the most telling, overarching insight of literary animal studies and ecocriticism and the environmental humanities is that texts are not straightforwardly human artefacts that express creativity as a distinguishing mark of an exceptional species. Rather, they are points of contact between the human and the more-than-human that – in multifarious ways – capture the ultimate predication of human cultures on forms of relationship beyond the human. To put it in the plainest terms: if there weren't any animals, there would be no books about animals. Without a forest, there are no stories about forests (even if the forest is long gone). There could be no *Moby Dick* without the ocean and the whale. Literary history contains an inexhaustible array of interpretations and speculations on the shape of human interactions with the more-than-human, framed at every scale. To activate this history for the present crisis is not to scour the archive for a single answer or a straightforward template for a new politics. Yet, the consistent demand made by the environmental humanities and animal studies in response to the ubiquitous crises of the age to nurture alternative or new narratives (or indeed old narratives reconfigured for the present) is still a demand to inhabit the world differently. As Wood puts it, the 'point of reading (and thinking) is not simply to understand, using the handrail of existing meaning, but to open possibilities'.[2] The urgency of the task is constructed by the continuing entrenchment of a political and economic system that has, as Adrienne Buller phrases it, 'diminished our collective ability to imagine alternatives'.[3] Buller's analysis leads her to the pivotal question: 'What could lie beyond the constraints within which we have been needlessly confined'?[4] Each of the subdisciplinary fields at work in this book is premised on this challenge. The point of vegan studies is to open the possibility of new conceptions of human–animal relations that move beyond commodification and objectification, and particularly beyond the violence of carnism, both material and epistemic, which is to say not just the harm done to animals but also the way that harm is sustained discursively through the cultural reproduction of animals as food. For the energy humanities, new possibilities are opened by the understandings of the (partly) concealed cultural operations of petroculture and the meanings of its alternatives. What world, what forms of life come after oil? Extinction studies, in its analysis of the distinct and competing discourses around species loss, opens possibilities for a deepened ethical commitment to the world and its creatures via an understanding of the processes and implications of living on a simplified planet. Each of these positions is a challenge to sustainable transition as it is formulated in our political moment, but none offers a straightforward programme for action, and this is the point. If a new politics might somehow come from this, it would need to come precisely from the tensions and contradictions that emerge within and around these modes of enquiry.

If natural capital approaches to ecological crisis hinge on a naïve faith in calculation, the meaning of arts and the humanities is closer to an experience of or commitment to what Derrida sees as the 'undecidable'. As Derrida writes in 'Force of Law', a 'decision that didn't go through the ordeal of the undecidable would not be a free decision, it would only be the programmable application or unfolding of a calculable process'.[5] This process maps with uncanny precision onto the operations of natural capital as the 'programmable application' of neoliberal ideology. If we run the programme of global capital over and over, the argument goes, eventually it will hit upon the solution to the problems that are hardwired into its structure. The upside of this calculation is that it removes the uncomfortable necessity of making decisions that run against the status quo; the downside is that it isn't going to work. Critical reading, by contrast, is a mode of thought 'foreign to the order of the calculable'.[6] To think of literary criticism, or artistic creation in these terms, is to confront the multiplicity, the complexity and the contradictoriness of the act of understanding the world and mitigating for a liveable future. Evidently, this task leads to and beyond the limits of capital to ideas at an angle to mainstream politics, conceptions and traditions irreducible to economic determinations like the beautiful or, perhaps most challengingly, the sacred. As the UK government's *Dasgupta Review on the Economics of Biodiversity* noted with resolute clarity, 'The sacred is not negotiable.'[7] It is a theme Schumacher emphasizes in the text that gives the world the term 'natural capital': 'There can be nothing sacred in something that has a price.'[8] To move beyond calculation in the name of a 'free decision' is to bring out from the shadows modes of signification that are routinely repressed in neoliberalism's calculable processes and to embrace the cultural diversity of the world as a corollary of its biological diversity. Here we might think of the dialogues of animal studies and the environmental humanities with Indigenous studies as a way of interrogating the discourse of sustainable transition from specific perspectives attuned to its history of (neo)colonialism.

If Derrida's formulation of the limits of calculability can be applied to neoliberal environmentalisms, it also carries ramifications for the intersection of animal studies and the environmental humanities. For Derrida, the undecidable 'is not merely the oscillation between two significations or two contradictory and very determinate rules ... not merely the oscillation or the tension between two decisions'.[9] The question of the relationship between ecological and animal ethics would not, from this perspective, be a case of asserting the priority of one position over the other or even of choosing one over the other in certain predetermined circumstances. As Derrida puts it:

> The undecidable remains caught, lodged, at least as a ghost – but an essential ghost – in every decision, in every event of decision. Its ghostliness deconstructs from within any assurance of presence, any certitude or any supposed criteriology that would assure us of the justice of a decision.[10]

Thinking about the relationship between animal studies and the environmental humanities is not to try to squeeze out certitude or criteriology. Resisting the calculations of green capitalism is not just to march towards another form of calculation but rather to linger with the ghost of the undecidable. In any case – and in an appropriately Derridean mode – neither position is internally consistent nor consistent in its operation in contradistinction to the other term. The proliferation of subfields within and at the edges of animal studies and the environmental humanities carries precisely the deconstructive force of a complex play of positions and priorities. So rather than providing a programme for decisions, the contact between ecological and pro-animal ethical positions provides a space for the unfolding of a just decision as the expression of responsibility, or as what is 'owed to the other, before any contract, because it has come'.[11] The issue at the animal–ecology intersection is, to follow Derrida's image, that no other ever comes alone but as an entity that exists in myriad relationships with other others and with the environment with which it interacts. A just decision can never be an act of responsibility to a singular other alone, though it also cannot subordinate or marginalize that other to some other criteria.

The relationship between pro-animal and ecological thought (and between animal studies and the environmental humanities as far as it is possible to characterize these enterprises in the singular) might thus be characterized, in Derridean terms, as an aporia. In Derrida's thought, the idea of aporia suggests, as Aidan Tynan summarizes, that 'the impasses of dualisms, oppositions, contradictions and paradoxes are neither dissolved dialectically nor endured passively, but used to account for ethical and political problems'.[12] A free decision requires that pro-animal and ecological ethics, aesthetics and politics are taken together, precisely because that act refuses a programmatic oversimplification of the issues. There are situations that appear intractable at the junction of animal studies and the environmental humanities. Should invasive species be eradicated to save native species from extinction? There is no good answer to this, though it is worth pondering the historical processes of colonial expansion that create this impossibility in the first place. Thinking aporetically about the tension between animals and ecology thus presents possibilities for a navigation of the meanings of global capital that emerge from a further, deconstructive reflection on the theme of holism.

To recap, holism presents a complex ethical question about the just point of ethical consideration. It constructs the problem of scale as perhaps the most obvious point of distinction between pro-animal and ecological thinking (though it is one that can be held onto only intermittently and unreliably); the question is how to find a just decision between the being and the world or between the part and the whole. The logic of a priority created by this terminology – the idea that the whole is more important than its constituents – should not, however, be taken as a matter of course. As Timothy Morton argues, '*The whole is literally less than the sum of its parts*' (original emphasis). In football, Morton explains, there is 'one team' but 'eleven players'; 'one is not "greater" than the other'.[13] For Morton, this insight provides the basis for a 'whole new kind of holism'.[14] As they explain, 'If we want to talk about global economics and ecology, we need to think in wholes ... But we need to think of wholes as "less", as fragile and contingent.' Moreover, 'ecological beings such as lifeforms ... are also wholes whose parts outnumber them and are disparate not "greater"'.[15] This line of argument is directed in part towards an old-school position in ecocriticism and environmental philosophy that sees the transcendental meaning of Nature as the defining criterion of ecological thought, a view which Morton's work has been particularly influential in debunking and which was used in the early work of Callicott (to go back to Chapter 2) as an environmentalist stick with which to beat animal liberationists. The deconstructive consequence of Morton's adjustment of conceptions of the part and the whole is that it becomes harder to hold on to the operation of these terms as stable points on which to base a politics or an ethics, which is to say to hold onto an ecological or an animal ethics over and above the other.

A key implication of this questioning of the logic of holism as a gathering of parts into a transcendental whole is a reconceptualizing of the central problematic of the human. 'Humans', Morton explains, 'are made from all kinds of nonhuman bits and pieces' as an effect of the co-evolution of life forms.[16] In this sense, holism penetrates to the deepest level of ontology; think of evolution as the mixing up of beings into an interrelated whole in which everything is part of everything else. This can be taken, as Tynan argues, as 'ecology's central insight': the realization that 'everything is connected'.[17] To realize this interconnection, however, is to step out of it by the imposition of 'narratives ... that cannot avoid reducing the complexity of ecological connectedness and thus removing us from what we call "nature" altogether'.[18] Tynan (following Jason W. Moore) identifies this paradox as part of a 'general tendency of "Green Thought" to recognise on one level that humanity is a species within "the web of life" while, on another level, treating human activity as separate to, and often destructive of nature'.[19] Resaint's death in *Venomous Lumpsucker* encapsulates something like this paradox. On the one hand, nothing says holism like being eaten alive; her flesh returns at the novel's conclusion to the flesh of the world. In this sense, her fate expresses the ecological theme of interconnectedness in exemplary form. At the same time, she is consumed by an eldritch collection of displaced beings, assembled by Barka, the embodiment of capitalism's alienation from the Earth. The appearance of holism at the novel's end is in fact the materialization of the disentanglement Beauman imagines in the world of extinction credits and informational topology. Resaint can only arrive at this holistic integration with the world through her separation from it.

In an eco-deconstructive reading, the ecological (holism, interconnection) is necessarily inseparable from the anecological, 'where interconnectedness is not merely given but destroyed'.[20] The human is both part and not part of nature; conversely, in the Anthropocene (if that is what we are to call the current epoch), nature is both part and not part of the human. For Tynan, this line of thought has political force in the task of thinking beyond capital. In the first instance, 'the accumulation of capital has depended on representations of nature as something external to society'.[21] Consequently, 'escaping the nature–society dualism ... requires the argument that nature has historical existence only through its internalisation by human acts of environment making'.[22] Nature is what capital is *about* to appropriate in its interminable expansion. Crucially, then, anti-capitalist resistance necessitates an interrogation of the idea of the human or at least an interrogation of the function of the idea of the human in the production of an idea of nature that legitimates its appropriation for capital.

Recourse to the idea of the human cannot, in this sense, provide a solution to the problems this book explores, even if it remains a crucial element of the way these problems are formed and articulated. To decentre the human as the basis of ethics and politics is to recentre the human as the subject of critical enquiry. Again, the question of meat appears centrally as a ready-made example of this trajectory. Is meat the birthright of the human? The recurrent carnist argument that meat-eating can be ethically sustained by the idea of the human (it is 'natural' for 'us' to eat meat) is to approach the question the wrong way round. A more productive line of enquiry is to ask how discourses of carnism produce a conception of the human that is serviceable to global capital. It might be possible to think of automobility – as a phantasmagoric sign of infinite freedom – as part of the birthright of the human, though this again would demand a deeper reflection on the work the idea of the human does in this context. Similarly, conservation could be taken as a uniquely human act of care for the world in the context of extinction, though this invites the counter-argument that extinction is generated by the violence of humanity in the first place. Think back here to Resaint's reflection in *Venomous Lumpsucker* that 'human beings were (as far as anyone knew) the only living things with the capacity to appreciate [the] majesty [of evolution], and yet human beings were also the ones who were stamping that majesty out' (107). These questions are haunted by the wider conservative claim that capitalism is a political and economic system harmoniously tuned to a taken-for-granted conception of human nature. The human should not be taken as a secure starting place from which to investigate any of these problems. It is here that animal studies questioning of the binary of the human and the animal provides a crucial challenge to the politics of green capitalism. If violence is enabled by creating an ethical line between the human and the animal that facilitates what Derrida famously called a 'noncriminal putting to death',[23] there is an enduringly radical force for a refiguring of the human or even a refusal of what McKay calls a 'compulsory humanity'.[24] For McKay, the discourse of species functions as a 'regulatory ideal' that 'forecloses all those practices of the self, practices of any self (and selves, certainly, are not human), that are not predicated on species boundaries as they are conventionally drawn'.[25] Thinking back to Wood's point that the 'point of reading (and thinking) [is] to open possibilities', one such avenue might be, following McKay, to formulate a reconstruction of the terms of being.

The ultimate stakes for Tynan, as for other thinkers in eco-deconstruction, is how to live with a 'lesser violence' against the 'worst violence of biological annihilation and environmental destruction' wreaked in the name of capitalism and imperialism.[26] Again, Tynan's response to this question involves clear resonances with the realm of natural capital accounting: the 'worst violence in an ecological sense would be an Earth on which every relationship, every form of life, is made calculable or quantifiable in advance' and in which 'the otherness of those others with whom we share the Earth through a myriad of interconnections has been abolished through technological and economic systems'.[27] Resistance to capital may exist in the formation of a 'life that constantly confronts the conditions of dwelling at the very limits of terrestrial hospitality, a life lived in the dangerous and precarious spaces beyond any ontologically secure relationship to an *oikos*'.[28] It is possible to gloss Tynan's confronting of 'the conditions of dwelling' as a mode of attention to the more-than-human that again directs us towards the arts and humanities as forms of experience foreign to mechanisms of calculation and also to the animal–ecological crux as the aporia in which this confrontation takes place. The aporetic structure of this crux means that there is no programmatic answer, though there are some positive, if compromised positions: veganism and altermobility have ethical and political force even if there are inevitably complicities (as the familiar routine of the vegan gotcha reveals).

The rejection of the terms of sustainable transition in this book and the contrasting investment in an undecidability that emerges at animal–ecology crux undeniably begs a lot of questions. It is easy to imagine lines of questioning that expose a position based in the humanities to mockery from a position that insists on capital as realpolitik. What are the literary critics going to do about it then? For sure, this book is dominated by a hermeneutics of suspicion. It is one thing to criticize the formations of green capitalism but another to set out an alternative pathway. And if veganism and altermobility might be contributions to a lesser violence, might not the techno-financial machinations of green capitalism be partial contributions too, in the way that proponents of natural capital approaches often express the caveat that such policies are best seen as a part of a portfolio of forms of value? Evidently, a resistance to technology per se is not a helpful position to adopt in response to the rise of neoliberal environmentalism; you don't have to be a luddite to contest the way that sustainable transition is being formulated or to contend with CM and EVs as not so much a lesser violence as a perpetuation of regimes of violence. Okorafor's emphasis on the ideological situatedness of technology in Chapter 6 is a salutary point here (even if her attention to the materiality of petroculture and inattention to the materiality of EVs are also telling). My reasons for ruling out green capitalism take us back to the start of the book; the evidence is clear that for all the agitation about the state of the world, attempts to address global heating, and other associated forms of crisis, are failing. And as Buller phrases it, 'We are currently travelling fast in the wrong direction'; 'at best, green capitalist solutions are a deadly distraction from the urgent task of actually slowing, reversing, and adapting to climate and ecological crisis'.[29] It would be an act of bad faith to end this book without my own provisional thoughts – which cannot be read as a programme or a form of calculation – on living with a lesser violence and even participating in the collective task of working against the despoilation of the planet and the ongoing subjection of animals to routines of violence and displacement.

The question is not just what to do but where to start: how to build a positive reparative movement out of critical thinking's necessary hermeneutics of suspicion. This framing of the task is not simply to indicate a generalized uncertainty, or anxiety about how to begin to address vast processes from a position (or the feeling of a position) of relative powerlessness, though of course this would be entirely justified. The point, rather, is a more specific one about the cultural or institutional location from which one might set out. As an academic, one facet of this task is a consideration of the role of the university in contributing to the kind of radical shift that the current situation demands. This is a question with many dimensions. How to balance the simultaneous function of universities as communities of research, sites of activism (for students and also for staff) and as institutions intimately affiliated with the project of neoliberalism? A substantial amount of work has explored the way in which universities have been reconfigured by neoliberalism. As a broad illustration of the contours of these debates, Alex Usher suggests that the neoliberalization of universities has four main aspects: the increasing 'role of markets, the role of competitions ... the role of performance data and the role of management'.[30] These ideas are complex, contentious and by no means exhaustive. A detailed discussion of them is beyond the scope of this chapter, but there is another key element that Usher omits.

Igea Troiani and Claudia Dutson note that the 'ideological shift' performed by universities in response to neoliberalism means that they changed not just their cultures of work, management and organization (in the terms that Usher outlines) but also 'their physical and urban form':

> In order to reimage and rebrand themselves in their physical form, many UK universities undertook or are in the process of undertaking ambitious real-estate developments including opening up overseas campuses, and expanding national property portfolios with new buildings in which can be found an excess of 'spaces for collaboration', 'vibrant meeting points' and multi-colored, office-style soft furniture.[31]

My own engagement with this process has come via my experience as a tree advocate, contending with developments that would result in the felling of significant numbers of trees in a city with a powerful recent history of tree activism. What I have learned from this is the enthusiasm with which institutions have embraced the emergence of biodiversity offsetting and biodiversity net gain as ways to legitimize the remaking of urban space in the image of neoliberal aesthetics and how this has seemingly justified an inattention to the diverse and complex reasons a community might value its trees. I have also learned about the creativity, curiosity, resilience, imagination and determination of student activists (nourished by a sense of intellectual community), which have in turn produced dynamic and respectful connections with the wider community, not in the terms instrumentalized by knowledge exchange or public engagement programmes but in the spirit of a shared opposition to institutional power and a commitment to the more-than-human world.

In terms of where to start the task of opening new possibilities in the wake or at the edges of exhausted and exhausting hegemonic visions of sustainable transition, the university's function is ambivalent as both an institution that inscribes neoliberal agendas onto the fabric of the spaces it occupies and as the site for a proliferation of activities that contest that agenda, through research, teaching and activism. Accordingly, of all the rhizomatic links between animal studies and the environmental humanities to other areas of enquiry, a connection to critical university studies would be a direction that allows fuller scrutiny of these themes. The value for me of experiencing the university not just as an academic has been to provide the impulse for a direction of flight deeper into grass roots (or tree roots) activism, not just through the contestation of the relentless attacks on the more-than-human world but also in the more reparative modes of community gardening and guerilla planting. These are moments of deep attention to the world and explorations of shared poeisis with the more-than-human which are slow and local enough to allow space to attend patiently to the aporia between animal and ecological ethics. Inevitably, the question of scale surfaces again. What claims can be made about the force of such local actions when the world is on fire? I have come to think of these local forms of activism – naively no doubt – as the beginning of a shadow world, growing, as the term grass roots implies, like a weed through the membrane of capital. This shadow world contains the possibility of not only autonomously determined forms or production, of food most obviously, but also altermobile communities of transportation and in time forms of community-owned renewable energy. These are extendible and adaptable; they are not a solution but a place at least to start. Community gardening is the frontline of the revolution.

Notes

1 Theodor Adorno, 'Sociology and Empirical Research'. Translated by Glyn Adey and David Frisby, 1976 [1957], http://isr.press/Adorno_Sociology_and_Empirical_Research/index.html, accessed 10 May 2025. For a fuller discussion of the connection of Adorno's thought to neoliberal environmentalisms see Malm and Carton, *Overshoot*, 220.
2 David Wood, 'The Eleventh Plague: Thinking Ecologically after Derrida'. In *Eco-Deconstruction: Derrida and Environmental Philosophy*. Edited by Matthias Fritsch, Phillippe Lynes and David Wood, 31 (New York: Fordham University Press, 2018).
3 Buller, *The Value of a Whale*, 5.
4 Buller, *The Value of a Whale*, 15.
5 Jacques Derrida, 'The Force of Law: The "Mystical Foundation of Authority"', *Cardozo Law Review* 11.5–6 (1990), 919–1045, 963.
6 Derrida, 'The Force of Law', 363.
7 Partha Dasgupta, *The Economics of Biodiversity: The Dasgupta Review* (London: HM Treasury, 2021), 309.
8 Schumacher, *Small Is Beautiful*, 31.
9 Derrida, 'The Force of Law', 963.
10 Derrida, 'The Force of Law', 965.
11 Derrida, 'The Force of Law', 965.
12 Aidan Tynan, 'Aporias of Ecological Thought', *Theory, Culture and Society* 39.5 (2022), 3–21, 4.
13 Timothy Morton, *Spacecraft* (London: Bloomsbury, 2022), 15.
14 Morton, *Spacecraft*, 14.
15 Morton, *Spacecraft*, 14.
16 Morton, *Spacecraft*, 18.
17 Tynan, 'Aporias of Ecological Thought', 3.
18 Tynan, 'Aporias of Ecological Thought', 4.
19 Tynan, 'Aporias of Ecological Thought', 4.
20 Tynan, 'Aporias of Ecological Thought', 4.
21 Tynan, 'Aporias of Ecological Thought', 12.
22 Tynan, 'Aporias of Ecological Thought', 13.
23 Jacques Derrida, '"Eating Well", or the Calculation of the Subject: An Interview with Jacques Derrida'. In *Who Comes after the Subject?* Edited by Eduardo Cadava, Peter Connor and Jean-Luc Nancy, 96–119, 112 (New York: Routledge, 1991).
24 Robert McKay, '"Identifying with the Animals": Language, Subjectivity, and the Animal Politics of Margaret Atwood's Surfacing'. In *Figuring Animals: Essays on Animal Images in Art, Literature, Philosophy and Popular Culture*. Edited by M.

S. Pollock and C. Rainwater, 207–27, 218 (New York: Palgrave Macmillan, 2005).

25 McKay, 'A Vegan Form of Life', 254.

26 Tynan, 'Aporias of Ecological Thought', 18.

27 Tynan, 'Aporias of Ecological Thought', 18.

28 Tynan, 'Aporias of Ecological Thought', 18–19.

29 Buller, *The Value of a Whale*, 277.

30 Alex Usher, 'What People Mean When They Talk about Neoliberal Universities', *Higher Education Strategy Associates*, 20 November 2017, https://higheredstrategy.com/what-people-mean-when-they-talk-about-neoliberal-univesities-part-1/, accessed 14 May 2025.

31 Igea Troiani and Claudia Dutson, 'The Neoliberal University as a Space to Learn/Think/Work in Higher Education', *Architecture and Culture* 9.1 (2021), 5–23, 6.

BIBLIOGRAPHY

Adams, Douglas. *The Hitch Hiker's Guide to the Galaxy*. London: Pan, 1979.

Adams, Douglas, and Mark Carwardine. *Last Chance to See*. London: Arrow, 2009.

Adams, John. 'Vogon Economics and the Hyperspace Bypass'. *New Scientist*, 18 September 1993. https://institutions.newscientist.com/article/mg13918915-200-forum-vogon-economics-and-the-hyperspace-bypass-john-adams-on-a-debate-in-which-scientific-uncertainty-is-being-transformed-into-economic-farce/. Accessed 2 April 2025.

Adams, John Joseph. 'Author Spotlight: Nnedi Okorafor'. *Lightspeed*, March 2011. https://www.lightspeedmagazine.com/nonfiction/author-spotlight-nnedi-okorafor/. Accessed 3 March 2025.

Adekola, Olalekan, and Gordon Mitchell. 'The Niger Delta Wetlands: Threats to Ecosystem Services, Their Importance to Dependent Communities and Possible Management Measures'. *International Journal of Biodiversity Science, Ecosystem Services & Management* 7.1 (March 2011): 50–68.

Adorno, Theodor. 'Sociology and Empirical Research'. Translated by Glyn Adey and David Frisby, 1976 [1957], http://isr.press/Adorno_Sociology_and_Empirical_Research/index.html. Accessed 10 May 2025.

Alaimo, Stacy. 'The Anthropocene at Sea: Temporality, Paradox, Compression'. In *The Routledge Companion to the Environmental Humanities*. Edited by Ursula K. Heise, Jon Christensen, and Michelle Niemann, 153–61. London: Routledge, 2021.

Alpers, Paul. *What Is Pastoral?* Chicago, IL: Chicago University Press, 1996.

Amnesty International. 'Niger Delta Negligence', 16 March 2018. https://www.amnesty.org/en/latest/news/2018/03/Niger-Delta-Oil-Spills-Decoders/. Accessed 3 March 2025.

Amnesty International. 'Shell Must Clean Up Its "Toxic Mess" in Niger Delta', 13 February 2025. https://www.amnesty.org.uk/press-releases/london-shell-must-clean-its-toxic-mess-niger-delta. Accessed 3 March 2025.

Apostolopoulou, Elia. *Nature Swapped and Nature Lost: Biodiversity Offsetting, Urbanization and Social Justice*. Cham: Palgrave Macmillan, 2020.

Armstrong, Philip. '"The Wonderment of This Taxonomy". Animals and Wonder from the Pre-Modern to the Modern'. In *Exploring the Animal Turn: Human–Animal Relations in Science, Society and Culture*. Edited by Erika Andersson Cederholm, Amelie Björck, Kristina Jennbert and Ann-Sofie Lönngren, 155–70. Lund: Pufendorfinstitutet, 2014.

Atwood, Margaret. *Oryx and Crake*. London: Virago, 2004.

Australian Conservation Foundation. 'Set and Forget Offsets Are Killing Biodiversity'. https://www.acf.org.au/set-and-forget-offsets-are-killing-biodiversity. Accessed 2 April 2025.

Baer, Hans A. *Motor Vehicles, the Environment and the Human Condition*. Lanham, MD: Lexington Press, 2019.

Baker, Brian. 'The Resurrection of Desire: J. G. Ballard's *Crash* as a Transgressive Text'. *Foundation* 29.80 (2000): 84–96.

Baker, Graeme. 'Sunak Vows to Stop 20mph Zones'. *BBC News*. https://www.bbc.co.uk/news/uk-politics-66965714. Accessed 6 November 2024.

Ballard, J. G. *The Concrete Island*. London: Fourth Estate, 2011 [1974].

Ballard, J. G. *Crash*. London: Vintage, 2004 [1973].

Ballard, J. G. *The Crystal World*. London: Fourth Estate, 2014 [1966].

Ballard, J. G. 'Don't Crash: The J. G. Ballard Interview'. https://jgballard.ca/media/1995_kjb.html. Accessed 14 February 2025.

Ballard, J. G. *The Drought*. London: Flamingo, 2001 [1965].

Ballard, J. G. *High Rise*. London: Fourth Estate, 2014 [1975].

Ballard, J. G. *The Wind from Nowhere*. London: Penguin, 1967 [1962].

Ballinger, Benjamin et al. 'The Vulnerability of Electric Vehicle Deployment to Critical Mineral Supply'. *Applied Energy* 255 (2019): 113–44.

The Bank of Natural Capital. 'The Economics of Ecosystems and Biodiversity Study (TEEB)'. 8 January 2012. n.p. http://bankofnaturalcapital.com/. Accessed 14 June 2014.

Banks, Brett, Jethro Kayat and Jean Rossman. 'Future Frontiers: Ontological Osmosis and Africanfuturist Cyborgs in Nnedi Okorafor's *Lagoon*'. *Image and Text* 37 (2023): 1–20.

Bate, Jonathan. *The Song of the Earth*. London: Pan Macmillan, 2001.

Baudrillard. Jean. 'Ballard's *Crash*'. *Science Fiction Studies* 18.3 (1991): 313–20.

Beauman, Ned. *Venomous Lumpsucker*. London: Sceptre, 2022.

Beckman, Frida. 'J. G. Ballard's Dark Ecologies: Unsettling Nature, Animals and Literary Tropes'. In *Animalities: Literary and Cultural*

Studies beyond the Human. Edited by Michael Lundblad, 60–79. Edinburgh: Edinburgh University Press, 2017.

Belasco, Warren. *Meals to Come: A History of the Future of Food*. Oakland: University of California Press, 2006.

Bennett, Carys et al. 'How Chickens Became the Ultimate Symbol of the Anthropocene'. *The Conversation*, 12 December 2018, https://theconversation.com/how-chickens-became-the-ultimate-symbol-of-the-anthropocene-108559. Accessed 17 April 2023.

Bennett, Carys et al.. 'The Broiler Chicken as a Signal of a Human Reconfigured Biosphere'. *Royal Society Open Science* 5 (2018): 180325.

Bergthaller, Hannes. 'Fossil Freedoms: The Politics of Emancipation and the End of Oil'. In *The Routledge Companion to the Environmental Humanities*. Edited by Ursula Heise, Jon Christensen and Michelle Niemann. London: Routledge, 2017.

Berry, Tanya Amyx. *For the Hog Killing*. Lexington: University of Kentucky Press, 2019.

Berry, Wendell. 'Aldo Leopold: A Reader's Testimony'. In *Aldo Leopold: His Life and Work*, xi–xvi. Madison: University of Wisconsin Press, 2010.

Berry, Wendell. *A Continuous Harmony*. San Diego, CA: Harcourt Brace, 1972.

Berry, Wendell. *The Farm*. Berkeley, CA: Counterpoint, 1995.

Berry, Wendell. *Wendell Berry: Collected Poems, 1957–1982*. New York: North Point Press, 1987.

Berry, Wendell. *What Are People For?* Berkeley, CA: Counterpoint, 2010.

Berry, Wendell. *The World-Ending Fire*. London: Penguin, 2018.

Black Panther [feature film]. Dir. Ryan Coogler. Walt Disney Studios, 2018.

Böhm, Steffen et al. 'Introduction: Impossibilities of Automobility'. In *Against Automobility*. Edited by Steffen Böhm, Campbell Jones, Chris Land and Matthew Patterson, 3–16. Oxford: Blackwell, 2006.

Bonneuil, Christophe, and Jean-Baptiste Fressoz. *The Shock of the Anthropocene: The Earth, History and Us*. London: Verso Books, 2016.

Borkfelt, Sune. 'Veganism and Animals'. In *The Edinburgh Companion to Vegan Studies*. Edited by Laura Wright and Emilia Quinn, 93–106. Edinburgh: Edinburgh University Press, 2022.

Bould, Mark. *The Anthropocene Unconscious: Climate, Catastrophe, Culture*. London: Verso, 2021.

Braun, Robert, and Richard Randell, *Post-Automobility Futures: Technology, Power and Imaginaries*. Lanham, MD: Rowman and Littlefield, 2022.

Brock, Andrea. 'Securing Accumulation by Restoration – Exploring Spectacular Corporate Conservation, Coal Mining and Biodiversity Compensation in the German Rhineland'. *Environment and Planning E: Nature and Space* 6.4 (2023): 2134–65.

Bruckner, Donald A. 'Strict Vegetarianism Is Immoral'. In *The Moral Complexities of Eating Meat*. Edited by B. Bramble and B. Fisher. Oxford: Oxford University Press, 2015.

Buell, Laurence. *The Environmental Imagination*. Princeton, NJ: Princeton University Press, 1995.

Buller, Adrienne. *The Value of a Whale: On the Illusions of Green Capitalism*. Manchester: Manchester University Press, 2022.

Buxton, Jayne. *The Great Plant-Based Con*. London: Piatkus, 2022.

Calarco, Matthew. *Animal Studies: The Key Concepts*. London: Routledge, 2021.

Calarco, Matthew. 'Animals, Mobility and the Future of Meat'. In *The Future of Meat without Animals*. Edited by Brianne Donaldson and Brian Carter. Lanham, MD: Rowman and Littlefield, 2016.

Calarco, Matthew. *Reflections on Roadkill between Mobility Studies and Animal Studies: Altermobilities*. London: Palgrave, 2023.

Calarco, Matthew. *Zoographies: The Question of the Animal from Heidegger to Derrida*. New York: Columbia University Press, 2008.

Callicott, J. Baird. 'Animal Liberation: A Triangular Affair'. *Environmental Ethics* 2.4 (1980): 311–38.

Castle, Nora, and Graeme Macdonald. 'Introduction: Food Futures'. *Science Fiction Studies* 49.2 (2022): 209–16.

Cawardine, Mark. '*Last Chance to See*'. https://www.markcarwardine.com/last-chance-to-see.html. Accessed 11 October 2019.

Chandler, James. 'Critical Disciplinarity'. *Critical Enquiry* 30.2 (2004): 355–60.

Chrulew, Matthew, and Rick de Vos. 'Extinction'. In *The Edinburgh Companion to Animal Studies*. Edited by Lynn Turner, Undine Sellbach and Ron Broglio, 181–97. Edinburgh: Edinburgh University Press, 2018.

Churchill, Winston. 'Fifty Years Hence'. *Popular Mechanics* 57.3 (1932): 393.

Clark, Timothy. *The Value of Ecocriticism*. Cambridge: Cambridge University Press, 2019.

Clarke, Jim. 'Reading Climate Change in J. G. Ballard'. *Critical Survey* 25.2 (2013): 7–21.

Clean Meat Hoax. 'About Us'. https://www.cleanmeat-hoax.com/about.html. Accessed 1 August 2023.

Clean Meat Hoax. 'Green-Washing & Vegan-Washing Evil Companies'. https://www.cleanmeat-hoax.com/green---vegan-washing.html. Accessed 1 August 2023.

Cole, Matthew. 'From "Animal Machines" to "Happy Meat"? Foucault's Ideas of Disciplinary and Pastoral Power Applied to "Animal-Centred" Welfare Discourse'. *Animals* 1.1 (2011): 83–101.

Cole, Stewart. 'Poetry'. In *The Edinburgh Companion to Vegan Studies*. Edited by Laura Wright and Emilia Quinn, 193–202. Edinburgh: Edinburgh University Press, 2022.

Cooper, Melinda. *Life as Surplus: Biotechnology and Capitalism in the Neoliberal Era*. Seattle: University of Washington Press, 2008.

Cusworth, George et al. 'Green Rebranding: Regenerative Agriculture, Future-Pasts, and the Naturalisation of Livestock'. *Transactions of the Institute of British Geographers* 47.4 (2022): 1009–27.

Darwin, Charles. *On the Origin of Species*. New York: Collier and Sons, 1909 [1859].

Dasgupta, Partha. *The Economics of Biodiversity: The Dasgupta Review*. London: HM Treasury, 2021.

DEFRA. 'New Plans Promise Flourishing Future for the Natural Environment'. 7 June 2011. https://www.gov.uk/government/news/new-plans-promise-flourishing-future-for-the-natural-environment. Accessed 1 April 2025.

DeKoven, Marianne. 'Why Animals Now?' *PMLA* 124.2 (March 2009): 361–9.

DeMello, Margo. *Animals and Society: An Introduction to Human–Animal Studies*. New York: Columbia University Press, 2012.

Derrida, Jacques. *The Animal That Therefore I Am*. Translated by David Wills. New York: Fordham University Press, 2008.

Derrida, Jacques. '"Eating Well", or the Calculation of the Subject: An Interview with Jacques Derrida'. In *Who Comes after the Subject?* Edited by E. Cadava, P. Connor and J.-L. Nancy, 96–119. New York: Routledge, 1991.

Derrida, Jacques. 'The Force of Law: The "Mystical Foundation of Authority"'. *Cardozo Law Review* 11.5–6 (1990): 919–1045.

Dery, Mark. 'Black to the Future: Afro-Futurism 1.0'. In *Afro-Future Females: Black Writers Chart Science Fiction's Newest New-Wave Trajectory*. Edited by Marleen S. Barr, 6–13. Columbus: Ohio State University Press, 2008.

Dini, Rachelle. '"Things Playing a More Important Part Than People": Waste in J. G. Ballard's Urban Disaster Trilogy'. *Deep Ends* (2016).

Donaldson, Sue, and Will Kymlicka. *Zoopolis: A Political Theory of Animal Rights*. Oxford: Oxford University Press, 2011.

Dutkiewicz, Jan. 'Socialize Lab Meat'. *Jacobin*, 8 November 2019. https://jacobin.com/2019/08/lab-meat-socialism-green-new-deal. Accessed 9 January 2023.
EAT. 'EAT-Lancet Commission Brief for Everyone'. https://eatforum.org/lancet-commission/eatinghealthyandsustainable/. Accessed 1 August 2023.
Edwards, Karen L., Derek Ryan and Jane Spencer. 'Introduction'. In *Reading Literary Animals: Medieval to Modern*. Edited by Karen L. Edwards, Derek Ryan and Jane Spencer, 1–10. London: Routledge, 2020.
Ellison, Ralph. *The Invisible Man*. London: Penguin, 1965 [1952].
Emmett, Robert S., and David E. Nye. *The Environmental Humanities: A Critical Introduction*. Cambridge, MA: MIT Press, 2017.
The Environment Bank. 'About Us'. https://www.environmentbank.com/more/about-us/. Accessed 1 April 2025.
The Environment Bank. 'Biodiversity Units'. https://www.environmentbank.com/what-we-do/biodiversity-units/. Accessed 4 April 2025.
Escobar, Arturo. *Encountering Development: The Making and Unmaking of the Third World*. Princeton, NJ: Princeton University Press, 2011.
Espiner, Tom. 'BP Set to Scale Back Green Investments as Profits Drop Sharply'. *BBC News*, 11 February 2025. https://www.bbc.co.uk/news/articles/c30d4ernzqjo. Accessed 14 February 2025.
EVA England. 'Benefits of EVs'. https://www.evaengland.org.uk/about-electric-vehicles/benefits-of-evs/. Accessed 6 November 2024.
The Extinction Studies Working Group. 'About Us'. http://extinctionstudies.org/about/. Accessed 2 May 2025.
FAIRR, 'ESG Risks and Opportunities of Clean Meat'. https://www.fairr.org/resources/knowledge-hub/key-terms/clean-meat. Accessed 1 September 2024.
Fassler, Joe. 'The Revolution That Died on Its Way to Dinner'. *New York Times*, 9 February 2024. https://www.nytimes.com/2024/02/09/opinion/eat-just-upside-foods-cultivated-meat.html. Accessed 24 June 2024.
Faunalytics, 'Global Animal Slaughter, Statistics and Charts: 2022 Update'. https://faunalytics.org/global-animal-slaughter-statistics-charts-2022-update/. Accessed 17 April 2023.
Feeding Ourselves Thirsty. 'Meat: Overview'. https://feedingourselvesthirsty.ceres.org/index.php/industry-scorecards/meat. Accessed 23 June 2023.
Fiddes, Nick. *Meat: A Natural Symbol*. London: Routledge, 1991.
Fisher, Mark. *Capitalist Realism: Is There No Alternative?* London: John Hunt, 2022.

Flint, Grainger. 'Afrofuturism in Food'. *English @ SUNY Genesco*. https://morrison.sunygeneseoenglish.org/2018/09/23/afrofuturism-in-food/. Accessed 31 March 2025.
Freeman, C. P. 'Lisa and Phoebe, Lone Vegetarian Icons: At Odds with Television's Carnonormativity'. In *How Television Shapes Our Worldview: Media Representations of Social Trends and Change*. Edited by Deborah A. Macey et al., 193–212. Lanhan, MD: Lexington Books, 2014.
Freund, Peter, and George Martin. 'Hypermobility, the Social Organisation of Space and Health'. *Mobilities* 2.1 (2007): 37–49.
FSIS Case No. 2018. https://downloads.regulations.gov/FSIS-2018-0016-0001/content.pdf, p. 1. Accessed 1 August 2023.
Garrard, Greg. *Ecocriticism*, 2nd edn. Abingdon: Routledge, 2012.
Garrard, Greg. 'Introduction'. In *The Oxford Handbook of Ecocriticism*. Oxford: Oxford University Press, 2014, 1–24.
Gerola, Alessia. 'Vibranium Dreams and Afrofuturist Visions: Technology, Nature and Culture'. In *Black Panther and Philosophy: What Can Wakanda Offer the World?* Edited by Edwardo Pérez and Timothy E. Brown, 176–83. Hoboken, NJ: Wiley, 2022.
Ghosh, Amitav. 'Petrofiction: The Oil Encounter and the Novel'. *The New Republic* (2 March 1992): 29–33.
Giraud, Eva Haifa. *What Comes after Entanglement? Activism, Anthropocentrism, and an Ethics of Exclusion*. Durham, NC: Duke University Press, 2019.
Giraud, Eva Haifa. *Veganism: Politics, Practice and Theory*. London: Bloomsbury, 2021.
Global Carbon Project. 'Fossil Fuel CO_2 Emissions Increase Again in 2024'. https://globalcarbonbudget.org/fossil-fuel-co2-emissions-increase-again-in-2024/. Accessed 14 February 2025.
Glotfelty, Cheryl. 'Introduction: Literary Studies in an Age of Environmental Crisis'. In *The Ecocriticism Reader: Landmarks in Literary Ecology*, xv–xxxvii. Athens: University of Georgia Press, 1996.
Good Food Institute. 'Cultivated Meat'. https://gfieurope.org/cultivated-meat/. Accessed 1 September 2024.
Greenfield, Patrick, Daisy Dunne and Giuliana Viglione. 'More Than Half of Countries Are Ignoring Biodiversity Pledges'. *The Guardian*, 24 February 2025. https://www.theguardian.com/environment/2025/feb/24/countries-biodiversity-pledges-rome-cop16-aoe. Accessed 27 February 2025.
Gunster, Shane. '"You Belong Outside": Advertising, Nature, and the SUV'. *Ethics and the Environment* 9.2 (2004): 4–32.

Hanchey, Jenna N. 'Desire and the Politics of Africanfuturism'. *Women's Studies in Communication* 43.2 (2020): 119–24.
Haraway, Donna J. *Staying with the Trouble: Making Kin in the Chthulucene*. Durham, NC: Duke University Press, 2016.
Haraway, Donna J. *When Species Meet*. Minneapolis: University of Minnesota Press, 2007.
Hardy, Thomas. *Jude the Obscure*. London: Penguin, 1978 [1896].
Heidegger, Martin. *Basic Writings*. San Francisco, CA: Harper, 1993.
Heise, Ursula. *Imagining Extinction: The Cultural Meanings of Endangered Species*. Chicago, IL: Chicago University Press, 2016.
Helm, Dieter. *Natural Capital: Valuing the Planet*. New Haven, CT: Yale University Press, 2015.
Helm, Dieter, and Cameron Hepburn. 'The Economic Analysis of Biodiversity'. In *Nature in the Balance: The Economics of Biodiversity*. Edited by Dieter Helm and Cameron Hepburn, 7–32. Oxford: Oxford University Press, 2014.
HM Government. *The Natural Choice: Securing the Value of Nature*. 2011. https://assets.publishing.service.gov.uk/media/5a7cb8fce5274a38e57565a4/8082.pdf. Accessed 2 April 2025.
Hubbell, J. Andrew, and John C. Ryan, *Introduction to the Environmental Humanities*. London: Routledge, 2021.
Huggan, Graham. 'Editorial'. *Green Letters* 23.1 (2019): 1–4.
Huggan, Graham. *Extreme Pursuits: Travel/Writing in an Age of Globalization*. Ann Arbor: University of Michigan Press, 2009.
Hume, Angela, and Gillian Osborne. 'Ecopoetics as Expanded Critical Practice'. In *Ecopoetics: Essays in the Field*, 1–16. Iowa City: University of Iowa Press, 2018.
Iovino, Serenella, and Serpil Oppermann. 'Introduction: Stories Come to Matter'. In *Material Ecocriticism*, 1–21. Bloomington: Indiana University Press, 2014.
Jameson, Fredric. *The Seeds of Time*. New York: Columbia University Press, 1994.
Jolly, Jasper. 'Most New Cars Sold in UK Will Have to Be Fully Electric by 2030'. *The Guardian*. https://www.theguardian.com/environment/2023/sep/28/majority-of-newscars-sold-in-uk-will-have-to-be-fully-electric-by-2030-government-confirms. Accessed 6 November 2024.
Jose, Shibu, and Jeanne Dollinger. 'Silvopasture: A Sustainable Livestock Production System'. *Agroforestry Systems* 93 (2019): 1–9.
Joy, Melanie. 'Understanding Neocarnism: How Vegan Advocates Can Appreciate and Respond to "Happy Meat", "Locavorism" and "Paleo Dieting"'. https://www.onegreenplanet.org/lifestyle/understanding-neocarnism/. Accessed 1 August 2023.

Joy, Melanie. *Why We Love Dogs, Eat Pigs and Wear Cows*. San Francisco, CA: Conari Press, 2010.
Jue, Melody. 'Intimate Objectivity: On Nnedi Okorafor's Oceanic Afrofuturism'. *Women's Studies Quarterly* 45.1–2 (2017): 171–88.
Kara, Siddharth. *Cobalt Red: How the Blood of the Congo Powers Our Lives*. London: St Martin's Press, 2023.
Kirksey, Eben, and Stefan Helmreich. 'The Emergence of Multispecies Ethnography'. *Cultural Anthropology* 25.4 (2010): 545–76.
Knickerbocker, Scott. *Ecopoetics: The Language of Nature, the Nature of Language*. Amherst: University of Massachusetts Press, 2012.
Knowles, Thomas. 'J. G. Ballard and the "Natural" World'. *Green Letters* 22.4 (2018): 341–53.
Ko, Aph, and Syl Ko. *Aphro-ism: Essays on Pop Culture, Feminism and Black Veganism from Two Sisters*. New York: Lantern Books, 2017.
Koistinen, Katariina et al. 'Sustainable Transition'. *Encyclopedia of Sustainable Management*. https://link.springer.com/referenceworkentry/10.1007/978-3-031-25984-5_434. Accessed 14 February 2025.
Ladkin, Sam, and Robert McKay. 'Against Value'. https://occursus.wordpress.com/2012/02/14/against-value-23-2-2012/. Accessed 1 May 2025.
Lane, Mary Bradley. *Mizora: A Prophecy*. New York: Syracuse University Press, 2007 [1881].
Lasswitz, Kurd. *Two Planets*. Carbondale: Southern Illinois University Press, 1971 [1895].
Leopold, Aldo. *A Sand County Almanac, with Essays on Conservation from Round River*. New York: Ballantine Books, 1966.
Lero. 'Electric Cars More Likely to Cause Accidents, Research Shows'. *Sci Tech Daily*. https://scitechdaily.com/electric-car-drivers-more-likely-to-cause-accidents-research-shows/. Accessed 6 November 2024.
Lestel, Dominique. *Eat This Book: A Carnivore's Manifesto*. New York: Columbia University Press, 2016.
Lippit, Akira Mizuta. *Electric Animal: Toward a Rhetoric of Wildlife*. Minneapolis: University of Minnesota Press, 2000.
Lundblad, Michael. 'From Animal to Animality Studies'. *PMLA* 124.2 (2009): 496–502.
Macdonald, Graeme. 'Impossibility Drives: The Energy of Sf'. *Paradoxa* 26 (2014): 111–44.
Macdonald, Graeme. 'Oil and World Literature'. *American Book Review* (March–April 2012): 7–31.
Macfarlane, Robert. 'Introduction'. In *The Crystal World*. London: Fourth Estate, 2014 [1966]).
Machovina, Brian et al. 'Biodiversity Conservation: The Key Is Reducing Meat Consumption'. *Science of the Total Environment* 536 (December 2015): 419–31.

Malm, Andreas, and Wim Carton. *Overshoot: How the World Surrendered to Climate Breakdown*. London: Verso, 2024.
Manisalidis, Ioannis et al. 'Environmental and Health Impacts of Air Pollution: A Review'. *Frontiers in Public Health* 8 (2020): 14, 1–13.
March-Russell, Paul. 'Après le Déluge'. *Foundation* 53.147 (2024): 76–82.
Maron, Martine et al., 'Biodiversity Offsets, Their Effectiveness and Their Role in a Nature Positive Future'. *Nature Reviews* 1 (March 2025): 183–96.
The Marvel Database. 'Vibranium'. https://marvel.fandom.com/wiki/Vibranium#Wakandan_Vibranium. Accessed 3 March 2025.
The Marvel Database. 'Wakanda'. https://marvel.fandom.com/wiki/Wakanda#Technology. Accessed 3 March 2025.
Marvin, Garry. 'Wild Killing: Contesting the Animal in Hunting'. In *Killing Animals*. Edited by the Animal Studies Group, 10–29. Urbana: University of Illinois Press, 2006.
McGregor, Don, Rich Buckler, Billy Graham, Stan Lee and Jack Kirby. *Black Panther*. London: Penguin, 2022.
McKay, Robert. '"Identifying with the Animals": Language, Subjectivity, and the Animal Politics of Margaret Atwood's *Surfacing*'. In *Figuring Animals: Essays on Animal Images in Art, Literature, Philosophy and Popular Culture*. Edited by M. S. Pollock and C. Rainwater, 207–27. New York: Palgrave Macmillan, 2005.
McKay, Robert. 'Read Meat'. In *Animal Remains*. Edited by Sarah Bezan and Robert McKay, 129–57. London: Routledge, 2022.
McKay, Robert. 'A Vegan Form of Life'. In *Thinking Veganism in Literature and Culture: Towards a Vegan Theory*. Edited by Emilia Quinn and Benjamin Westwood. London: Palgrave, 2018.
McKibben, Bill. *The End of Nature*. New York: Random House, 1989.
McKibben, Bill. 'Prophet in Kentucky'. *New York Review of Books* (14 June 1990).
McLelland, James. 'Why the Left Loves Trains (and Hates Cars)'. *Challenge Magazine*, 29 January 2023. https://challenge-magazine.org/2023/01/29/why-the-left-loves-trains-and-hates-cars/. Accessed 29 April 2025.
Melsom, Blair. 'Is Wakanda a Real Place? Building Smart Cities within Africa'. https://www.bcs.org/articles-opinion-and-research/is-wakanda-a-real-place-building-smart-cities-within-africa/. Accessed 3 March 2025.
Middelhof, Frederike, and Sebastian Schönbeck. 'Coming to Terms: The Poetics of More-Than-Human Worlds'. In *Texts, Animals, Environments: Zoopoetics and Ecopoetics*. Edited by Frederike Middelhof and Sebastian Schönbeck, 11–40. Berlin: Rombach Verlag, 2019.

Milburn, Josh. 'The Best Argument against Veganism'. *ShARC Blog*. https://sharc.sites.sheffield.ac.uk/blog/the-best-argument-against-veganism. Accessed 6 November 2024.

Milburn, Josh. 'Is Lab-Grown Meat Good News for Animals'. *The Conversation*. https://theconversation.com/is-lab-grown-meat-good-news-for-animals-151610. Accessed 1 August 2023.

Miller, John. 'The Literary Invention of *In Vitro* Meat: Ontology, Nostalgia and Debt in Pohl and Kornbluth's *The Space Merchants*'. In *Literature and Meat since 1900*. Edited by Seán McCorry and John Miller, 9–110. London: Palgrave, 2019.

Miner, Patrick et al. 'Car Harm: A Global Review of Automobility's Harm to People and the Environment'. *Journal of Transport Geography* 115 (2024): 103817, 1–17.

Moe, Aaron. *Zoopoetics: Animals and the Making of Poetry*. Lanham, MD: Lexington Books, 2014.

Monbiot, George. '"Let Them Eat Lentils" Won't Save Us from Animal Farming – We Must Embrace Meat Substitutes'. https://www.theguardian.com/commentisfree/2023/feb/01/environmentalists-animal-free-meat-livestock-farming. Accessed 17 April 2023.

Monbiot, George. *Regenesis: Feeding the World without Devouring the Planet*. London: Allen Lane, 2022.

Mooney, Attracta, and Jim Pickard. 'UK Climate Activists Jailed for At Least Four Years over Road Blocks'. *The Financial Times*, 18 July 2024. https://www.ft.com/content/efa11ff6-555d-44a4-84f9-469e5e58c37d. Accessed 14 February 2025.

Moore, Jason W. 'The Capitalocene, Part I: On the Nature and Origins of Our Ecological Crisis'. *Journal of Peasant Studies* 44.3 (2017): 594–630.

Morris Viveca, and Jennifer Skene (hosts). 'Episode 51 – Novelist Ned Beauman on Venomous Lumpsuckers and the Price of Extinction' [audio podcast]. *When We Talk about Animals*. https://www.whenwetalkaboutanimals.org/2023/04/11/ep-51-ned-beauman/#more-2030. Accessed 1 May 2025.

Morton, Timothy. 'Ecology as Text, Text as Ecology'. *Oxford Literary Review* 32.1 (2010): 1–17.

Morton, Timothy. *Ecology without Nature: Rethinking Environmental Aesthetics*. Cambridge: Harvard University Press, 2007.

Morton, Timothy. 'How I Learned to Stop Worrying and Love the Term *Anthropocene*'. *Cambridge Journal of Postcolonial Literary Inquiry* 1.2 (2014): 257–64.

Morton, Timothy. *Spacecraft*. London: Bloomsbury, 2022.

Natural Capital Committee. 'Advice on Using Nature Based Interventions to Each Net Zero Greenhouse Gas Emissions by 2050'. 6 April 2020. https://assets.publishing.service.gov.uk/media/5e986365d3bf7f4123758926/ncc-nature-based-interventions.pdf. Accessed 1 April 2025.

Natural Capital Committee. 'Information Sheet'. https://webarchive.nationalarchives.gov.uk/ukgwa/20130822074033/http://www.defra.gov.uk/naturalcapitalcommittee/files/NCC-Information-Sheet.pdf. Accessed 1 May 2025.

Natural England, Press Release. '"Nature Is the National Wealth Service": Natural England Chair Calls for New Approach in Major Report'. 9 October 2024. https://www.gov.uk/government/news/nature-is-the-national-wealth-service-natural-england-chair-calls-for-new-approach-in-major-report. Accessed 10 May 2025.

Nature Blog Network. 'The Top 10 Most Useless Animals on the Planet'. https://www.hummingbirdsplus.org/nature-blog-network/the-top-10-most-useless-animals-on-the-planet/. Accessed 2 April 2025.

Niman, Nicolette Hahn. *Defending Beef: The Case for Sustainable Meat Production*. White River Junction, VT: Chelsea Green, 2014.

Nocella II, Anthony J. et al. 'Introduction: The Emergence of Critical Animal Studies'. In *Defining Critical Animal Studies: An Intersectional Social Justice Approach for Liberation*. Edited by Anthony J. Nocella II, John Sorenson, Kim Socha and Atsuko Matsuoka, ix–xxxvi. New York: Peter Lang, 2014.

Nuri, Mohammed Ataullah. 'Three Waves of Ecocriticsm: An Overview'. *Horizon*, 2.5 (2020): 253–68.

Oatman, Rachael. 'Future Meat Rebrands to Believer Meats'. *Food Business News*. https://www.foodbusinessnews.net/articles/22657-future-meat-rebrands-to-believer-meats. Accessed 1 August 2023.

Okrafor, Nnedi. 'Africanfuturism Defined'. https://nnedi.blogspot.com/2019/10/africanfuturism-defined.html. Accessed 3 March 2025.

Okrafor, Nnedi. *Lagoon*. London: Hodder and Stoughton, 2014.

Okrafor, Nnedi. *Noor*. New York: Daw, 2021.

Okrafor, Nnedi. 'Organic Fantasy'. *African Identities* 7.2 (2009): 275–86.

Okrafor, Nnedi. *The Shadow Speaker*. New York: Daw Books, 2023 [2007].

Okrafor, Nnedi. 'Spider the Artist'. In *Kabu-Kabu*. Germantown, MD: Prime Books, 2013, 100–15.

Oliver, Catherine. *What Is Veganism For?* Bristol: Bristol University Press, 2024.

O' Riordan, Kate. *Unreal Objects: Digital Materialities, Technoscientific Projects and Political Realities*. London: Pluton Press, 2017.

Ossana, Eugenia. 'Decolonizing the Desert: From Necropolitical Dynamics to Ubuntu Communal Re-Imaginings in Nnedi Okorafor's *Noor* (2021)'. *ISLE* (2024): 1–20.

Parham, John. 'With or without Us: Literature and the Anthropocene'. In *Cambridge Companion to Literature and the Anthropocene*. Edited by John Parham, 1–33. Cambridge: Cambridge University Press, 2021.

Parr, Adrian. *The Wrath of Capital: Neoliberalism and Climate Change Politics*. New York: Columbia University Press, 2013.

Parry, Jovian. 'Speculative Fiction'. In *The Edinburgh Companion to Vegan Studies*. Edited by Laura Wright and Emilia Quinn. Edinburgh: Edinburgh University Press, 2022.

Percival, Rob. *The Meat Paradox: Eating, Empathy and the Future of Meat*. London: Little, Brown, 2022.

PETA. 'The Future of Food'. https://prime.peta.org/news/the-future-of-food-is-vegan/. Accessed 17 April 2023.

PETA. 'Is It Really Natural? The Truth about Humans and Eating Meat'. https://www.peta.org/living/food/really-natural-truth-humans-eating-meat/. Accessed 1 August 2023.

Pfaelzer, Jean. 'Introduction'. In *Mizora: A Prophecy*. New York: Syracuse University Press, 2007.

Pfaelzer, Jean. *The Utopian Novel in America, 1886–1896: The Politics of Form*. Pittsburgh, PA: University of Pittsburgh Press, 1985.

Pick, Anat. *Creaturely Poetics*. New York: Columbia University Press, 2011.

Plumwood, Val. 'Animals and Ecology: Towards a Better Integration'. 2003. https://openresearch-repository.anu.edu.au/bitstream/1885/41767/3/Vegpap6.pdf, 1. Accessed 1 May 2025.

Plumwood, Val. *The Eye of the Crocodile*. Canberra: ANU Press, 2012.

Pohl, Frederick, and Cyril Kornbluth. *The Space Merchants*. London: Penguin, 1984 [1952].

Power, Kevin. '*Venomous Lumpsucker* by Ned Beauman Review – a Cerebral Eco-Thriller'. *The Guardian*, 14 July 2022. https://www.theguardian.com/books/2022/jul/14/venomous-lumpsucker-by-ned-beauman-review-a-cerebral-eco-thriller. Accessed 1 May 2025.

Price, Kiley. 'Will the Drive for EVs Destroy Earth's Last Ecosystem'. *Live Science*. https://www.livescience.com/planet-earth/climate-change/mining-crystals-locked-in-the-deep-sea-could-help-fight-climate-change-it-may-also-destroy-earths-last-untouched-ecosystem. Accessed 6 November 2024.

Quinn, Emilia. 'Notes on Vegan Camp'. *PMLA* 135.5 (2020): 914 –30.

Radcliffe, James. *Green Politics: Dictatorship or Democracy?* Basingstoke: Macmillan, 2000.

Reid, Carlton. '20mph Zones "Against British Values" Rishi Sunak Says Prior to Unveiling Pro-Motorist Policies'. *Forbes*. https://www.forbes.com/sites/carltonreid/2023/09/29/20mph-zones-against-british-values-rishi-sunak-says-prior-to-unveiling-pro-motorist-policies/. Accessed 6 November 2024.

Reuters. 'Swordfish Attack Angolan pipeline'. 2 February 2010. https://www.reuters.com/article/oukoe-uk-angola-crude-idAFTRE6113BU20100202/. Accessed 3 March 2025.

Richards, Morgan. 'Global Nature, Global Brand: BBC Earth and David Attenborough's Landmark Wildlife Series'. *Media International Australia* 146.1 (February 2013): 143–54.

Rignall, Karen and Nnedi Okorafor. 'Energy Politics and Africanfuturism – a Conversation with Nnedi Okorafor'. *Middle East Research and Information Project* 311 (Summer 2024). https://merip.org/2024/07/energy-politics-and-african-futurism-a-conversation-with-nnedi-okorafor/. Accessed 8 April 2025.

Rogers, Heather. *Green Gone Wrong: Dispatches from the Front Line of Eco-Capitalism*. London: Verso, 2010.

Rose, Deborah Bird, Thom van Dooren and Matthew Chrulew, eds. *Extinction Studies: Stories of Time, Death, and Generations*. New York: Columbia University Press, 2017.

Rueckert, William. 'Literature and Ecology: An Experiment in Ecocriticism'. *The Iowa Review* 9.1 (1978): 71–86.

Salaudeen, Aisha. 'R & B singer Akon Is Building a "Real-Life Wakanda" Worth $6 Billion in Senegal'. *CNN News*, 2 September 2020. https://edition.cnn.com/travel/article/akon-city-senegal-wakanda-intl/index.html. Accessed 3 March 2025.

Sayre, Gordon. 'Automobile'. In *Fueling Culture: 101 Words for Energy and Environment*. Edited by Imre Szeman, Jennifer Wenzel and Patricia Yaeger, 54–6. New York: Fordham University Press, 2017.

Scarborough, Peter et al. 'Vegans, Vegetarians, Fish-Eaters and Meat-Eaters in the UK Show Discrepant Environmental Impacts'. *Nature Food* (2023): 1–10.

Schumacher, E. F. *Small Is Beautiful: A Study of Economics As If People Mattered*. London: Vintage, 1993 [1973].

Schwägerl, Christian. *The Anthropocene: The Human Era and How It Shapes the Planet*. London: Synergetic Press, 2014.

SciFi Foods. https://scififoods.com/. Accessed 1 August 2023.

Secretariat of the Convention on Biological Diversity. *Handbook of the Convention on Biological Diversity*. London: Earthscan, 2001.

Selborne, Lord John. 'Foreword'. In *Synthesis of the Key Findings. UK National Ecosystem Assessment*. Cambridge: UNEP-WCMC, 2011.

Shelley, Mary. *Frankenstein*. London: Colburn and Bentley, 1831.

Shepherd, W. Andrew. 'Afrofuturism in the Nineteenth and Twentieth Centuries'. In *The Cambridge History of Science Fiction*. Edited by Gerry Canavan and Eric Carl Link, 101–9. Cambridge: Cambridge University Press, 2019.

Shiva, Vandana. *Monocultures of the Mind: Perspectives on Biodiversity and Biotechnology*. London: Zed Books, 1993.

Shotwell, Alexis. *Against Purity: Living Ethically in Compromised Times*. Minneapolis: University of Minnesota Press, 2016.

Shukin, Nicole. *Animal Capital: Rendering Life in Biopolitical Times*. Minneapolis: University of Minnesota Press, 2009.

Simon, John. *Animal Rights and the Politics of Literary Representation*. London: Palgrave, 2002.

Singer, Peter. *Animal Liberation: A New Ethics for Our Treatment of Animals*. London: Pimlico, 1995 [1975].

Slovic, Scott. 'On the Third Wave of Ecocriticism'. *Ecozon@* 1.1 (2010): 4–10.

Slow, Oliver. 'Sunak Orders Review of Low Traffic Neighbourhoods in Pro-Motorist Message'. *BBC News*. https://www.bbc.co.uk/news/uk-politics-66351785. Accessed 6 November 2024.

Smith, F. E. *The World in 2030*. London: Hodder and Stoughton, 1930.

Smith, Kimberley A. *Wendell Berry and the Agrarian Tradition: A Common Grace*. Lawrence: University Press of Kansas, 2003.

Solnick, Sam. *Poetry and the Anthropocene: Ecology, Biology and Technology in Contemporary British and Irish Poetry*. Abingdon: Routledge, 2016.

Space Is the Place [feature film]. Dir. John Coney, 1974.

Stecopoulos, Harilaos. 'The Heat of Modernity: The Great Gatsby as Petrofiction'. In *The Cambridge Companion to American Literature and the Environment*. Edited by Susan Ensor and Susan Scott Parrish, 81–92. Cambridge: Cambridge University Press, 2022.

Stephens, Neil. 'In Vitro Meat: Zombies on the Menu?' *SCRIPTed: A Journal of Law, Technology & Society* 7.2 (2010): 394–401.

Stoekl, Allan. *The Three Sustainabilities: Energy, Economy, Time*. Minneapolis: University of Minnesota Press, 2021.

Sukhdev, Pavan, Heidi Wittmer and Dustin Miller. 'The Economics of Ecosystems and Biodiversity (TEEB): Challenges and Responses. In *Nature in the Balance: The Economics of Biodiversity*. Edited by Dieter Helm and Cameron Hepburn, 135–50. Oxford: Oxford University Press, 2014.

Swanson, Heather Anne. 'The Banality of the Anthropocene'. *Fieldsights*, 22 February 2022. https://culanth.org/fieldsights/the-banality-of-the-anthropocene. Accessed 1 May 2025.

System of Environmental Economic Accounting, 'What Is the SEEA?'. https://seea.un.org/content/homepage. Accessed 4 April 2025.

Szeman, Imre. 'Introduction to Focus: Petrofictions'. *American Book Review* 33.3 (2012): 3.

Szeman, Imre. 'On the Energy Humanities; or, What Can Philosophy Tell Us about Oil?' *European Union Centre of Excellence Papers* no. 1 (2015): 4–23.

Szeman, Imre. *On Petrocultures: Globalisation, Energy, and Culture*. Morgantown: West Virginia University Press, 2019.

Szeman, Imre, and Dominic Boyer. 'Acknowledgments'. In *Energy Humanities: An Anthology*. Edited by Imre Szeman and Dominic Boyer, vii–viii. Baltimore, MD: John Hopkins University Press, 2017.

Szwed, John F. *Space Is the Place: The Life and Times of Sun Ra*. New York: Da Capo Press, 1998.

Tait, Adrian. 'Nature Reclaims Her Own: J. G. Ballard's *The Drowned World*'. *Australian Humanities Review* 57 (2014).

Taylor, Josephine. *The Nonhuman Narratives of Energy: Multispecies Encounters in Extraction Zones*. London: Palgrave, 2025.

Taylor, Nik, and Richard Twine. 'Introduction: Locating the "Critical" in Critical Animal Studies'. In *The Rise of Critical Animal Studies*. Edited by Nik Taylor and Richard Twine, 1–15. Abingdon: Routledge, 2014.

Thomas, Mark. 'The Rules of Autogeddon: Sex, Death and Law in JG Ballard's *Crash*'. *Griffith Law Review* 20.2 (2011): 333–61.

Trexler, Adam, and Adeline Johns-Putra. 'Climate Change in Literature and Literary Criticism'. *Wiley Interdisciplinary Reviews: Climate Change* 2.2 (March/April 2011): 185–200.

Troiani, Igea, and Claudia Dutson. 'The Neoliberal University as a Space to Learn/Think/Work in Higher Education'. *Architecture and Culture* 9.1 (2021): 5–23.

Tynan, Aidan. 'Aporias of Ecological Thought'. *Theory, Culture and Society* 39.5 (2022): 3–21.

UK Government. 'Biodiversity Net Gain'. 21 February 2023. https://www.gov.uk/guidance/understanding-biodiversity-net-gain. Accessed 4 April 2025.

UK Government. 'Biodiversity Offsetting'. 9 April 2013. https://www.gov.uk/government/collections/biodiversity-offsetting. Accessed 2 April 2025.

UK Government. 'Enabling a Natural Capital Approach (Guidance)'. 4 February 2025. https://www.gov.uk/government/publications/enabling-a-natural-capital-approach-enca-guidance/enabling-a-natural-capital-approach-guidance. Accessed 2 April 2025.

UK National Ecosystem Assessment: Technical Report. http://uknea.unep-wcmc.org/LinkClick.aspx?fileticket=QLgsfedO70I%3d&tabid=82. Accessed 2 April 2025.

United Nations. 'United Nations Conference on Environment and Development, Rio de Janeiro, Brazil, 3–14 June'. https://www.un.org/en/conferences/environment/rio1992. Accessed 27 February 2025.

United Nations. 'What Is Sustainable Development?' https://www.un.org/sustainabledevelopment/blog/2023/08/what-is-sustainable-development/. Accessed 14 February 2025.

United Nations Development Programme. 'Food Systems Transformation'. https://www.undp.org/facs/food-systems-transformation. Accessed 15 September 2025.

United Nations Environment Programme. 'Natural Capital Declaration'. http://www.naturalcapitaldeclaration.org/the-declaration/. Accessed 1 April 2025.

United Nations Environment Programme. 'TEEB: Approach and Timeline'. https://www.unep.org/topics/teeb/about-teeb/teeb-approach-and-timeline. Accessed 2 April 2025.

United Nations Food and Agriculture Organization. 'Key Facts and Findings'. https://www.fao.org/news/story/en/item/197623/icode/. Accessed 17 April 2023.

United Nations Sustainable Development. 'Agenda 21'. June 1992. https://sustainabledevelopment.un.org/content/documents/Agenda21.pdf. Accessed 4 April 2025.

Upside Foods. 'Meet the New Meat'. https://upsidefoods.com/. Accessed 1 August 2023.

Urbi, Jason. 'The Fight against "Fake Meat" Has Officially Begun'. *CNBC*. https://www.cnbc.com/2018/02/23/the-fight-against-fake-meat-has-officially-begun.html. Accessed 1 August 2023.

Urry, John. 'The System of Automobility'. *Theory, Culture & Society* 21.4–5 (2004): 25–39.

Usher, Alex. 'What People Mean When They Talk about Neoliberal Universities'. *Higher Education Strategy Associates*, 20 November 2017. https://higheredstrategy.com/what-people-mean-when-they-talk-about-neoliberal-univesities-part-1/. Accessed 14 May 2025.

Valeriote, Elena. 'Italy's Ban on Cultured Meat Raises Questions about Innovation versus Tradition'. *Modern Farmer*. https://modernfarmer.com/2023/05/italys-ban-on-cultured-meat/. Accessed 1 August 2023.

Van Dooren, Thom. *Flight Ways: Life and Loss at the Edge of Extinction*. New York: Columbia University Press, 2014.

Van Dooren, Thom, Eben Kirksey and Ursula Münster. 'Multispecies Studies: Cultivating Arts of Attentiveness'. *Environmental Humanities* 8.1 (2016): 1–23.

Vegan Land Movement. 'Vegan Agriculture Land Buyout 8'. https://veganlandmovement.com/animal-agriculture-land-buyout/. Accessed 1 September 2024.

Virgil. *The Georgics: A Poem of the Land*. Translated by Kimberley Johnson. London: Penguin, 2009.

Waldau, Paul. *Animal Studies: An Introduction*. Oxford: Oxford University Press, 2013.

Walker, Ian et al. 'Motonormativity: How Social Norms Hide a Major Public Health Hazard'. *International Journal of Environment and Health* 11.1 (2023): 21–33.

Wells, Ione. 'Amazon Forest Felled to Build Road for Climate Summit'. *BBC News*, 12 March 2025. https://www.bbc.co.uk/news/articles/c9vy191rgn1o. Accessed 30 April 2025.

Westling, Louise. *The Logos of the Living World: Merleau-Ponty, Animals, and Language*. New York: Fordham University Press, 2013.

'Why Hunt?' https://why-hunt.org/. Accessed 1 May 2025.

Wilcox, Johnnie. 'Black Power: Minstrelsy and Electricity in Ralph Ellison's *Invisible Man*'. *Callaloo* 30.4 (Fall 2007): 987–1009.

Williams, Heathcote. *Autogeddon*. London: Jonathan Cape, 1991.

Wilson, E. O. 'Editor's Foreword'. In *Biodiversity*. Edited by E. O. Wilson and Smithsonian Institution Staff, v–vii. Washington, DC: National Academy Press, 1988.

Wilson, E. O. 'Living on Earth: Interview with E. O. Wilson'. *E. O. Wilson Biodiversity Foundation*. https://eowilsonfoundation.org/eowbf-archive/listen-living-on-earth-interview-with-e-o-wilson-on-how-to-save-the-most-species/. Accessed 4 April 2025.

Winters, ed. *This Is Vegan Propaganda*. London: Ebury, 2022.

Wolfe, Cary. 'Human, All Too Human: "Animal Studies" and the Humanities'. *PMLA* 124.2 (2009): 564–75.

Wolfe, Cary. *What Is Posthumanism?* Minneapolis: University of Minnesota Press, 2010.

Wood, David. 'On Being Haunted by the Future'. *Research in Phenomenology* 36 (2006): 274–98.

Wood, David. 'The Eleventh Plague: Thinking Ecologically after Derrida'. In *Eco-Deconstruction: Derrida and Environmental Philosophy*. Edited by Matthias Fritsch, Philippe Lynes and David Wood, 29–49. New York: Fordham University Press, 2018.

The World Commission on Environment and Development. *Our Common Future*. Oxford: Oxford University Press, 2009.

World Health Organisation. 'Air Pollution'. https://www.who.int/health-topics/air-pollution#tab=tab_3. Accessed 6 November 2024.
Wurgaft, Ben. *Meat Planet: Artificial Flesh and the Future of Food.* Berkeley: University of California Press, 2020.
Yaeger, Patricia. 'Literature in the Ages of Wood, Tallow, Coal, Whale Oil, Gasoline, Atomic Power, and Other Energy Sources. *PMLA* 126.2 (2011): 305–26.
Yaszek, Linda. 'Afrofuturism, Science Fiction and the History of the Future'. *Socialism and Democracy* 20.3 (2006): 41–60.
Yin Han, Lisa. *Deepwater Alchemy: Extractive Mediation and the Taming of the Seafloor.* Minneapolis: University of Minnesota Press, 2024.
Youngquist. Paul. *A Pure Solar World: Sun Ra and the Birth of Afrofuturism.* Austin: University of Texas Press, 2016.
Yusoff, Kathryn. 'The Valuation of Nature: The Natural Choice White Paper'. *Radical Philosophy* 170 (November/December 2011): 1–6.

INDEX